The Rhythm Method, RaZZmatazz, and Memory

How to Make Your Poetry Swing

W
WRITER'S DIGEST BOOKS
www.writersdigest.com
Cincinnati, Ohio

KEITH FLYNN

Visit our Web sites at www.writersdigest.com and www.wdeditors.com for information on more resources for writers.

To receive a free weekly e-mail newsletter delivering tips and updates about writing and about Writer's Digest products, register directly at our Web site at http://newsletters.fwpublications.com.

11   10   09   08   07   5   4   3   2   1

Distributed in Canada by Fraser Direct, 100 Armstrong Avenue Georgetown, Ontario, Canada L7G 5S4, Tel: (905) 877-4411; Distributed in the U.K. and Europe by David & Charles, Brunel House, Newton Abbot, Devon, TQ12 4PU, England, Tel: (+44) 1626 323200, Fax: (+44) 1626 323319, E-mail: postmaster@davidandcharles.co.uk; Distributed in Australia by Capricorn Link, P.O. Box 704, Windsor, NSW 2756 Australia, Tel: (02) 4577-3555

Library of Congress Cataloging-in-Publication Data

Flynn, Keith.

The rhythm method, razzmatazz, and memory : how to make your poetry swing / by Keith Flynn. -- 1st edition.

    p. cm.

Includes bibliographical references and index.

ISBN-13: 978-1-58297-404-0 (pbk. : alk. paper)
ISBN-10: 1-58297-404-7 (pbk. : alk. paper)

1. Poetry. I. Title.

PN1031.F59 2007

808.1--dc22

                  2006038712

Edited by Lauren Mosko
Designed by Claudean Wheeler
Cover and interior illustrations by Michelle Thompson
Production coordinated by Mark Griffin

fw
F+W PUBLICATIONS, INC.

PERMISSIONS

Lifshin, Lyn: "BB King" from *Asheville Poetry Review* (Vol. 11, No. 1, 2004). Reprinted by permission of the author.

Liner, Amon: "A Mondrian Poem…," from *Rose, A Color of Darkness* (Durham, NC: Carolina Wren Press, 1981). Reprinted by permission of the publisher.

Lux, Thomas: "There Were Some Summers," from *New and Selected Poems 1975-1995* (New York, NY: Mariner Books, 1999). Reprinted by permission.

Matthews, William: "Mingus In Diaspora" and "Unrelenting Flood" from *Search Party: Collected Poems* ed. Sebastian Matthews and Stanley Plumly (New York, NY: Houghton Mifflin Company, 2004). Reprinted by permission of the publisher and the Estate of William Matthews.

Niedecker, Lorine: "How white the gulls," and "Remember my little granite pail" from *The Granite Pail: Selected Poems* (Frankfort, KY: Gnomon Press, 1985, 1996). Reprinted by permission.

Reverdy, Pierre: "Memory," (trans. Patricia Terry), "The Poets" and "The Traveler and His Shadow," (trans. Mary Ann Caws) from *The Selected Poems of Pierre Reverdy* (Winston-Salem, NC: Wake Forest University Press, 1991). Reprinted by permission.

Rilke, Rainer Maria: "Moving Forward," from *Selected Poems of Rainer Maria Rilke* ed. Robert Bly (New York, NY: Harper and Row, 1981). Reprinted by permission.

Rimbaud, Arthur: "Morning of Drunkenness" (trans. Louise Varèse) from *Baudelaire, Rimbaud, Verlaine: Selected Verse and Prose Poems* (New York, NY: Citadel Press, 1990). Reprinted by permission of Citadel Press.

Rivera, R. Flowers: "Vera Genera, 1939," from *Asheville Poetry Review* (Vol. 9, No. 1, 2002). Reprinted by permission of the author.

Roberts, Stephen Morris: "Sex," from *A Space Inside a Space* (Laurinburg, NC: St. Andrews College Press, 1999). Reprinted by permission of the author.

Sandburg, Carl: "Jazz Fantasia," from *Smoke and Steel* (New York, NY: Harcourt Brace Jovanovich, 1948). Reprinted by permission.

Shapiro, Karl: "Lower the Standard: That's My Motto," from *Collected Poems 1940-1977* (New York, NY: Random House, 1977). Reprinted by permission of the publisher.

Spicer, Jack: "A Letter to Lorca" from *The Collected Books of Jack Spicer* ed. Robin Blaser (Los Angeles, CA: Black Sparrow Press, 1975). Reprinted by permission.

Stevens, Wallace: "Men Made Out of Words," from *The Collected Poems* (New York: Alfred A. Knopf, 1999). Reprinted by permission of Alfred A. Knopf, Inc.

Wainio, Ken: "Getting Rid of the Ego," from *Asheville Poetry Review*, (Vol. 2, No. 2, Fall/Winter, 1995). Reprinted by permission of the author.

White, Mike: "Murder," from *Asheville Poetry Review* (Vol. 12, No. 1, 2005). Reprinted by permission of the author.

Williams, William Carlos: "To Elsie" and "The Yachts" from *Selected Poems*, ed. Charles Tomlinson (New York: New Directions, 1985). Reprinted by permission of New Directions Publishing Co.

Wilbur, Richard: "A World Without Objects is a Sensible Emptiness," from *Collected Poems: 1943-2004* (New York, London, Toronto, etc.: Harcourt, 2004). Reprinted by permission of the publisher.

Young, Kevin: "Locomotive Songs" from *Jelly Roll: A Blues* (New York, NY: Alfred A. Knopf, 2005). Reprinted by permission of the author.

For Denise Petrey
and Twicket Glorium

ABOUT THE AUTHOR

Keith Flynn is the author of five books, including four collections of poetry: *The Talking Drum*
(1991), *The Book of Monsters* (1994), *The Lost
Sea* (2000), and *The Golden Ratio* (2007). From
1987–1998, he was lyricist and lead singer for the
nationally acclaimed rock band The Crystal Zoo,
which produced three albums: *Swimming Through
Lake Eerie* (1992), *Pouch* (1996), and the spoken-
word and music compilation *Nervous Splendor*
(Animal Records, 2003).

His poetry has appeared in many journals
and anthologies around the world, including *The
Colorado Review*, *The Cuirt Journal* (Ireland),
Word and Witness: 100 Years of NC Poetry, *Poetry Wales*, *Rattle*, *The Southern
Poetry Review*, *Margie*, *Shenandoah*, and *Crazyhorse*.

He has been awarded the Sandburg Prize, the ASCAP Emerging Songwriter
Prize, and the Paumanok Poetry Award and was twice named the Gilbert-Chap-
pell Distinguished Poet for North Carolina. He is the founder and managing
editor of *Asheville Poetry Review*.

ACKNOWLEDGMENTS

The author wishes to express gratitude to his fearless editor and defender of
the faith, Lauren Mosko, and to Jane Friedman, who believed.

The author also wishes to thank Luke Hankins, Thomas Rain Crowe,
Patrick Bizzaro, Sebastian Matthews, Stephen Roberts, and Jay Bonner for
their helpful guidance through the formative process of this manuscript,
and the motivational forces of The Mars Volta, Johnny Winter, and the Great
Trane, who steered me through many sleepless nights of research and composition in the service of the Muse.

CONTENTS

PART 1: *Learning to Listen*

PART 2: *Learning to Observe*

PART 3: *Learning to Speak*

PART 1

Learning to Listen

THE RHYTHM METHOD

"It don't mean a thing if it ain't got that swing ..."

—IRVING MILLS AND DUKE ELLINGTON

INTRODUCTION

From the Beginning:
The Body Is Nourished by the Word

This book must begin with water, like all life forms bubbling out of their buried wells. And make no mistake, a poem is a living organism, capable of great permutations—but only if it is built with a carefully considered architecture of sounds that create an indispensable flow. There are amazing parallels between our bodies and the Natural World. The planet Earth is almost entirely covered with water; about 70 percent of the planet's surface is constructed of vast oceans and seas. Surprisingly, our bodies are also about 70 percent water, and thus we are liquid beings, flowing through the world seeking rhythm; blood rolls through every limb, propelled by the constant thump and engine of our heart. From the way we close the door to the pace of our breath; from the movement of our eye as it follows the wind rippling the shutter to the way we style our hair or shave our face; from the way we walk to the voice we affect, then take on and perfect; even the way our fingers flutter the pages of this book—all speak to our sense of personal rhythm and style, the basic building blocks of the poet's most cherished possession: his voice.

Water is pure in a river because it is always moving. When water or energy becomes stagnant, it dies. Therefore, water and energy constantly seek to circulate. A poem and its rhythms are an energy-driven turbine of vibrations. The body is made of water, propelled by rhythm, in constant perfect circulation, flowing through the world. Homeopathy is based on the idea that water has the ability to copy and memorize information, since the greater the dilution, the greater effectiveness in flushing out the toxin; therefore, water knows the poison's characteristics and overwhelms it in direct proportion to the density of the pollutant. Water circulates around the globe, carrying vibrations and seeking perfect rhythmic harmony. "The Buddhists," says Dr. Masaru Emoto, a doctor of alternative medicine who has conducted numerous experiments regarding water's response to sound, "believe that the human being is born with 108 earthly desires (such as confusion, attachment, jealousy, and vanity), which torture us throughout our lives. I think it is logical to conclude that these 108 earthly desires have counterparts in the 108 elements contained in the human body." It therefore seems reasonable to think that certain emotions would vibrate toward equivalent elements—irritation, anger, or sorrow might be caused by the presence of mercury, lead, or aluminum. Uncertainty, despair, and stress could be related to levels of cadmium, copper, and zinc. It is fascinating to me to think that water crystals change shape based on the musical vibrations they are exposed to. Melodic, complex, classical music almost always created beautiful, balanced water crystals in Dr. Emoto's experiments. The more frenzied vibrations showed dissonant, unrelated crystal structures that corresponded to the tempos of the hardcore rock music or rhythms that were chaotic in nature.

A poem is a musical structure and will enter the reader's body; its construction will dictate how long it stays there. William Pitt Root is a poet and teacher whose work has shown a beautiful kinship and consideration of the vibrations in nature, and I first heard him speak about the remarkable breeding habits of humpback whales. We know that they sing the longest and most complex of all animal songs, a baffling medley of moans, groans, roars, snores, squeaks, beeps, and whistles. Most singing takes place at the breeding grounds, where another extraordinary thing occurs. Two males chase a female through miles of sea and one begins to imitate every movement and sound she makes until he begins to completely replicate her, parallel her swimming patterns, achieving a shadowlike congruency that makes him vanish. He continues alongside, invisible and silent except as an echo, moving in harmony with her and inhabiting the same vibratory space. The second male then swims under her, holding her aloft and out of the water, as she is a mammal and must breathe periodically. Thus the primary male, who has mimicked her to perfection, slips inside her almost imperceptibly and they consummate the act, becoming one being. As makers of poems, could we but create structures that enter our readers, quiet and perfectly poised in our rhythm and construct, and dwell there.

THE PRIMACY OF THE READER

Memorable poems—with their romantic readiness, the ones we can most readily recite—are shot through with a sense of music, a rhythm that insinuates into the reader's physical body and resonates. Pablo Neruda said, "In the house of poetry, nothing is permanent except that which has been written in blood to be heard by blood."

One of the most fascinating things about the living line, the ability of the poem to cohere regardless of what the poet takes away, is watching two stanzas move toward one another as a middle one is omitted. The space where the stanza existed before is still there, but it is now invisible, at the service of the poem's new flow. If you take at face value that a poem is a living thing born whole cloth from the imagination, then its assimilation into the reader's body makes the poem's history alive, and it becomes true. Most of our thoughts of poetry are made of memories or a worldview filled with snapshots that string out along the clothesline of our consciousness; but memories deceive, and poetry, like all living things, must change as memories do in order to survive.

Poetry is language with a shape. It communicates by giving, and yet, as it elicits answering energies from the reader, more energy is poured back into a poem by its various readers than the energy taken to create it in the first place. In fact, the reader may not know the difference between a villanelle or an ode, but she can come to know more about a poem than the poet does and to experience it more fully. In order to set the poem free, the reader must hear it as well as feel it, more than merely understand the words. Understanding what a line means in literal terms may actually limit the experience for the reader. As a poet develops, his textures change. As a reader develops, his world changes, and consequently so does his relationship to the poem as it is suspended in the world.

A poet's first need, said Seamus Heaney, "is to make works that seem all his own work," or to find his voice, the one he alone can sing with and through. The poet's second need is harder, though, because he has to go be-

The Rhythm Method, Razzmatazz, and Memory

yond himself and take on "the otherness of the world in works that remain his own, yet offer right-of-way to everybody else." In other words, we can never believe that anything we write is sacred and is not subject to change. Robert Lowell continued to re-write his poems until his death. Paul Valéry believed that the poem is never finished, but abandoned, the poet having poured all he knows into it and seeing no other possibilities, releases it into the world. Thus, there are no famous writers, only famous re-writers who become professional or published or famous by their force of will upon the words, unwilling to settle for the first thought or effort and committed to the lifelong process of honing and sharpening their tools. In this respect, the poet can never settle for easy or quick satisfaction. The idea of gratification comes from the surrender to the process, the internal drive to make sentences so tight that "a mosquito couldn't squeak through" (to borrow a phrase from John Berryman), to make poems where the artifice of labor disappears and the seams dissolve. The search, not the arrival, is the thing. "Poetry is right," Jack Spicer said, "even when the poet is wrong."

CHAPTER

Honoring the Condensary

C ondensation is the final frontier for the poet, after the pulses of the syllables, the break of the lines, the word choices and punctuation and stanza order; what we take away is as important as what we leave. "All art," said Pablo Picasso, "is the elimination of the unnecessary." Just as a foggy or repetitive tone can become an emulsion, or a caul over the head of the poem, the beats and arpeggios of breath inside the poem rescue it from monotony by their variance. So too can the negative space be used just as forcefully. The singer Shirley Horn used silence in her singing style to create a sound with astounding drama and weight. "I want the listener with me," she said, "to feel what I feel, to be touched by the lyric, to be beside me, then inside me." Songs are lucky when certain singers choose them. Horn's voice isn't full of fireworks, but she controls the mic with breath and nuance, whispers and nimble caresses, allowing the lyric to embody the silences between chords and, using the stillness like Miles Davis did, giving the negative space such life and prominence that the quiet continues to grow and shimmer by contrast, making the places where no notes exist as heavy as the active intervals.

Ballads were originally designed to make audiences dance, and players gave the chords a bounce, keeping the tempo lively to keep the hips in line, even if the song was being played at half speed. But Shirley Horn put the molasses in *sssssllllllooooooowwww*, eschewing vibrato and transitional sounds. She wanted to induce the forces of the world, to have gravity pause and catch the willing listener in a trance. Even now, I can feel Horn hush-ing the band, stirring the silence like a drummer, the almost imperceptible scrape of cymbals and velvet lushness of the brushes on the snare's taut skin. "The poet is the priest of the invisible," said Wallace Stevens. The poet sings inside the form he chooses, attempting the impossible by embracing the things unseen.

EVERY WORD, EVERY BREATH

If you think of each word as a note, then language is like an enormous piano, and wherever it is, the poet has a medium, just as the painter has his variety of colors and the sculptor the physical presence of wood or stone. On the poet's keyboard, each note or word is also a breath inside the reader and refers to or stands for something that is not physically present and that is not itself. Nouns seem to carry the most weight and space because we can see, smell, touch, and feel the deer, the tree, the water. They can also be taken anywhere and merged with anything. The tree beneath the water, the water leaping like a deer, the wind stalled in the tree. Words represent and are weightless; the material world they represent is bulky, unmovable. As space yields to nouns, time and pace are controlled by verbs and their various tenses and energy, and it is valuable to try and replace those verbs that lack heft or energy. Being small and learning what to take away is one of the hardest things for a young poet to practice. Learning how to leave our ego at the door and get out of the way of the poem's transmission is essential and sometimes arbitrary, I admit. One poet whose lifelong commitment to the condensary yielded some of the most beautiful small poems in American letters was Lorine Niedecker, whose reputation is still in the process of spreading. Listen as her words flit quickly across the page:

> How white the gulls
> in grey weather
>   Soon April
> the little
> yellows

Niedecker's commitment to pare away all but the essence of her poems allows each poem to grow into its own identity and power, letting the color nudge up at the end just like small flowers in the underbrush, or the return

---

of chickadees, their little yellow breasts whipping from branch to branch as the weather warms. Niedecker's needs as a poet are simple, and her boundaries are firm, but there is a bounty in her discipline.

> Remember my little granite pail?
> The handle of it was blue.
> Think what's got away in my life—
> Was enough to carry me thru.

Ezra Pound believed that each line was a minor component of the poem and must be tested for its authority and rightful place. He advocated a line-by-line examination; after the poet is certain that he has accomplished his purpose, he should move to the top of the poem and remove the first line. If the music or meaning of the poem is not altered, then that line has no place and must be deleted. Then the weight of the second line is judged and again, if it does not alter the music or meaning, it has no place. Line by line, the poem is thus trimmed of excess fat so that its essence is distilled.

This removal of dross may take a long time. I've had poems that took a decade to finally be pared down to their strongest representation. One poem, "The Piano Lesson," took twenty-three years before it showed its true face. My method is to take copious notes and build poems from the top down. An eighteen-line poem may have begun as a hundred lines or more, but it is slowly whittled away as the poem reveals its identity. Sometimes several fragments may begin to move toward one another and be judged as family, letting me know that they were the idea I was seeking all along. This way, I track the poem among hundreds of ideas word by word. "Ideas in poetry," said Stéphane Mallarmé, "are what we return to when we leave the music as one returns to the comfort of a wife, leaving the mistress we desire." When the poet accepts that nothing he may first compose is sacred, his surrender will allow the poem's true nature to emerge.

Condensation may be painful, requiring extreme discretion and almost brutal self-examination. We think of our poems as our children and no matter their condition, if they have two heads or four arms or three legs or don't act right, they are our creation and we love them and find it hard to let them go or to be pruned for their own preservation. The audience of the poem will apply its own bias and worldview to the end result, and so the poet's primary responsibility is to communicate, not equivocate or obfuscate or

The Rhythm Method, Razzmatazz, and Memory

imbue the poem with an overdose of ambiguity, obscuring the real meaning. The meaning and the sound may merge, and the best poems remind us of our place in the universe and make manifest the mystery and machinations of the larger system that surrounds us.

OUR TOOLS AND THE TASK AT HAND

Each poet develops his own system and technique. The purpose of this book is to share my tools with other poets, and they may place in their own toolbox whatever tools they find useful and discard the others. We come to poetry for different reasons and may never know if poetry is all we need until it is all we have. John Keats was moved to create poems out of a state of bliss. Vladimir Mayakovsky was moved by clear social need. John Milton began by imitating Virgil before his ambition and Christian faith gave him deeper reasons to create. George Orwell believed that there were always lies that he needed to expose, and so he began there. Frank O'Hara and many others simply thought that poetry afforded them a way to record their life, a vessel in which they might pour all the grievances, transgressions, exultations, and discoveries essential to their existence. Robert Lowell thought this was the difference between "raw" and "cooked" poetry. He was accepting the National Book Award in 1960 when he gave a speech delineating the difference between what he believed to be over-elaborate method, such as Richard Wilbur or A. E. Housman or Dylan Thomas, and the need for confessional reflection, culminating in the personal unraveling of the Beats or the torrid emotional states of Sylvia Plath, John Berryman, Anne Sexton, W. D. Snodgrass, and a host of others. The former are engaged with negotiations of the various states of desire in illuminated, controlled moments; the latter are immersed suddenly in chaotic revelations upon which they seem to career out of control, allowing indecision and fragmentary language to enter the poem.

Compare Dylan Thomas's deliberate movement to Plath's herky jerky, emotional roller coaster in the samples below. Listen to the sureness of Thomas's words marching through the final stanza hand in hand with one of his favorite themes, death, in this justifiably famous poem from 1936, "And Death Shall Have No Dominion." Here is the last stanza:

Where blew a flower may a flower no more
Lift its head to blows of the rain;
Though they be mad and dead as nails,
Heads of the characters hammer through daisies;

Break in the sun till the sun breaks down,
And death shall have no dominion.

Now witness the frenzied nature of Plath's long striptease for death in lines 28–36 of her poem, "Fever 103°":

Darling, all night
I have been flickering, off, on, off, on.
The sheets grow heavy as a lecher's kiss.
Three days. Three nights.
Lemon water, chicken
Water, water make me retch.
I am too pure for you or anyone.
Your body
Hurts me as the world hurts God. I am a lantern—

See how Plath's personal references and sexual undertow are weaved together to create tension, mostly negative, casting her husband in the role of a benign cuckold? She is not casting about for another lover but is open to the experience of her own longing. She makes the language deliberately violent, convincing herself that the suffering is worth it and will eventually free her from her self-destructive habits and, possibly, the need for a man at all. The syncopated two-beat words and phrases stab out at the reader in a violent manner. *Dar-ling, all night, off on, off on, The sheets, hea-vy, Three days, Three nights, le-mon, wat-er, chick-en, wat-er, I am, too pure, for you, bo-dy, Hurts me, I am, lant-ern.* The confessional poets eventually won out, the emotional heights of their language matched the intensity of the nation's events in the late 1950s and '60s, creating a poetry that became public property. In its wake, the audience was wedded to the poets, feeling a kinship with their struggle and an intimacy that was probably artificial (however deeply felt), making the tragic nature of these poets into myths that threatened to circumvent the attention to their poetry.

CHAPTER 2

The Poem as Momentum: Building the Flow

One way to ramp up the creative juices, or one technique that works for me, is the simple act of reading aloud a poem by a poet whose work I admire and picking out the points where the sound of the consonants is most closely aligned. Here are lines 6–23 of Thomas Lux's poem "There Were Some Summers":

So calm the slow sweat existing
in half-fictive memory: a boy
wandering from house, to hayloft, to coop,
past a dump where a saddle rots
on a sawhorse, through the still forest
of a cornfield, to a pasture talking to himself
or the bored, baleful Holsteins nodding
beneath the round shade of catalpa, the boy
walking his trail towards the brook
in a deep but mediocre gully,
through skunk cabbage and pop-weed,
down sandbanks (a descending
quarter acre Sahara), the boy wandering,
thinking nothing, thinking:
Sweatbox, sweatbox, the boy
moving towards a minnow whose slight beard
tells the subtleties of the current, holding there,
in water cold enough to break your ankles.

I could have been that boy wandering through a neighbor's farm down to the magic, isolated, slow-moving, and shaded stretch of creek where you caught minnows and crayfish. Notice the soft s sounds in the first five lines—*so, slow, sweat, existing, house, past, saddle rots, sawhorse*—and then the b's—*bored, baleful, beneath, boy, brook, cabbage*—the repetition of *boy*, which echoes through the poem, never losing sight of his central place in the narrative even as Lux surrounds him with a revolving landscape of motion and imagery. It is a slow and lazy rhythm, slow like summer walks with nothing on your mind but discovery, and then comes the cold shock of the icy creek water at the end. Sound loves proximity, and pushing any of these like sounds too far apart from one another will dull them, too close together and you have a staccato effect that will kill the lilt of the lines. Balance the two-beat words and the poem takes a pulse that quickens closer to the water: *cabbage, pop-weed, sandbanks, quarter acre, thinking nothing, thinking, sweatbox, sweatbox, moving, minnow.* This subtle piling up of beats pushes the momentum of the poem toward its conclusion, and the poet makes no value judgments about the boy's intentions, letting the subjects find the boy and vice versa, with an emphasis on the precision of the tone that takes the poem over.

I will sometimes use a metronome as a base for jumping into the rhythm of writing, or I will take a sheet of paper and write down as many words as I can think of that start with the letter A, then the letter B, then C, and so on. This bunching of words with like sounds will usually lead to sentences seeking a balance between the consonants, but if I begin to write sentences, then I've accomplished my aim to trigger a rhythm in my body that my mind can follow.

THE ONE

I want to discuss now the concept of the One, the initial beat or downbeat in the timing of a poem or song. I've always been a singer—the front man, given the responsibility to talk to the audience and direct the band. It would be easy to feel as if I were in charge, but that would be a false assumption, because the true director of any ensemble is the drummer—the timekeeper, the guardian of the One. The One is the first beat and the last, and all the beats between. It is the pulse of the poem. Every syllable can count as a beat. Music is the universal language because it is mathematical. One means one

The Rhythm Method, Razzmatazz, and Memory

in every language, two means two, and so on. Rhythm is encoded in our molecular structure and constantly seeks other rhythms that the body may respond to. This exchange of energy creates the inner life of the poem.

After the outpouring of emotion, when the tempest of inspiration is spent, the real work begins: knowing how many beats there are in your lines, how many lines should form the poem into stanzas. Where the line breaks or ceasuras must occur in the lines are indications of breath and manner, for sure, but more importantly, they signal that the poet is in control of his lines, that they have a particular intention. A poem should be a long piece of angular hungry momentum, a flow with authority, admitting no impediments. It is important to acknowledge inspiration's worth here; we have to let our emotions have free reign at the outset, just as there are necessary obstacles that enable one to pause and make changes, to alter and improve the words. To deny the existence or the worth of the obstacle, or to give it too much importance, is to empower it or make it sacred. Most writing impediments are either technical problems obstructing the poem's flow or psychological problems blocking the writer from his recognition of the true impulse. Not the first impulse, mind you; *first thought, best thought* is a worthless conceit. The best thought may not be the first one available. And a lazy writer is as apparent as a desperate salesman; neither one can close the deal.

It's really the same process for a singer. Some singers have a more lovely tone than others, but a singer has to sell the song, make the listener feel its authenticity. Regardless of the magnificence of the singer's instrument, if the song doesn't arise out of his core being, we will not believe him. Tom Petty is not the most brilliant singer in the world, but he is always convincing, giving the listener the sense that he is participating in the act of creation, inhabiting the narrative of the song as it uncurls inside the rapt, listening body. All fine singers know how to sing behind the beat, laying the melody just behind the initial attack of the One. The listener, who is counting the One whether he knows it or not, tapping his toe or drumming his fingers or nodding his head, is bloated with expectancy after each strike of the One as if he were following a clock buried deep in his head. That mournful interval between the attack of the snare and the moan of the singer is where the soul resides, in the space between beats, elongating the listener's expectation, then meeting it.

This is the same way a verse operates with a chorus. The verse is full of information, and then the chorus becomes the hook that draws the listener in by its repetition. The listener is given information, then satisfied by the assurance of the chorus, the repeated hook. Every songwriter I know keeps a notebook filled with pithy or memorable comments that were overheard and can be condensed into a single phrase or a hook to base a chorus upon. That is the starting place for a black sound, the intervals between the universal truth of the hook and the moments of contemplative information gathering. Between the attack and satisfaction is the convincing *duende* of Federico Garcia Lorca, where soul music gets its affecting, memorable platform inside its listeners, reminding them of their human condition with a cry that is the basis for the blues.

> Ernest Hemingway said, "There is no going backward in pleasure." A poem's flow has to continue unabated.

Poetry, like jazz, is a sophisticated display of energy and expertise, admired by a small percentage of the culture and understood fully by far less. It is practiced and maintained by a select group of committed indispensables. When I told an editor friend of mine that fewer than 1,500 poets in America actually made money from their work in 2005, his voice was incredulous, tinged with awe, as he asked, "That many?" Poetry, unlike jazz, however, is something everyone believes they can do. The golden age of American songwriting occurred between 1920 and 1960, when most of the pop standards were composed for movies and the stage. A standard is a "chestnut," able to stand the test of time and be somewhat malleable with soaring melodies, interesting chord changes, and lyrics that appeal to every year and every ear. The golden age of song—however great the Hoagy Carmichael or Ellington-Strayhorn compositions were—would not have been possible without jazz. The interpretation of Cole Porter and others could only be accomplished by musicians of a certain sophistication and discernment, who saw the possibilities that the song structures presented. Just as much as the achievement of the initial song structures were appreciated and mastered by each successive group of players and singers, so too was the reflected experience magnified as each musician added his or her style to it and poured it out, conversely lengthening the shadow of the classics.

The Rhythm Method, Razzmatazz, and Memory

Music and poetry began to truly intermingle in the 1940s and '50s when jazz musicians like Charlie Parker, Dizzy Gillespie, and Thelonius Monk began to hang with the poets and painters of the period. Several poets wrote pieces that were destined to be set to jazz accompaniment. Jack Kerouac's characters from *On The Road* were constantly talking about one musician or another, Sonny Rollins or Chet Baker or John Coltrane. Kerouac prefaced his book of poetry *Mexico City Blues* with the note, "I want to be considered a jazz poet, blowing a long blues in an afternoon jam session on Sunday…" Allen Ginsberg's famous *Howl* performance was one long riff punctuated by Kerouac screaming from the audience, "Go, man, go!" The great jazz tenor Jimmy Scott—who influenced Nancy Wilson, Billie Holiday, and Marvin Gaye—said, "I try to deal with songs that bring forth thoughts about life, thoughts that we live with every day. There are love stories, hate stories, the gamut, but to me the lyric must mean something; just singing a lyric where the words just go along with the melody, that doesn't interest me. The lyric has to be telling a story."

The primary difference between a poem and a song is the restrictions of the melody on the lyric. In a song, one must stick strictly to the beat and craft the shorter lines accordingly, respecting the restraint of the groove and the melody line. In a poem, one must create the music by the sonic arrangement of the words themselves, varying the beat, stresses, and line breaks to reflect the poem's purpose. In a song, the notes and their application to the melody restrict the freedom of the lyricist but free the players and the singer, depending upon their interpretation. We'll explore these possibilities more fully in Part III, when we chart the course poets and musicians have taken together across the arc of the twentieth century.

Marina Tsvetaeva wrote that "the condition of creation is a condition of being overcome by a spell. Until you begin, it is a state of being obsessed; until you finish, a state of being possessed. Something, someone lodges in you … that which through you wants to be." Rhythm is what "lodges" in a poet, for language and rhythm cannot be separated, just as the same word in voodoo means drum and dance simultaneously. The proximity of music and language extends its understanding even when the symbols seem to change. Take, for example, the United Nations: Many of the interpreters either sing part time or have a background as musicians, which aids them, as they immediately must recognize not only the meaning and nuance of sentences but also the rhythm and vibration of the speech pattern itself. One mistake for these keen listeners is critical, just as an entire musical composition may fall apart if a single wrong note is played. Every poem is filled with an endless amount of decisions. One of my favorite things is to find a writer thinking inside the poem for a moment as he suspends time and then roars forward. The ancient Greeks used to build gazebo-like structures, usually reserved to speak to Apollo, but more to the point, to meditate or pray inside. These were usually constructed at crossroads or forks in the road so that the weary traveler could pause inside and consider which direction he should take. We have many forks in the road when writing, but decisions should be made that propel the force of the music or narrative. Ernest Hemingway said, "There is no going backward in pleasure." A poem's flow has to continue unabated.

The Rhythm Method, Razzmatazz, and Memory

CHAPTER 3

Being Called to the Tribe

For the beginning poet, there is always the moment he can recall when the words began to come out of him, the moment he knew that something unusual and unexpected was taking place inside his thought process—and a compulsion was formed requiring him to take notes and listen to the way words fit themselves together. This is how poetry begins: out of nothingness, out of darkness and silence as right and mysterious as the Great Master who some say is responsible for the voices that reside in poets' heads and tell them: Write it down; say it aloud; give it wings. I was the skeptical child in Sunday school, unable to cast aside logic for the lessons of Genesis. "But who made God?" I asked. "Where did Cain's wife come from?" "Were the dinosaurs in Eden?" How could the progenitor of such creative designs be such a poor editor of his book? Nevermind that it's the biggest selling tome of all time. I needed answers. Being called to be a poet for me was not unlike the altar call of my childhood; both required a belief in things unseen, a witness for the invisible, and a willingness to surrender to a life of the mind, to the unrolling requests of the creative intuition. One of my first poems, written about twenty-five years ago, is called "The Book of Deliverance," which appeared in my second book, *The Book of Monsters*:

> Afflicted with a Zen rhetoric,
> men die in the privacy of their rooms,
> not from a lack of love received,
> but from an inability to return it.
> Death leaves tributes where it can,

---

swimming in the center

of the woods at night,

tirelessly holding up the sky.

Below our nature, a hundred laughing natures lie,

patiently aging in the kingdom of instinct,

waiting for a sudden seizure of conscience,

as God turns in his hiding place,

silently stewing,

like smoke trapped brooding in a glass.

The property of the mind is frail,

filled with wreckage and unmarked trails,

more vows than we can ever remember.

The first page in the book

of deliverance reads **surrender**.

Learning to listen, learning to surrender, learning how to get out of the way of the poem as it manifests itself in the creative process—these tenets would lead the young creator to believe that writing poems was investigative work, tracking the sequence of meaning as the music of the words reveals itself. The only other spiritual presence I had experienced was religious in nature; therefore, the presence of poetry coursing through me was difficult to decipher in purely evidentiary ways. I began to feel that explanations actually derailed the train of thought; to ask for requisite meaning was the same as asking God to reveal himself, to give me the cosmic striptease. I had "no more worth than the birds," as Thomas Merton said, and deserved no more than my allotment of grace, or poetry, which, when properly accomplished, feels akin to grace. The tracings of frost, the architecture of webs, the multitude of miniature lives and purposes that lived within and without me led me to feel the hidden connections between beings, animate and inanimate, many hidden in plain sight. Poetry, I thought, was the language of these hidden things in commerce with one another. "Starfish" was an early poem of mine, written in college under the influence of Rainer Maria Rilke and Pierre Reverdy:

Furry
mounted by light

a myriad desert silence
is carried by your little jets

You are the nucleus of prayer
drifting like faith

layer upon layer
toward a God you cannot see

A prop twirling in the blue heaven
pulls your delicate hand

waving slowly adieu

You are a flower
circling in the foamy orchard

In the calm expanse
you tinkle like a shy comet

you sigh
inside
the reef

All the rage and confusion and violence inside me was appeased when the voices came in clusters and language crystallized on a page, evidence of apostasy, a range of knowing corralled into code, and a longing for membership in the brotherhood of poets who also heard voices stretching back hand-in-hand to the beginning of time—witnesses taking down the history of the tribe, poetry cleaning the dust of the everyday from their spirit. Suddenly, the songs made sense, the imperiled, unheralded, and hidden music rose out of the murk and revealed a vast architecture of sound. Suddenly, that protein molecule in its ninth configuration had a divine spark and life kindled from it, like the beginnings of rhythm in the newborn finding voice to tell the story that is already within him. I was born—naked, naive, and nineteen years old—and all my life, I swore, would be devoted to poetry.

This is how poetry arrives for many young students, a gush overwhelming the uninitiated, an outpouring of their deepest feelings, the collapse of held secrets, the blown-open vault. Poetry, when it announces itself, is inextricably tied to overweening emotional states, the abundance of feeling. Perhaps this is why poets have a higher suicide rate than any other artist; these tsunamis of empathy that struggle forth from the psyche can bring about great extremes of mental turbulence—the addictive, roller coaster ride of language and ideas blossoming, and then the raw thud of nothing to say, no sense to be made of your surroundings, an emptiness. And there is always the pressure to condense, condense, condense, making yourself amenable to the process of taking words away, straining the gold specks and silt out of a vast river of mud and clay and waste. The discipline required to patiently edit and pare away the dross is where the continental divide between mediocrity and meticulous accomplishment is clearly rooted, I believe. This is part of the calling.

I wrote my first poems when I was eight years old. In retrospect, it now makes sense to me that this was also the year of my "spiritual" awakening and baptism. I was already a news junkie and had spent the previous day glued to the TV, upset by the imagery and special reports being beamed from the other side of the world in Vietnam. It was 1970, and Nixon had begun the systematic prosecution of the bombing campaign in Cambodia. As a boy with a deepening artistic sensibility, my instinct said to protest with the only tools available to me—the force of words. I went up on the hillside at the edge of a stand of young poplars and spent two straight days making poems in opposition to the war. I do not remember them, but I cannot forget the overwhelming need to write my feelings down in order to make sense of the chaos and to establish and record my thoughts on this pageant of mutual destruction.

What struck me most was my mother's reaction when I showed her the poems. She wrapped them carefully in wax paper to preserve them and placed them in her cedar hope chest. Thus, she legitimized my creative impulse, lending worth to my imagination and giving me the sense that what I wrote was valuable, and that poetry, built out of sincere conviction, was prized by others and would capture their attention. It was, as it turned out, exactly the right response. I didn't begin to compose poems again until I was a freshman in college and took a creative writing course from a woman named Margaret Verhulst, whose immediate and enthusiastic encouragement of my efforts changed the course of my life. I would not finish my basketball scholarship and go on to law school; my compass point was fixed. I was a poet.

For better or worse, I'd spend every day in service to my ideal of what a poet should be and do. I was flooded with projects and possibilities, intoxicated by the ideas in "The Love Song of J. Alfred Prufrock," the power and sound of Milton's Samson, Robert Browning's first-person monologues, William Blake's visionary reshaping of the world. I will never forget the concussive effect of Blake's "Proverbs Of Hell": "In seed-time learn, in harvest teach, in winter enjoy. Drive your cart and your plough over the bones of the dead. The road of excess leads to the palace of wisdom. Prudence is a rich ugly old maid courted by incapacity. He who desires, but acts not, breeds pestilence. The cut worm forgives the plough. Prisons are built with stones of law, brothels with bricks of religion. Sooner murder an infant in its cradle than nurse unacted desires. Exuberance is beauty. Energy is eternal delight." Already in love with books, I was seduced all over again by the sound of well-made sentences, the buzz, hum, and resonance of words. I was learning to speak an entirely new language and was enthralled by the perfection of it.

AT THE MERCY OF WORDS

We are what we read. This is never more true than when we begin to forge a course as a writer. The books that lodge in your development never leave you. Like rungs in a ladder, each book marks a step forward and upward in the possibilities for your own work, another piece of the world's puzzle snapped into place.

Rainer Maria Rilke's *Duino Elegies*; Arthur Rimbaud's *Illuminations*; Henry Miller's *Colossus at Maroussi*; Jean Genet's *Lady of Our Flowers*; Galway Kinnell's *The Book of Nightmares*; Anne Sexton's *Transformations*; Delmore Schwartz's *In Dreams Begin Responsibilities*; Lawrence Ferlinghetti's *Coney Island of the Mind*; Ralph Waldo Emerson; Charles Dickens; Robert Browning's dramatic monologues; Jorges Luis Borges's *Dreamtigers*; T. S. Eliot's *Four Quartets*; D. H. Lawrence's *Sons and Lovers*; Gerard Manley Hopkins's *Notebooks*; Carl Sandburg's *Chicago Poems*; E. E. Cummings; the Cranes (not Ichabod, but Stephen and Hart); Langston Hughes; Emily Dickinson; Walt Whitman; Dylan Thomas; Josephine Miles; Charles Olson's *Maximus;* Robert Creeley's Minimus; Joseph Conrad's *Heart of Darkness*; John Berryman's *Dream Songs*; Larry Levis's *Winter Stars*;

Gwendolyn Brooks's *Sadie and Maud*; James Dickey's *Buckdancers*; Pablo Neruda's *Odes*; Theodore Roethke's *Far Field* (which I first stole from a college library by throwing it out the window and retrieving it, because I could not bear to be apart from it); the Wrights (Richard, James, and Charles—triple-threat brothers from another mother); John Keats; Colette; Jean-Paul Sartre; Jean Cocteau; Charles Baudelaire; Percy Shelley; Edna St. Vincent Millay; Maximilien Robespierre; Honoré de Balzac; Emile Zola; John Dos Passos; Umberto Eco; John Ruskin; Samuel Taylor Coleridge; Edgar Allan Poe; Thomas Pynchon; William Butler Yeats; William Stafford's *Stories That Could Be True*; Gary Snyder's *Myths & Texts*; Augustine's *Confessions*; Pierre Reverdy; Paul Verlaine; Yvgeny Yevtushenko; Marcel Proust's *Remembrance*; Michael Ondaatje's *Billy the Kid*; the Morrisons (Jim and Toni); Norman Mailer; Louis-Ferdinand Céline; Blaise Cendrars; Vladimir Mayakovsky; Truman Capote; John Steinbeck; and thousands of others are cast members in the movie of poetry that my mind could make. We are always students. As Dylan said (Bob, that is), "He not busy being born is busy dying."

The reason the poems of Dr. Seuss will live for a thousand years in the mouths of schoolchildren is because many times these are the first poems that young children are exposed to. Sound over sense, they say—with some of his books containing no more than a hundred words, finely tuned, endlessly arranged for greatest sonic effect. Our first memories are crowded around words, songs, prayers, and pledges of allegiance. We learn from the earliest years to love the feel of words in our mouth, to mimic the cow's moo, the bird's tweet and whistle, the dog's bark, driving our little red wagons around, growling like car engines. Dylan Thomas, in answer to why and how he began to write poetry, gives a response familiar to most poets in their early stages:

> The first poems I knew were nursery rhymes, and before I learned I could read them for myself I had come to love just the words of them, the words alone. What the words stood for, symbolized, or meant was of very secondary importance; what mattered was the sound of them as I heard them for the first time on the lips of the remote and incomprehensible grown-ups who seemed, for some reason, to be living in my world. And these words were, to me, as the notes of bells, the sounds of musical instruments, the noises of wind, sea, and rain, the rattle of milk carts, the clopping of hooves

on cobbles, the fingering of branches on a windowpane ... I did not care what the words said, overmuch, nor what happened to Jack and Jill and the Mother Goose rest of them; I cared for the sound that their names, and the words describing their actions, made in my ears ... I fell in love—that is the only expression I can think of—at once, and I am still at the mercy of words ...

The disdain for poetry is an unnatural act, helped along at the secondary school level by a curriculum that force-feeds the students Shakespeare and Milton and Dryden and Donne before their little gullets are fully formed enough to digest Mother Goose. It is important to find the poems that speak to the worldview of the student, appropriate to his or her cultural maturity. Poems are everywhere, in every style and language, seeking the readers for whom the poems were born in the first place, whose need for the poem is invisible and unrelenting until the connection is made, and the unknown expectations are satisfied.

CHAPTER 4

The Anxiety of Influence: Borrowing the Mask of the Master

Surrendering to the will of the work and learning to listen require a capacity for extreme patience and discipline. But, in the beginning, it is typical to imitate the writers we admire. Wallace Stevens and William Carlos Williams shunned T. S. Eliot for fear of imitating his unique tone. Eliot himself said, "Bad writers imitate, great writers steal." Imitation is part of the process, but the truly great writers make what they find their own. They seize upon ideas and unsnarl them, pulling out the golden threads for their own spool. Objectivity shifts depending on the purpose of the work at hand, and the same idea through separate filters can be made new. All poets borrow and fret about the weight of their predecessors upon the poems they create. Richard Hugo worried about the influence of his great teacher, Theodore Roethke, but later Hugo wrote, "Every poem a poet writes is a slight advance of self and a slight modification of the mask, the one you want to be. Poem after poem, the self grows more worthy of the mask, the mask comes closer to fitting the face. After enough poems, you are nearly the one you want to be, and the one you want to be closely resembles you."

William Butler Yeats believed that poems serve as masks through which the submerged self might escape. "Given a mask," said John Ruskin, "we will speak the truth." To borrow the mask of a master is to sing freely with a legitimized and accepted vehicle, a posture bearing no real risk. Yeats, through his various masks, tried to show as many sides of himself as he could, and through his investigations into the supernatural, he hoped to find other sides he did not know existed. To create poems is to reveal one's

The Rhythm Method, Razzmatazz, and Memory

self completely, especially if the task is undertaken for the long haul. But poems are art, not confession, and to read too much biography or persona into a poem is to smother it. If all we have to fear from the poet is the truth, then he might as well be a juror or a clerk—both noble undertakings, but they are not conduits to greater understanding. A lie in art is just as interesting as the truth; naked eyes that reflect the majesty of the Sierras in the cornea's tiny mirrors are still a pair of eyes reflecting something greater (or larger) than themselves. There are no mountains in there. But if I write that those mountains are everywhere, within and without, and that I carry those mountains inside me always, you will believe it. When a poem speaks its truth to you, it feels like a sunken shipwreck that continues to send its radio signals from the deep. You will find yourself constantly going back to it, attracted and obsessed by its mystery and music.

Robert Browning was twenty-six years old when he wrote the interminable six thousand line poem *Sordello*. Alfred Lord Tennyson said there were only two lines in the whole poem that he could follow—the first and the last. The first was "Who will, may hear Sordello's story told." The last was "Who would, has heard Sordello's story told." Both lines, said Tennyson, were lies. Discouraged though he was, Browning did not cease writing and even insisted writing for the stage. Several of his plays were produced but garnered little praise. It was during his study of Shakespeare and the master's dramatic monologues that Browning began to develop his ideas about personality and the angle of the poem and began to experiment with first-person narratives. Reaching back to the master led Browning to his greatest achievements as a poet. The dramatic monologues—"My Last Duchess," "In a Gondola," "Soliloquy of the Spanish Cloister," "The Pied Piper of Hamelin," "How They Brought the Good News from Ghent to Aix," "Incident of the French Camp," "The Glove," "Fra Lippo Lippi," and several others—made Browning one of the nineteenth century's most successful poets and secured his place in the literary canon.

Great writing always reserves the right to mix its myths with its reality and to take responsibility for neither. The poet is constantly threatened by, and in constant flight from, his own superficiality. A persona becomes insupportable the minute the puppeteer understands the lie upon which his power is based. His control is supported by those most in need of his illusion. Without some form of illusion or grandeur, the writer will hang himself upon the strings with which he sought to control his subjects. "Sumjects and omjects," Samuel Coleridge would say, his lips slurry from laudanum. Objectivity and the power of persona requires distance and time and the response of an audience, even an audience of one. The most valuable ally to the poet is a reader who will tell him the truth, warts and all. Most times, a mentor will serve in that capacity, but not always. The powerful attraction that masters exert upon their students comes from the recognition and acceptance of a unique sound. And sound in a poem can be replicated without using the same word choices or ideas. Poetry therefore layers itself by borrowing from what came before and by seeing that each new layer is repaid with a better life and fresher context. W. H. Auden himself was a magpie and extended his poetry into the future through his readings of Wilfred Owen, Gerard Hopkins, Laura Riding, Robert Graves, and Yeats. Where would Robert Creeley be without Dr. Williams and Charles Olson? Where would Mark Strand be without W. S. Merwin? Dylan Thomas without Yeats?

> *Great writing always reserves the right to mix its myths with its reality and to take responsibility for neither.*

Sonny Stitt, a virtuoso sax player, was constantly minimized by critics for his close readings of the solos by Charlie Parker. But Stitt was trying to extend the vocabulary of the solo, and Parker was the means to that end, the best medium that Stitt could find. The poet's ultimate loyalty is to the poem, and the poet can only find himself by reading everything he can. We must *aspire*. Whether we will become a Homer or Shakespeare or Keats is another matter, for others to decide. But whether we find our place in the long river of literature that came before us can only be possible by knowing *what* came before and familiarizing ourselves with the history of poetry. The very fact that we are supported by a tradition or mentor enables us to more fully be ourselves, or more than ourselves, by extending the tradition through innovation. This muscle memory that evolves out of repetition takes great courage and time; the pursuit of excellence in literature is not a sprint, it is a marathon, and the race goes not to the swift, but to the diligent. We must go back in order to go forward, and as Donald Revell wrote in *Arcady*, "A poem is a toy car, I pull it backward, it goes forward twice as far."

A contract with poetry inevitably involves listening in a deeper manner than we believed possible. We listen, we interpret or misinterpret, no matter, for the capacity to hear into the intentions and strategies of our for-bears will add fragment upon fragment to the textures of our own creative landscape, the ability to pull out of previous experiments our own mystical sense of the poem. Eventually, the acolyte settles into his own instinctual and original technique. "Only a poet of experience," said Robert Graves, "can hope to put himself in the shoes of his predecessors, or contemporaries, and judge their poems by re-creating technical and emotional dilemmas which they faced while at work on them." Graves recommended copying out the texts of poems by hand, to discover where the strengths and weaknesses are located. "Analeptic mimesis," he called it. Visitors who spent time with Dylan Thomas remarked on the piles of poems, copied in his own careful handwriting, he carried with him—works from Thomas Hardy, John Crowe Ransom, A. E. Housman, John Davies, Edward Thomas, Yeats, and others who had been placed under the microscope and carefully dissected. Dylan felt he could never get inside the skin of a poem, to get at its guts, until he had done this. And loyalty for him was to the poem, not the poet, for indeed, each poem has its own individual life and must be accepted as a separate offering, regardless of where the poem might fit in its author's ideology.

CHAPTER

Chance Favors the Prepared Mind

5

As Stanley Kunitz has said, "the page is a cold bed," and poetry has to live in the air, or not at all. Reading your favorite poems aloud will uncover whether they creak or fly. In my office, in the middle of my desk, is an ancient cassette recorder. As I compose a poem, I recite it aloud into the recorder, over and over, and listen to the recording for fault lines in the sonic structure of the piece. I walk round and round that old table, circling the poem like a vulture, ready to pounce on and eradicate any dead parts of the poem that do not lift. It is a painstaking, never-ending process, and the faded track of my worn carpet shines like a deer trail in my office, a path I climb onto and silently follow, listening to the voice in the recorder that lilts back and no longer belongs to me. "Sound brings us to our senses," said Henry David Thoreau, and learning to listen, for a poet, should become a lifelong preoccupation. Sound affects our bodies more than any other of our senses, even when we are asleep and we are dulled in our capacity to taste, smell, touch, or see; our ears are wide open and absorbing the sounds around us.

The capacity for continuous transformation means being an open vessel through which new sounds and ideas may pass. What seem to be the tricks or techniques of today will be the truths and tools of tomorrow. Learning to be wholly yourself requires patience and a dutiful ability to listen and observe. If you're talking half as much, then you're listening doubly, reflecting the attitudes of your time and, more importantly, assimilating the bourbon of the world's words, the colloquial, unguarded communications. Some po-

The Rhythm Method, Razzmatazz, and Memory

ets, like George Oppen or Bob Kaufman, feeling thwarted in their artistic missions, lapsed into long periods of silence. They were not suffering from writer's block but became transparent in their dealings with the world, allowing the world to pour through them, and both re-emerged more vital and vivid than before. For them, the more the universe seemed comprehensible, the more it seemed pointless, and the writer who claims to have no fear of writing in a vacuum is either a fool or a robot.

It has been said that we compose out of a fear of death, to create something that will remain beyond our mortal coil, but death is something we can never grasp or define. History, with its newspapers and testimonies, uses numbers to define death, but death must be the loss of anything remarkable to think about or do. And if so, our culture is permeated with the stink of that. Belief is a form of expectation; without it, roadblocks are everywhere. The poet must believe that the next best work lies ahead, but if asked what's next, must be willing to acknowledge that they have no idea what to expect.

Chance, however, favors the prepared mind, and most young poets lack the store of knowledge that comes from the frequent reading of good poetry and the daily adherence to a writing schedule, regardless of convenience. Convenience is the world's most prevalent addiction, especially in America,

Learning to be wholly yourself requires patience and a dutiful ability to listen and observe.

where dreaming is no cinch, and children are rarely taught to listen without prejudice. There is a contented cynicism that comes with the open and creative mind, a willingness to challenge the pat answers of the status quo. The permanence of poetry has always been the work of a minority, and poetry seeks not immortality in the market place but resurrection. Technology is not an image of the world or its mirror; it is a praxis whose purpose is to change the world or cast it aside. Poetry is our best vision of the world as it exists, and what is good is always rare. The proliferation of writing programs in America has created a huge canopy of competence, and so, many young poets, in a hurry to be published or professional, know the process and begin to go about the business of a career long before they have anything to say or the discipline and patience to work long enough to say it. Lawrence Kasdan has written, "A writer is someone condemned to do homework for the rest of his life." And for most writers, they must perfect their voice while trying to earn a living, giving forty hours a week to the mundane task of making money, because poetry only pays if you teach. And thus the vicious cycle is repeated.

But it is not my purpose here to denigrate the system, or the Poetry Biz, as William Matthews called it; facing the self so large and pervasive is to invite ruin enough for the young maker. The most frightening thing I recall about my conversion to poetry was having to face my father and tell him I wasn't going to law school after all. I was a poet, I said, and about to start a rock band, and I hope you understand.

"The one thing in the world of value, is the active soul," said Ralph Waldo Emerson in "The American Scholar." When we are influenced, we are disturbed, lifted out of the ordinary, and forced to act. Poets, by their very nature in this world, are neglected, and so, faced with neglect and teeming with voices, they write. Let us now examine the phenomenon of the act of poetry from the ground up, because poems are made of words, not ideas, according to Stéphane Mallarmé, and should be constructed with these basic building blocks as a starting point, one careful word at a time.

The Rhythm Method, Razzmatazz, and Memory

CHAPTER 6

The Action Verb and Beautiful Accidents

If a poem is dynamic, its rhythm headlong, then the tiny turbines of this momentum are the verbs. Action verbs muscle up a sentence and help its propulsion. They may also create unexpected astonishment for the reader. When we believe a poem is finished, we should examine every single verb for a more powerful alternative. Rhythm is the *entire* movement of the poem, the recurrence of stress and unstressed syllables as they relate to the pitch and texture of the sentences, one against the next. You can also play against the pattern to create tension, what William Blake called "the bounding line," such as these variations in his poem "A Poison Tree":

> I was angry with my friend:
> I told my wrath, my wrath did end.
> I was angry with my foe:
> I told it not, my wrath did grow.

This is simple but instructive. Watch how lines two and four stop with a comma in the middle and then double the rhythm, making the line leap forward and gather in intensity. Over the course of several stanzas, this momentum would be like a snowball rolling downhill, gaining size and speed as it picks up more and more lines.

Another method to make the sentence more lively is to turn a noun into a verb, and to relax the use of adjectives. Look at the moment of surprise at the end of Stephen Roberts's poem "Sex," when the noun *maple* becomes a verb:

Each love creates
its own final cause.
Crimson, orange,

pink and violet
wisps arch behind
the oak and pine

draped mountain's
distant, unseen slope.
The gray, creaky,

board-warped dock
projects from the reed
rimmed shore into

the spectral lake.
Leaves sink surface
to sediment while

unending, wind
driven waves maple
out into darkness.

You can see the fingers of the waves curling down along the shoreline
like the branches of a tree and receding out against the darker surf. The unexpected word *maple*, turned into a verb, is a moment of quiet surprise that
also provides the sentence's motion. The poem turns into itself and then
follows the motion of the waves as it releases. It only takes a single verb,
cleverly chosen, to set a poem upon, like a balloon balanced on the tip of a
pin. See how Lorine Niedecker makes the cold come alive in this tiny poem,
animating it by her choice of an unexpected verb that is usually thought of
as a noun:

Popcorn-can cover
screwed to the wall
over a hole
so the cold
can't mouse in

The Rhythm Method, Razzmatazz, and Memory

The choice of *mouse* here in the last line almost makes us *see* the cold as it sticks its nose into every crevice of the house, searching for a way in. A mouse is insistent, just like the cold, and that aids us in the feeling of the cold as a pervasive foe, not one to be easily deterred. It's a liberating choice, allowing the poem a final motion, as the lines find their way inside the reader to slowly nestle and resonate.

MUSCULAR VERBS, CAREFULLY CHOSEN

Everyone has access to a dictionary. All the words are there. But their order and distillation are what the show-stopping, life-altering sentences are all about. When Sylvia Plath writes, "Love set you going like a fat gold watch," or Walt Whitman begins, "Out of the cradle endlessly rocking," and then ends with, "the sea whispered me," you have the sense of unusual words, especially the verbs, carefully chosen.

There are more sounds in the English language than any other language, and we are blessed with about two hundred irregular verbs that can test our patience. If, for instance, I describe a rumble in the jungle by saying, "Foot by silent foot, the lion (choose your verb) closer to the unsuspecting pig." Creeped closer? Crept closer? Sneaked closer? Snuck closer? Perhaps this was a Disney lion and he slinked closer. Or slunk closer. What does the lion do then? He leaped upon his prey. I prefer leapt upon his prey, but semantically there is very little difference. It is the sound that matters. If a knight must greet queens and kill dragons, how would this be accomplished? He kneeled before or knelt before her? He slayed a dragon. Or slew it? Does his head change sizes in that steel helmet? Would that mean his head shrunk? Or shrank? Drug or dragged? Weaved or wove? Strided or strode? Could it be that a stride piano strode down the street on the back of a Mardi Gras float? These choices are instinctual for the most part, but the decision must be based on the sounds before and behind the choice.

There are writers for whom the action verb choice is transcendent. Among novelists, I truly admire Toni Morrison, E. L. Doctorow, Thomas Pynchon, Margaret Atwood, Michael Ondaatje, and John Steinbeck for their verb choices. Steinbeck especially, more than William Faulkner or F. Scott Fitzgerald or Ernest Hemingway or Norman Mailer, makes sentences where the verbs are unexpected and the participles minimized. Consider this short paragraph from Steinbeck's brilliant novel of short bursts, *Of Mice and Men*:

> From his pocket Carlson took a little leather thong. He stooped over and tied it around the old dog's neck. All the men except Candy watched him. "Come boy. Come on, boy," he said gently. And he said apologetically to Candy, "He won't even feel it." Candy did not move or answer him. He twitched the thong. "Come on, boy." The old dog got slowly and stiffly to his feet and followed the gently pulling leash.

The simple verb in the middle sets up the movement at the end. The verb *twitched* has a balanced sound, but it is also sinister, foreboding, and a simple foreshadowing of the fate to befall the animal. Michael Ondaatje's book *The Collected Works of Billy the Kid* is chock full of surprising and powerful action verbs whose sound and muscularity are of equal importance. This passage refers to Tom O'Folliard, whose rifle had blown up in his face while on a hunting trip alone:

> When he finally got to a doctor he found all the muscles on the left side of his face had collapsed. When he breathed he couldn't control where the air went and it took new channels according to its fancy and formed thin balloons down the side of his cheek and neck. Those fresh passages of air ricocheted pain across his face every time he breathed. The left side of his face looked as though it had melted by getting close to fire. So he chewed red dirt constantly, his pockets were full of it. But his mind was still sharp, the pain took all the drug. The rest of him was flawless, perfect. He was better than me with rifles. His feet danced with energy. On a horse he did tricks all the time, somersaulting, lying back. He was riddled with energy. He walked, both arms crooked over a rifle at the elbows. Legs always swinging extra.

For modern and contemporary poets, I think Wallace Stevens is an excellent and consistent example, but also read Theodore Roethke, Galway Kinnell, Robert Lowell, Adrienne Rich, James Merrill, Gwendolyn Brooks, Heather McHugh, and Yusef Komunyakaa for the verbs you may pocket without incrimination. César Vallejo, Federico Garcia Lorca, Guillaume Apollinaire, and Stéphane Mallarmé also leap to mind, but it's always hard

The Rhythm Method, Razzmatazz, and Memory

to know what their actual choices would be in a language not their own. Reading a poem in translation is like kissing through a shower curtain. You get all the thrust without any of the nuance.

TOUCH 'EM ALL

The muscular verb that works its way into the reader is like a sharp elbow to the ribs after a long home run leaves the nighttime ballpark and soars into the mist. As a matter of fact, describing the physical nature of a home run with abstract language is an exercise in description that is fun for the student and the teacher. *It's gone. That pumpkin seed is popped. That ball was scorched. That's a laser into the cheap seats. Boo yow. Cancel that ticket. Rock that, Amadeus. That's a bomb, a blast, a dinger, a jack, a moonshot, a swat, a lash, a monster, a tater, a wallop, a goner, a gotcha, a smack. He's going yard. He's leaving. Adios. That's good eatin'. Bye-bye, baby. That's a twister. Forget it. Holy cow. Holy Toledo. Touch 'em all. It could be—it might be—it is. That one ain't coming back. Back, back, back, back, gone. How 'bout that. Slam-a-lama, ding dong. Get up, get up, get outta here. Splash.*

I particularly like the last one here; that's the call the announcer makes for the San Francisco Giants when Barry Bonds drives a ball over the right field wall into McCovey Cove, which is filled with boats floating in the bay. The home run call is a distinctive bit of Americana, encapsulating an act, a thing, a moment, and the personality of the speaker all at once. Some of these calls are from famous broadcasters, others I made up for our purposes here, but it is a fun and useful exercise for students to make up their own home run calls. Another favorite is "You're not the boss of me," which, of course, must be called at just the right instant. I imagine pitchers particularly hate this call, but it's funny nonetheless.

One exercise with a sports theme that was used frequently by Kenneth Koch in his writing classes was to envision any sporting event—Super Bowl, Final Four, World Series—and replace the participants with members of your own family. The possibilities for hilarity are obvious ("Aunt Frances stiff-arms Uncle Herbert and bowls her way into the end zone tying the score"), but anything that forces the student's mind out of his preordained patterns is helpful to his progression as a writer. Koch also used to bring comic books to his classes with the speech balloons whited out and then have his students fill them in. This exercise takes into account the student's ability to listen and reorganize the important elements of speech, slang, and grammar at the same time. You may also use the exercise to help students spot and eliminate clichés, which are always the death of good writing.

Bob Dylan used to take clichés in his lyrics and invert them for his own strategies, as in "Ballad of a Thin Man" or "Tombstone Blues," usually as a means to illustrate our culture's willingness to embroider our lives with clichés or stereotypes as a form of intellectual laziness or narrow-minded shortcuts. What the reader craves, and I've spoken here already about the reader's primacy, are beautiful accidents, surprise and astonishment in the poem, doors opening outward to true vistas for the first time. Something built up from within, not merely extracted from the exterior. The connective tissue is the evanescent need to become part of something that is larger than humans or mere language, but parts of both compressed into radioactive poetry; the right words in the right order, lending light. A poem is an animal big enough to ride, teeming with unexpected energy, charting a course into the unknown, moments of agility and delight that do not throw the rider off its back but serve as reminders of the exquisite muscularity and nimbleness of the animal, and the reader is made more beautiful as well, by having ridden it.

THE VELVET FISH

If, as Franz Kafka suggested, art is an axe with which to break up the frozen sea within us, then the healing aspects of poetry should be the most accessible, its flow the easiest to recognize and drink from, its rhythm alive in us from the sound of the first word. It is helpful to enter a poem already in action; some event has already begun, and we bring the reader into the midst of the play without setting the stage or creating faux emotional states. One way to do this may be the use of a prepositional phrase which leads the reader directly to its subject. Another is the immediate juxtaposition of an unusual adjective-noun arrangement from the outset—like *velvet fish*, or *crystal zoo*, or *rum dagger*—an indication that the reader has immediately entered a new and more interesting terrain.

I've already mentioned a device I use to jump-start my creative process—forming columns of words starting with the same letter, like sounds which speak to one another. This technique may also be used by creating columns of nouns that could be used as verbs, or columns with strange combinations of adjectives and nouns. I use columns to create the movement vertically down the page ("the white bull we face," said Hemingway), in order to avoid the making of sentences before the list is complete. It also allows for the negative space on the page to be considered, a key component when allowing the proximity of like sounds to fall into proper balance. A poet with a bad ear makes his consonants knock against one another like ungreased rods, pinging, then clicking, then rocking uncontrollably in a dying engine. The poem wobbles and will not gush, bumps but will not glide, for the author has no flight plan or headlong momentum and his words will not lift. Rhythm in songs and poems depends upon balance. The reader is baited and opened; he must be made to burn.

Although I've spoken of the prepositional phrase as a possible way to begin a poem, it can also have a negative effect in the body of the piece. Just as action verbs help a poem to muscle up and add dynamism to its musical architecture, so too can the overuse of gerunds or prepositional phrases bog down the momentum of the lines, creating an artificial music, false beats like unnecessary grace notes that flutter into the poem and create evasions, shadows of indirect melody, masking the poem's real strength and direct vitality. Sometimes, if a poem feels bulky or leaden, the problem lies in the connectives, passive constructions, surplus adjectives, or words that lack energy or sizzle. Roethke said that one of the tests of the poem was to judge every line as if it were a poem itself. That's a high standard indeed. But paring away the dross may mean putting the poem under that type of intense scrutiny, and line by line the poem, and thus the idea, comes to life. In the midst of an anguished asylum spent in New York City, Lorca gave these lines, from *In Search of Duende*, as part of a tribute to the classical Spanish dancer Antonia Merce. Notice the verb choices and their dramatic weight, one verb balanced on each line:

> While the poet wrestles with the horses in his brain
> and the sculptor wounds his eyes on the hard
> spark of alabaster, the dancer battles the air
> around her, air that threatens at any
> moment to destroy her harmony or to open
> huge empty spaces where her rhythm will be annihilated.

CHAPTER 7

The Poet as Engineer: Leading the Reader's Train of Thought

The pace of the poem is woven from the line as it stops and starts against the chosen punctuation and the intermittent pauses afforded by the abbreviated sentence structure. Imagine yourself with a lantern walking down a railroad track. You are the stationmaster and the reader is the train following your light as you move down the rails, switching the engine's direction by virtue of your choices. The lantern is the punctuation and break of the line, or *brake* on the line, depending on your purpose. A period should be read as a full stop, a comma as a pause or half-stop, a colon would be a full stop, a semicolon half, and so on. The reader's eye is moving down the page (we read with our eyes *and our ears*), careful to go where you are leading. Every writer carries a pack of punctuation marks in her pocket that she can draw like Doc Holliday and fire all over town. Some even become a style; witness this by the king of the colon, A. R. Ammons, in his poem "Anxiety's Prosody," published in 1989:

Anxiety clears meat chunks out of the stew, carrots, takes
the skimmer to floats of greasy globules and with cheesecloth

filters the broth, looking for the transparent, the colorless
essential, the unbeginning and unending of consommé: the

open anxiety breezes through thick conceits, surface congestions
(it likes metaphors deep-lying, out of sight, their airs misting

up into, lighting up consciousness, unidentifiable presences),
it distills consonance and assonance, glottal thickets, brush

clusters, it thins the rhythms, rushing into longish gaits, more
distance in less material time: it hates clots, its stump-fires

level fields: patience and calm define borders and boundaries,
hedgerows, and sharp whirls: anxiety burns instrumentation

matterless, assimilates music into motion, sketches the high
suasive turnings, mild natures tangled still in knotted clumps.

Ammons, whose run-on sentences are his trademark, uses the colon as
a signifier for the reader to *breathe*, to stop for a moment and pause before
the poem revs up again and continues pell-mell toward its conclusion. In his
longer poems "Corson's Inlet" and "Garbage," written decades apart, he uses
the comma and colon almost exclusively, breaking his sentences in as basic
a way as possible, with little pause for air. He has also composed his poems
on rolls of adding machine tape, which pushes the line into a particular
shape by limiting the margins left and right and forcing the poem into the
center of the page. In a typewriter, a roll of this tape could not be broken
and so the author must not stop and edit, but find new and inventive ways
to complete the sentences before and after the broken line.

Part of the joy in reading Ammons, in his wildly inclusive style unbro-
ken by pages, is to watch his mind as it actively operates on the poem. You
catch him thinking, whereas most poems are presented with the strategies
already completely sorted out. Ammons is the great Houdini of postmodern
poetry; time after time, we get to watch him escape cages he has built himself. Painted into a corner, he uses the language in unexpected ways to fly
over the still drying poem and land outside it, conveying to the reader the
mind's capacity to always be free of entanglements. As a result, the reader
begins to cheer him on, to get on his side as he challenges the language and
its seeming rigidity, as it quickly unbundles and holds him aloft, free from
the usual constraints faced by other poets. His tone is almost always wry
and he speaks with a disarming casualness, so when the poem develops and
the language intensifies, we find ourselves already seduced by the offhand
manner in which the poem first approached us. It's as if *The Catcher in the
Rye* suddenly becomes the theory of relativity, or the stranger sharing your
bus ride with offhand remarks begins to explain the necessity of string theory. Few poets have the intellectual acuity to balance these extremes.

Three great offenders, overused by poets in the quest for poignancy and import, are the hyphen, the slash, and the exclamation mark. Exclamation marks leap off the page with their chin out, daring you to deny their enthusiasm. Pack too many into a poem and it feels like the poet is screaming at you in a shrill voice. A slash never really tells you anything, the Nathan Hale of punctuation, "give me ambiguity or give me death." I myself am forced to admit the occasional overabundance of hyphens, that most promiscuous of punctuaters, available at a moment's notice to hook up with anything. It is tempting to create a spondaic effect by employing the hyphen between words and slur the two for punch effect, to create heavier successive accents. I'm guilty here, but we teach best what we most need to learn. Punctuation is the boat in front of the skier, and those marks alone slow or stall the headlong rush of the lines for the reader. Their careful placement can increase the control of the poet as he lets his line release itself, varying the tension by the intermittent stall of the comma or apostrophe, hitting the gas by allowing no punctuation at all to be displayed.

> *Punctuation is the boat in front of the skier, and those marks alone slow or stall the headlong rush of the lines for the reader.*

CHAPTER 8

Finding the Form:
The Open Field

Robert Frost famously said, "Free verse is like playing tennis with the net down." But most poets now feel the necessity to break out of decades of consistent iambic pentameter, so I am really not going to delve into sheer formalism. There are thousands of books that will give you instruction on the creation of the sonnet, sestina, or villanelle, the trochaic or dactylic effect as it concerns the haiku's seventeen syllables, but I am more interested in creating my own music, singing with my own breath and forms.

I take to heart the Robert Creeley idea that "form is never more than an extension of content," and following the beat is more creative, instinctive, and original than creating the appropriate stresses for my ghazal or pantoum. I do not want the vehicle to replace the tenor of the work or for the form "to be used as asbestos gloves, allowing me to handle subject matter too radioactive to handle otherwise," in the words of Adrienne Rich. I don't want to feel detached from my subject matter. I don't need a form for a father, to tell me what I may or may not do. I want the freedom to experiment, to create structures dictated by the pace of the poem itself, to recognize that every structure should erect its own particular scaffolding on the page, to recognize that the negative space is as important as the space that is used, that the silence between notes is as palpable as the notes themselves.

"When a writer once begins to work with his own material," said Willa Cather, "he realizes that, no matter what his literary excursions may have been, he has been working with it from the beginning—by living it ... He finds that he need have little to do with literary devices; he comes to depend

---

more and more on something else—the thing by which our feet find the road home on a dark night, accounting of themselves for roots and stones, which we had never noticed by day ..." I believe what she means is that, after a certain point, when the young writer has accumulated a great deal of experience and technique and is willing to do the work, the voice and abilities stay with him and come forth mysteriously and consistently when needed.

Formal verse can help the young poet locate things to say, but it can also obligate him to write things he wouldn't otherwise conceive except to fill out the form. It is not my aim to disparage Formalism or the tradition of writing with recognized formal structures. It is just that the New Formalism is the same as the Old Formalism, not a very maverick concept at the beginning of the twenty-first century. It requires the same diligence, discipline, and concentration—perhaps more—to build new forms as it does to flesh out and perfect lines whose rhythmic currents are filled with pre-ordained expectation. To outwit this expectation is spectacular in the extreme.

However one comes to his or her mature style, to deny one's self the practice of traditional forms is to limit your preparation for what is possible. Pablo Picasso first perfected his line drawing and portraits before he exploded into Cubism. To learn the metric pattern of the sonnet and practice its fourteen-line condensation is to begin the training that might one day enlarge the sonnet form in our thinking. The eight-year-old child throwing the rubber ball at a specific place on the wall is teaching himself to pitch and field at the same time. The college freshman imitating the sonnets of Shakespeare and Raleigh is preparing the latent musical architecture in his body to one day make poems that are vivid and singular, with an individualism born of rote memorization and trial. He is mastering the language as it moves through him from the voices of the masters, the way a filament fills a bulb with current and the lighted room is the end result.

"The difference is this," said Jorge Luis Borges. "If you attempt a sonnet, you already have something given to you, and the reader can anticipate the form, while if you attempt free verse, everything must come from within you. You have to be far more skillful technically to attempt free verse than to attempt what you may think of as being old-fashioned. So, my advice to young poets is to begin with the classical forms and only after that become more revolutionary. I remember an observation by Oscar Wilde—a prophetic

The Rhythm Method, Razzmatazz, and Memory

observation. He said, 'Were it not for the sonnet, the set forms of verse, we should all be at the mercy of genius.'"

There are exceptions to and exemplars of every rule, of course, and Richard Wilbur's *Collected Poems* are built from the ground up like Antoni Gaudi's *Sagrada de Familia* in Barcelona, a cathedral of forms created from a lifetime of focus. No American formalist has been as varied or prolific. The forms disappear in Wilbur's capable hands, and the preconceived meter hides itself behind the shimmering beauty of the sentences and ideas. Listen to the intricate internal music and end rhymes of "A World Without Objects Is a Sensible Emptiness":

> The tall camels of the spirit
> Steer for their deserts, passing the last groves loud
> With the sawmill shrill of the locust, to the whole honey of the arid
> Sun. They are slow, proud,
>
> And move with a stilted stride
> To the land of sheer horizon, hunting Traherne's
> Sensible emptiness, there where the brain's lantern-slide
> Revels in vast returns.
>
> O connoisseurs of thirst,
> Beasts of my soul who long to learn to drink
> Of pure mirage, those prosperous islands are accurst
> That shimmer on the brink
>
> Of absence; auras, lustres,
> And all shinings need to be shaped and borne.
> Think of those painted saints, capped by the early masters
> With bright, jauntily worn
>
> Aureate plates, or even
> Merry-go-round rings. Turn, O turn
> From the fine sleights of the sand, from the long empty oven
> Where flames in flamings burn
>
> Back to the trees arrayed
> In bursts of glare, to the halo-dialing run
> Of the country creeks, and the hills' bracken tiaras made
> Gold in the sunken sun,

Wisely watch for the sight
Of the supernova burgeoning over the barn,
Lampshine blurred in the steam of beasts, the spirit's right
Oasis, light incarnate.

James Longenback wrote, "Wilbur's great poems are always marked by a combination of the high wire and the homespun. They usually begin in an occasional, almost off-hand manner. He notices something in the world (sheets hanging on a wash line), then invites us to notice it too." Indeed, Wilbur almost always builds his poems around singular mundane events that gather in significance as the reader is pulled into the poem by the moving vortex of the language. Once hooked by the abiding image, the poem turns and swirls musically around this central tenet like a planet on its axis. Consider here the first two stanzas of "Love Calls Us to the Things of This World." The poem's title, borrowed from St. Augustine, is not an answer to a question, but, rather, a challenge to the reader, to see both worlds at once:

The eyes open to a cry of pulleys,
And spirited from sleep, the astounded soul
Hangs for a moment bodiless and simple
As false dawn.

Outside the open window
the morning air is all awash with angels.

Some are in bed-sheets, some are in blouses,
Some are in smocks: but truly there they are.
Now they are rising together in calm swells
Of halcyon feeling, filling whatever they wear
With the deep joy of their impersonal breathing

What Wilbur seeks are complex symmetries, which, once apprehended, he surrounds with the ceremony of writing. These symmetries are an abundance of images, each serving the other to fill the poem with action or reflected light, like a flashlight beam refracted in a hall of mirrors. First, he fills the poem with things—*eyes, pulleys, window, angels, bed-sheets, blouses, smocks*—and then contrasts them with abstract subjects, such as *sleep, soul, dawn, swells, feeling, joy, breathing*. This way, the concrete objects become dislocated among the spiritual elements, in much the same way the laundry stands in for angels. In both "Cigales" and "Exeunt," Wilbur praises the cricket and its song because it both puzzles and enchants. Even though it is not squarely or perfectly understood, it has a healing power. Paradoxically, the cricket itself is not soothed or relaxed, since, according to the naturalist Geoffrey Faber, they cannot hear their own song. This is a bow to poetry in its purest lyrical form.

Though Wilbur may at times be moved to social protest as a lifelong liberal thinker, he seems most at home juxtaposing the poet's contrary existence in two poles, of the spirit world and the world of things, grounded in fact. "One does not use poetry," he has said, "for its major purposes, as a means of organizing oneself and the world, until one's world somehow gets out of hand. A general cataclysm is not required; the disorder must be personal and may be wholly so, but poetry, to be vital, does seem to need a periodic acquaintance with the threat of chaos." Wilbur's methods endorse organization at all times, without feeling that the elements are corralled too easily.

WRITING AS CEREMONY

It is simpler to think of a poem as a ceremony if it is strictly in a form. Sometimes beautiful accidents occur outside the poet's sphere of influence. These accidents enter our writing because of our ability to listen and to be open to the possibilities of *any influence*. Be one of those people on whom nothing is lost, and all will be possible. "I want to be with those who know secret things or else alone," said Rainer Maria Rilke. The ceremony of writing takes place every day, by going constantly to the well. Once, when Jack Nicklaus overheard a fan yell "Lucky!" after a particularly well-placed shot upon the green, he turned to the gallery and said, "The more I practice, the luckier I get." Writing as a form of ceremony includes experimentation with every material the poet may find. Anything, any subject, is fit to be considered because all poetry is experimental at its inception. Franz Kafka talks about the possibilities made into poems in his piece "Leopards of the Temple": "Leopards break into the temple and drink up the contents of the sacrificial pitchers. This is repeated again and again; finally it can be calculated in advance, and it becomes part of the ceremony." All art is action, and poetry is the art of the imagination pressing back against the pressure of reality.

To help release that pressure, Wilbur asserted, the poet must find a blueprint; his formal dexterity therefore becomes an internal part of his self-expression. In a letter to John Ciardi in 1950, Wilbur explained his method more fully: "There are other, less metaphysical reasons for preferring strictness of form: the fact, for example, that subtle variation is unrecognizable without the pre-existence of a norm; or the fact that form, in showing and complicating the writing process, calls out the poet's full talents and thereby insures a greater care and cleverness in the choice and disposition of words. In general, I would say that limitation makes for power: the strength of the genie comes of his being confined in a bottle." Compression of language, therefore, would result (as the atom has also shown), in powerful nuclear combustion.

> *Be one of those people on whom nothing is lost, and all will be possible.*

SURFACE TENSION AND THE VARIABLE FOOT

"Imperfection," Robert Lowell asserted, "is intrinsic to every art form." He had come to this assertion after serving his apprenticeship under John Crowe Ransom and Allen Tate, old-world agrarian fugitives devoted to metric regularity. Lowell's *Life Studies* only became possible when he switched allegiance and fell under the hypnotic sway of the century's most influential poet, Dr. William Carlos Williams, who used to write his poems on prescription pads between rounds and is probably the only poet in literary history to deliver more babies (nearly 2,000) than poems. Williams understood that poetry in America had to be rescued from its British counterparts, and he envisioned a poetic that combined the natural speech rhythm of the worker with the musical rhythm of the poem in movement. He wanted to give up rhyme and meter completely and to introduce sound similarities that intruded less on the ear and felt like someone talking: "I have eaten/ the plums/ that were in/ the icebox/ and which/ you were probably/ saving/ for breakfast ..." Icebox and breakfast seem unrelated and plain, but when put together like this and severely enjambed, they make music with their *s*, *b*, and *k* sounds and trochaic half-rhyme. Williams was lengthening the task of Emerson, Thoreau, and, yes, Whitman, with whom it would seem he had little in common. All, however, were deeply immersed in the American vernacular. "Colleges and books only copy the language which the field and work-yard made," said Emerson. Williams claimed his English was "the speech of Polish Mothers," many that he had cared for in sickness and in health, intimately.

When Williams made the war cry, "no ideas but in things," he hoped to rescue poetry from the abstraction and generality of much academic verse in the 1920s and '30s. Emerson had said, "ask the fact for the form," and Thoreau had countered, "the roots of letters are things." As early as 1913, Williams had in his mind the idea of "the variable foot" and declared that he "did not believe in *vers libre*, this contradiction in terms. Either the motion continues or it does not continue, either there is rhythm or no rhythm." The variable foot was a unit of varying length, one word or several, which was supposed to have the same weight and duration in the poem. Grouped in threes to make up a triadic line, these variable feet allowed the poet to nudge through "the open field" of the page, in continuous motion. One of my favorite early examples of this form, "To Elsie," brings together all of Williams's concerns—the American speech pattern, the role of the underdog, and the surface tension of things:

> The pure products of America
> go crazy—
> mountain folk from Kentucky
>
> or the ribbed north end of
> Jorsoy
> with its isolate lakes and
>
> valleys, its deaf-mutes, thieves
> old names
> and promiscuity between
>
> devil-may-care men who have taken
> to railroading
> out of sheer lust of adventure—
>
> and young slatterns, bathed
> in filth
> from Monday to Saturday

to be tricked out that night
with gauds
from imaginations which have no

peasant traditions to give them
character
but flutter and flaunt

sheer rags—succumbing without
emotion
save numbed terror

under some hedge of choke-cherry
or viburnum—
which they cannot express—

Unless it be that marriage
perhaps
with a dash of Indian blood

will throw up a girl so desolate
so hemmed round
with disease or murder

that she'll be rescued by an
agent—
reared by the state and

sent out at fifteen to work in
some hard-pressed
house in the suburbs—

some doctor's family, some Elsie—
voluptuous water
expressing with broken

brain the truth about us—
her great
ungainly hips and flopping breasts

addressed to cheap
jewelry
and rich young men with fine eyes

as if the earth under our feet
were
an excrement of some sky

and we degraded prisoners
destined
to hunger until we eat filth

while the imagination strains
after deer
going by fields of goldenrod in

the stifling heat of September
Somehow
it seems to destroy us

It is only in isolate flecks that
something
is given off

No one
to witness
and adjust, no one to drive the car

    Though he would seem an unlikely revolutionary, Williams turned modern poetry on its head. His object was to communicate with the world directly and slough off all pretense of literary artifice. "I propose sweeping changes from top to bottom of the poetic structure," he said. "I take contact to mean: man without the syllogism, without the parody, without Spinoza's ethics, man with nothing but the things and the feeling of that thing ... the poet does not permit himself to go beyond the thought to be discovered in the context of that which he is dealing. The poet thinks with his poem." Octavio Paz has said of Williams, "The greatness of the poet is not to be measured by the scale, but by the intensity and perfection of his works. Also by his vivacity. Williams is the author of the most vivid poems of modern American poetry."

Williams believed that all art began in the local and that the senses would instinctively find their material there. To secure this contact, this immediacy and "radiant gist" of finality, meant that new forms must arise out of the language and its thrust, and that the forms, as both Charles Olson and Robert Creeley would attest, must come from the collision of music and its subsequent metaphors, each poem daring to be different and speaking from its own container. Watch how the poet's thought process unfurls in "The Yachts":

> contend in a sea which the land party encloses
> shielding them from the too-heavy blows
> of an ungoverned ocean which when it chooses
>
> tortures the biggest hulls, the best man knows
> to pit against its beatings, and sinks them pitilessly.
> Mothlike in mists, scintillant in the minute
>
> brilliance of cloudless days, with broad bellying sails
> they glide to the wind tossing green water
> from their sharp prows while over them the crew crawls
>
> ant-like, solicitously grooming them, releasing,
> making fast as they turn, lean far over and having
> caught the wind again, side by side, head for the mark.
>
> In a well guarded arena of open water surrounded by
> lesser and greater craft which, sycophant, lumbering
> and flittering follow them, they appear youthful, rare
>
> as the light of a happy eye, live with the grace
> of all that in the mind is fleckless, free and
> naturally to be desired. Now the sea which holds them
>
> is moody, lapping their glossy sides, as if feeling
> for some slightest flaw but fails completely.
> Today no race. Then the wind comes again. The yachts
>
> move, jockeying for a start, the signal is set and they
> are off. Now the waves strike at them but they are too
> well made, they slip through, though they take in canvas.

Arms with hands grasping seek to clutch at the prows.
Bodies thrown recklessly in the way are cut aside.
It is a sea of faces about them in agony, in despair

until the horror of the race dawns staggering the mind,
the whole sea become an entanglement of watery bodies
lost to the world bearing what they cannot hold. Broken,

beaten, desolate, reaching from the dead to be taken up
they cry out, failing, failing! their cries rising
in waves still as the skillful yachts pass over.

For a poet who wanted to abandon rhyme, Williams employs a remark-able amount of like sounds in balanced cooperation with each other. Just in the first seven lines, you can hear the poem begin to race its engine; *encloses, blows, ocean, knows* are interwoven like a chain with the sounds of *sea, shielding, too-heavy*, with an accent on the hard *e* sound and *beatings*, which are all a half-line or so away from each other. Then we're off with the gorgeous lines: "Mothlike in mists, scintillant in the minute/ brilliance of cloudless days, with broad bellying sails/ they glide to the wind tossing green water/ from their sharp prows while over them the crew crawls/ ant-like, solicitously grooming them, releasing ..." What a wonder this is, first with repeatedly echoed *s* sounds as the poem begins to move, keeping the *m* and *n* repeatedly to counter the slither and punch of *mists, scintillant, brilliance, cloudless, days, sails, sharp prows, crawls, solicitously, releasing*, and the two-beat internal compound words like a constant drumbeat and undertone: *mothlike, minute, cloudless, sharp prows, crew crawls, ant-like*. Moreover, there are only two sentences in the first twelve lines, so as the yachts break free, or yearn pointedly to get moving, there is nothing to stop the gravity of the sentences from falling headlong down the page. All that interlocking sound is found in the first third of the poem. Williams, by casting aside the old structures, relies more on his instinctive internal clock to set the timing of the poem. As a consequence, there is more sophistication in the way the poem is presented, with repeated moments of surprise for the reader. It has a higher purpose at work than the dutiful placing of certain sounds in certain slots.

Williams's recognition of the page as an open field was clarified and expanded by Charles Olson and his Black Mountain College acolytes. Olson's
essay on "Projective Verse" helped spawn a new way of thinking about
language, that the life of art was filled with intuitive moments of magic,
mystery, and discovery, that poets learn language to unleash the rhythms
that are already within them, not the other way around. Thus, the poet was
allowed to experiment more and more, and the ability to listen to the poem
as it manifested itself became as important as the ego forcing the poem into
a particularized shape, like the farrier or blacksmith forcing the shoes on a
horse. Williams was so impressed with Olson's essay that he quoted much
of it in his *Autobiography*. In place of inherited line, stanza, formal pattern,
all that he calls "closed form" or "verse that print bred," Olson offers "composition by field," open forms. "The voice is greater than the eye," he declared.
Perhaps with William Blake's dictum in mind, that "energy is eternal delight,"
Olson wrote, "A poem is energy transferred from where the poet got it (he
will have several causations), by way of the poem itself to, all the way over
to, the reader. Okay. Then the poem must itself, at all points, be a high en-
ergy-construct and, at all points, an energy-discharge."

Every poem, therefore, would ultimately have its own form. Edward Dahl-
berg insisted that "one perception must immediately and directly lead to a
further perception." The form becomes more a product of breath than of literary tradition. As such, many poems take on musical shapes, and the objects
inside them shimmer. The fact that all things are in transition or in constant
motion due to the movement of molecules and their invisible rhythm, the
idea of the poem as a living organism, filled with moving parts, has always
appealed to me. This is how great poems *feel* when I read them.

It is no wonder that Dr. Williams can claim his revolution complete; Louis
Zukofsky, George Oppen, Basil Bunting, Robert Duncan, Denise Levertov,
Robert Creeley, Lorine Niedecker, Allen Ginsberg, Robert Lowell, Lawrence
Ferlinghetti, W. S. Merwin, and many others acknowledge Williams as a
major influence. Creeley and Bunting, in particular, seem to have extended
his reach in their own poetry. Bunting, now almost forgotten, deserves better treatment and was early admired by Pound, Williams, and Zukofsky, who
numbered him among the Objectivists. His work is less a break with tradition
than others, but it stands as a reformulation of tradition. "To me it seems that
history points to an origin that poetry and music share," Bunting said, "in the

dance that seems to be a part of the makeup of *homo sapiens* and needs no more justification of conscious control than breathing." He adds, "The further poetry and music get from the dance and from each other, the less satisfactory they seem." As I have stated previously in this section, the source of the poem is the body and being of the poet, and the poet's creation, no longer his own, should engage the body and being of the reader. The result is a living architecture that requires precise and interesting subject matter to hold it upright. The plainer the language and the tighter the rhythm, the more concrete and substantial are the things, images, building blocks of the poem.

CHAPTER 9

Mastering the Art of Description

I am sometimes able to begin writing by listening to music, often jazz and usually instrumental, because hearing the words to a song may keep me from conjuring words myself. But I am most interested in anything that will jump-start my process, and rhythm is often the way. There are other times I can begin to compose through the process of description; by the act of acute observation I use my time carefully describing an object, and those perceptions lead to other associations or ideas. If the mind is forced, through a constellation of images, to pick out the details and give them relevance, so too will the object take on a sudden life and be forced to tell its story. This can be accomplished through the experience of viewing a piece of art or describing the circumstances of a movie—or, more to the point, stopping where you are and taking stock of your surroundings, defining your emotional state through the filter of your environment.

Poems should be filled with moments of concrete detail, which become the metaphors that stand in for our emotional upheavals and locate the poem in space. I'm reminded here of Rainer Maria Rilke carefully recording descriptions of sculptures and animals when working as a secretary for Auguste Rodin. It seemed to him that through his careful observation, the inner life of the observed thing began to speak, and the poet's own application of words became less important than the animation of his experience as it intimately co-existed with his subject.

In a letter to Lou Andreas-Salome in 1903, Rilke spoke of his strategy: "Somehow I too must find a way of making *things*; not plastic, written things,

The Rhythm Method, Razzmatazz, and Memory

but realities that arise from the craft itself. Somehow I too must discover the smallest constituent element, the call of my art, the tangible immaterial means of expressing everything." Rilke's ability to observe was honed by his associations with Rodin and Paul Cézanne, his poetic sensibility sharpened by utter devotion to the artistic achievements of others around him, assimilating their devotion to their subjects. "Not since Moses has someone seen a mountain so greatly," Rilke said of Cézanne's painting of the Montagne Sainte-Victoirie. The meetings and conversations between the poet and Pablo Picasso, Marc Chagall, and Paul Klee were deeply embedded in Rilke, and he gave up his immature search for narrative or lyrical context in their works. He sought instead the *saintliness* of merging and seeing inside the object, securing the smallest units of language, breath, pacing, space, and color, with absence of intention. The willingness to surrender the self and "praise," he said, "is the whole thing." The shock of recognition is what poetry should strive for, giving the readers new eyes through their participation with the poem. Rilke wrote of this moment in a poem called "Moving Forward," translated here by Robert Bly:

The deep parts of my life pour onward,
as if the river shores were opening out.
It seems that things are more like me now,
that I can see farther into paintings.
I feel closer to what language can't reach.
With my senses, as with birds, I climb
into the windy heaven, out of the oak,
and in the ponds broken off from the sky
my feeling sinks, as if standing on fishes.

Rilke was attempting a union of the senses, to emphasize that union and devotion are competent to every art form. He also believed that a poem should end in movement, that the suspended shiver of recognition is the means by which the poem had entered the reader's body and they "see." This intimacy with our subject matter creates a willing intimacy with the reader. The discovery, then, is twofold and resonates. All of these elementary encounters with the objects of our poetry force us to use our senses more fully. The accuracy and precision of the poem's description comes out of the textures, smells, tastes, and absence of moral judgment that the writer applies. Thus, the object enters the writer and then the world at large. All are momentarily one. Here is the fourth stanza of "The Man Watching," from Rilke's *Book of Pictures*:

> When we win it's with small things,
> and the triumph itself makes us small.
> What is extraordinary and eternal
> does not *want* to be bent by us.
> I mean the Angel who appeared
> to the wrestlers of the Old Testament:
> when the wrestler's sinews
> grew long like metal strings,
> he felt them under his fingers
> like chords of deep music.

Rilke ends the poems by saying, "Winning does not tempt that man." He knows that to insert the self here will block the poem's transmission to the reader, and that transmission is doubly accurate when surrendering to description and *taking control* of his own music. "This is how he grows," Rilke concludes, "by being defeated, decisively, by constantly greater beings."

In a letter to his wife Clara, Rilke stated, "I can tell you how I've been changed by the way Cézanne is challenging me now. I am on the way to becoming a worker, on a long way perhaps, and probably I've only reached the first milestone: but still, I can already understand ...Today I went to see the pictures again; it's remarkable what an environment they create. Without looking at a particular one, standing in the middle between two rooms, one feels their presence drawing together into a colossal reality. As if these colors could heal one of indecision once and for all. The good conscience of these reds, these blues, their simple truthfulness, it educates you; and if you stand beneath them as acceptingly as possible, it's as if they were doing something to you. You also notice a little more clearly each time, how necessary it was to go beyond love, too; it's natural after all, to love each of these things as one makes it: but if one shows this, one makes it less well; one *judges* it instead of *saying* it ..." (italics his).

Rilke also noticed when there was a turning point in the painting or poem, what Victor Hugo called the "trigger," and others describe as "the abiding image." This is the center around which the artwork circles, the interior that Johannes Vermeer hoped to establish through his use of light and its hidden lives. This is the heart that beats at the core of the poem, what it has to say, and the pulses of the lines are the vibrations of the core as they push the reader down the length of the line and the reader participates or resists the poem's decided thrust.

The need for this participation in the poet is acute and bloated with expectancy. Work, observe, listen, record, and wait. At times, inspiration comes like a hurricane and everything pours out. But it takes a lot of sludge to make a snowman, and we must constantly be on the hunt, gathering information, taking notes, perfecting our technique. In the winter of 1922,

> *The shock of recognition is what poetry should strive for, giving the readers new eyes through their participation with the poem.*

when Rilke was forty-seven years old, after more than ten years of waiting, he settled in a small house in Muzot and finished *The Duino Elegies* (begun ten years before) and wrote the fifty-nine *Sonnets to Orpheus* in less than a month. It is one of the great sustained inspirational moments in literary history. Here is the first half of the first stanza and part of the last stanza in "The First Elegy," as translated by Stephen Mitchell:

> Who, if I cried out, would hear me among the angels'
> hierarchies? And even if one of them pressed me
> suddenly against his heart: I would be consumed
> in that overwhelming existence. For beauty is nothing
> but the beginning of terror, which we still are just able to endure,
> and we are so awed because it serenely disdains
> to annihilate us. Every angel is terrifying.

Just a quick mention here of the poet's powerlessness in the face of the poem. The power comes later when the dilemma of its creation is overcome and the music unspools. Until then we are faced with silence. "A poem can kill a man," Wallace Stevens said. It's not the poem that is lethal, it's the waiting. I'm not sure if I believe in writer's block as a phenomenon. Even if uninspired, there is research to be done and so many more books to read. Even now, Rilke changes as I change. My perceptions of the poet alter as I age. T. S. Eliot, in his hope for the reward of heaven, knew that waiting must be done in the proper spirit, without the poet being enfolded upon himself. Eliot wrote:

> I said to my soul, be still and wait without hope,
> For hope would be hope for the wrong thing: wait without
> > love
> for love would be love of the wrong thing; there is yet faith
> But the faith and the love and the hope are all in the
> waiting.

Now, back to the last stanza of the Rilke's First Duino Elegy:

> In the end, those who were carried off early no longer need us.
> They are weaned from earth's sorrows and joys, as gently as children
> outgrow the soft breasts of their mothers ...

> Is the legend meaningless that tells how, in the lament for Linus,
> the daring first notes of song pierced through the barren numbness;
> and then in the startled space which a youth as lovely as a god
> had suddenly left forever, the Void felt for the first time
> that harmony which now enraptures and comforts and helps us.

Robert Hass has written that Rilke's project was the transformation of human longing into something else. But it is also besotted with furious oppositions, between living and death, between love and longing, between observation and invisibility. Anne Sexton wrote, "Sometimes the soul takes pictures of things it has wished for but never seen." Her own re-telling of fairy tales in her book *Transformations* takes well-known characters and imbues them with contemporary value systems, altering their motives and intentions forever and rescuing them for an adult audience. Here is the opening stanza for "Snow White and the Seven Dwarfs":

> No matter what life you lead
> the virgin is a lovely number:
> cheeks as fragile as cigarette paper,
> arms and legs made of Limoges,
> lips like Vin Du Rhone,
> rolling her china-blue doll eyes
> open and shut.

The Rhythm Method, Razzmatazz, and Memory

Open to say,
Good Day Mama,
and shut for the thrust
of the unicorn.

She is unsoiled.
She is white as a bonefish.

These opening lines are almost pure description, but they bring the reader into a collision with contemporary things. Sure, a unicorn struts through, but only for the purposes of sexual innuendo and only after the author has compared Snow White to a litany of modern materials. She takes other familiar fables and adorns them with sarcasm. Consider this final stanza from "Cinderella":

Cinderella and the prince
lived, they say, happily ever after,
like two dolls in a museum case
never bothered by diapers or dust,
never arguing over the timing of an egg,
never telling the same story twice,
never getting a middle-aged spread,
their darling smiles pasted on for eternity.
Regular Bobbsey Twins,
that story.

Sexton's use of metaphors and similes is counter-balanced here by the repetition of images connected with a modern marriage, and her tone is sarcastic, like a woman roped to a suburban lifestyle, perversely denigrating the pseudo-perfection of her neighbors. Her tone is unlike any other poet of the 1970s. *Transformations* is a singular work, hopelessly funny, but tragically so, as the characters wheel weightlessly from fable to suburban frontiers of droll and mundane consumerism and listless detachment.

CHAPTER 10

The Imagination as a Redemptive Force: The Power of Poetry

In "Asphodel, that Greeny Flower," William Carlos Williams wrote:

> It is difficult
>> to get the news from poems
>>> yet men die miserably every day
>>>> for lack
> of what is found there.

Dr. Williams probably never intended to substitute a poem for penicillin, but he understood how the imagination becomes thirsty for stimulation, longs to feel the tribal recognition of universal rhythm, to express itself in its own way. "It's just that boogie woogie," sang John Lee Hooker, "the boy's got it in him, and it's got to come out." Carl Sandburg, writing in the March 1923 issue of the *Atlantic Monthly*, described poetry in this way:

> Poetry is an art practiced with the terribly plastic material of human language, a journal of a sea animal living on land, wanting to fly in the air ... Poetry is a search for syllables to shoot at the barriers of the known and the unknowable ... Poetry is the cipher key to the five mystic wishes parked in a hollow silver bullet and fed to a flying fish ... Poetry is a fresh morning spider web telling a story of moonlit hours, of weaving and waiting during the night ... Poetry is the capture of a picture, a song, or a flair, in a deliberate prism of words.

The Rhythm Method, Razzmatazz, and Memory

In our culture, to describe some remarkable act or to give highest praise when no description will suffice—to measure excellence or virtuosity—is to call it *pure poetry* or to say that the utter graceful execution of a jump or dance was *poetry in motion.* The most lyrical, astute, or moving novels and movies are called *poetic.* Perfection, encapsulation, wholly-rendered operas, paintings, and stories are *tightly wound as a poem,* the language most apt. Saying or singing the most powerful thing in the fewest words possible, to reside in the evocative cadence of the listener's mind, is to give "... airy nothing a shape," wrote Shakespeare, "... a local habitation."

Poetry has long been memorized by the struck observer, to comfort in times of greatest distress or confusion—from Horace to Jesus to Alexander to Lincoln to Gandhi. Their favorite poems were nurtured and sustained by them, inside them, to bring forth as protection against the darker nights of the soul. Or, to illuminate and capture a room for the sole purpose of persuasion, the poem is the ultimate instrument of focus, fealty or empathy. "The cow is a poem of pity," said Gandhi, when seeking to describe the humility and sacrifice required for a life of non-violence, in service to those who cannot help themselves. "Injustice anywhere is a threat to justice everywhere," exclaimed Martin Luther King, Jr., an acolyte of Gandhi. King sometimes used the poetry of Langston Hughes in his sermons, seeking to truly engender in his listeners the sense of a local habitation, that all politics are local and personal, with personal responsibilities.

Poetry is what the world wants when its heart is broken, not a nickel and a beer to wallow in some tepid country song on the jukebox, but the majesty and gospel of language that reminds us of our human dignity, the highest expression of our inner beauty where "we contain multitudes," as Walt Whitman said, where the poem is the equivalent to the pyramids or the Taj Mahal, and poetry the primary force available to Pablo Neruda as he ascended into the heights of Machu Picchu and sought to capture the history of the Americas in his verse.

In October 1963, less than a month before his assassination, John F. Kennedy gave a speech at Amherst College in honor of the late poet Robert Frost, who had himself spoken at the president's inauguration. "When power leads man toward arrogance," Kennedy said, "poetry reminds him of his limitations. When power narrows the areas of human concern, poetry reminds him of the richness of his existence. When power corrupts, poetry cleanses, for art establishes the basic human truths which must serve as the touchstones of our judgment. The artist, however faithful to his personal vision of reality, becomes the last champion of the individual mind and sensibility against an intrusive society and officious state; the great artist is thus a solitary figure. He has, as Frost said, 'a lover's quarrel with the world.' In pursuing his perceptions of reality, he must often sail against the currents of his time ... I see little of more importance to the future of our country and our civilization than full recognition of the place of the poet. If art is to nourish the roots of our culture, society must set the artist free to follow his vision wherever it takes him."

> *Poetry is what the world wants when its heart is broken, not a nickel and a beer to wallow in some tepid country song on the jukebox, but the majesty and gospel of language that reminds us of our human dignity.*

Abraham Lincoln, another great president also tragically assassinated, often quoted from poems during his public appearances and spoke of poetry as a tonic to help soothe his melancholy. His law partner William Herndon said, "sadness dripped from him as he walked." Many times as a young man, Lincoln spoke of suicide, and as he grew older, he believed the world to be hard and grim. His depression, remarked upon frequently by those closest to him, was an integral part of his character. His suffering had lent him empathy, "clarity and conviction, creative skills in the face of adversity," wrote Joshua Shenk, "a faithful humility that helped him guide the nation through its greatest peril." Lincoln, perhaps our finest writing president, author of the Gettysburg Address and the Emancipation Proclamation, wrote poems in his twenties to ward off his self-destructive thoughts and was known to carry volumes of poetry with him in his travels. He once wrote of "that intensity of thought, which will some times wear the sweetest idea threadbare and turn it to the bitterness of death." One poem Lincoln wrote survives, attributed to him by the scholar Richard Lawrence Miller, and published by Lincoln's best friend at that time, Joshua Speed. The poem ran in the August 25, 1838, issue of *The Sangamo Journal* under the title "The Suicide's Soliloquy":

The Rhythm Method, Razzmatazz, and Memory

Here, where the lonely hooting owl
　　Sends forth his midnight moans,
Fierce wolves shall o'er my carcass growl,
　　Or buzzards pick my bones.

No fellow-man shall learn my fate,
　　Or where my ashes lie;
Unless by beasts drawn round their bait,
　　Or by the ravens' cry.

Yes! I've resolved the deed to do,
　　And this the place to do it:
This heart I'll rush a dagger through
　　Though I in hell should rue it!

To ease me of this power to think,
　　That through my bosom raves,
I'll headlong leap from hell's high brink
　　And wallow in its waves.

There is in this poem, besides the clear, degraded sense of futility, an overriding moral question for the Christian believer: whether Hell awaits the suicide. But Lincoln is also haunted by the desire to stop his spinning mind, which will not allow his physical body any real peace. Speed later recorded a conversation with Lincoln where the young Congressman told him that he was "not afraid to die, but that he possessed an 'irrepressible desire' to connect his name with the great events of his generation and that he 'desired to live for something that would redound to the interest of his fellow man.'" Lincoln resolved to improve himself and recast his energies from those of mere existence to *how* he would live and what he would live for. We now know, of course, that he was destined to abolish slavery and save a fractured nation from itself.

Well aware of the power of words even before he became the world's most famous athlete, Cassius Clay changed his name to Muhammad Ali in an effort, he said, to rid himself of his slave name, or the name white people had given his family. Ali, who was largely self-educated, used to compose poems before each of his boxing matches, many times belittling his opponent and predicting the round in which he would score a knockout. It was on-again, off-again corner-man Drew Bundini Brown who would join him as they screamed Ali's motto into the camera: "Float like a butterfly, Sting like a bee; Rumble, young man, rumble!" Later, during his wilderness years, when, as a conscientious objector, Ali was forbidden to box in the United States, he embarked on a speaking tour of colleges and universities where his courage and self-confidence inspired countless millions of young people, black and white, to stand up for their personal beliefs. It was during one of these lectures, at Harvard, that Ali extemporaneously composed the smallest couplet of all time. It has been transcribed variously, as Ali pointed to himself and said, "Me. Whee!" in the tradition of Walt Whitman, who wrote: "I celebrate myself ... I sing the body electric." Or perhaps it was "Me. We," a gesture of unity, brotherhood and universal justice, reaffirming the belief that all men are created equal.

"Heaven gives its glimpses only to those not in position to look too close," Frost wrote, well aware that real experience comes incidentally but must be sought. "I suppose," he once said, "you ought to write poetry to gratify some feeling that no one has gratified for you ... the primary thing is gratification ... you can't get any other way ... You gradually find what the particular craving of your own is—that the other poets haven't satisfied and you slowly eliminate them until there is nothing left but the pure you ... Poetry won't begin in thought. It may back up in thought. It begins in a haunted feeling that must be satisfied ... the first thing the mood picks up is not words ... it is some urge of an idea to embody itself in. The idea picks up the words. The words make the poem." Finding expression for our emotional states may lead us to poetry or a thousand other disciplines, but poetry makes meaning anywhere it is created. It gives poignancy to the humdrum routines of the everyday. It raises the buried flags, the heretofore unremarkable signifiers.

Frost compared the human imagination to the cambium layer, between the solid wood and the protective bark, in a tree. If school doesn't put us through the mill, our imagination is always between our subconscious mind and our awakened body shell, moving purposely through the world. All around the tree, from root to leaf and subsequent blossom or flower, is this thin inner sheath. Through it move the minerals and the sugar. It may sleep in winter, but the rest of the time it never ceases action, never ceases changing while the tree's alive. It is always solidifying and expanding; the inner side of the sheath hardens into a ring and rises—becoming stiff wood to lift the tree and hold it erect against storms, moving and changing beneath the outer bark. We see the history of the tree as its cambium layer rises in the cross section of the sawed-off stump. The poet's memory and experience lie on either side of the imagination as it hardens and expands. Memory informs our artistic expression and experience hones the movement of the shell—"the figure a poem makes,"wrote Frost,"it begins in delight and ends in wisdom."

Few poets are capable of calling all their tools into play at once without subduing the human element in the poem's construct. In other words, a highly technical or stylized poem may reflect the author's facility for language and yet not communicate effectively.

Much of this communication comes in the form of rhythm. Even if Shakespeare had not written some of the greatest dramas ever conceived, he would still be acclaimed as one of the world's finest poets. Besides the incomparable sonnets, his reputation could rest on the songs which intersperse his plays and are filled with sympathy for the human condition. Most were composed as theatrical devices. They were meant to emphasize a situation, relieve a crisis, prepare an entrance, or bring a scene to a close. The lyrics were sung, not recited, and the printed page probably does not offer them to full effect. Shakespeare and his contemporaries created a golden age of music. Many Elizabethan poets were also composers, and Shakespeare continually paid tribute to music's ability to persuade and heal. He wrote of music "with her silver sounds" (*Romeo and Juliet*, Act IV, scene V) and that "if music be the food of love, play on" (*Twelfth Night*, Act I, scene I) Here's an excerpt from *The Merchant of Venice* (Act V, Scene I):

> The man that hath no music in himself,
> Nor is not moved with concord of sweet sounds,
> Is fit for treasons, stratagems, and spoils.

Wallace Stevens, a contemporary of Frost and Williams, was an insurance executive for whom poetry bloomed in redemptive philosophical and visceral ways. His first book, *Harmonium*, sought to balance these extreme needs in the human animal. In his poem "Men Made Out of Words," Stevens added fear to the list of reasons men are moved to create: fear of dissolution, certainly, but more than that—fear of having not lived up to the promise of being human, of having missed the meaning that the pure imagination needs:

What should we be without the sexual myth,
The human revery or poem of death?

Castratos of moon-mash—Life consists
Of propositions about life. The human

Revery is a solitude in which
We compose these propositions, torn by dreams,

By the terrible incantations of defeats
And by the fear that defeats and dreams are one.

The whole race is a poet that writes down
The eccentric propositions of its fate.

Stevens believed in the imagination as a redemptive force, and in a time after the first World War when religion could no longer satisfy men, poetry was constructed to replace it. Poetry is, as Stevens said, "the supreme fiction" that provides and sustains "a freshening of life." Martin Heidegger called Friedrich Hölderlin the poet of the Time Between—between the departure and return of the gods—the midnight of the world's fall evening. Stevens, whose career stretched across half a century and two World Wars, was consciously a poet between the loss of faith and the belief in the imagination's ability to heal and sustain this fractured world.

Ralph Waldo Emerson, the greatest of American essayists, described The Poet as a kind of Pegasus: "Surprise and wonder always fly beside him. There is no poetry where they are not." Later, Emerson stated that "the discovery of Nature, the greater one that surrounds us and the smaller one inside, is linked to a plain sense of things, and the bridge between these two natures has a gatekeeper—that namer of things unseen who is also a guide." In his essay "Poetry and Imagination," Emerson wrote, "The poet accounts all productions and changes of Nature as the nouns of language, uses them representatively, too well pleased with their ulterior to value much their primary meaning. Every new object so seen gives a shock of agreeable surprise." SURPRISE = ENLIGHTENMENT = POWER, the sudden manifestation of the vital will. The Romantic dialectic of *ethos, logos,* and *pathos* in William Wordsworth, Percy Bysshe Shelley, John Keats, and Alfred Ten-

The Rhythm Method, Razzmatazz, and Memory

nyson pomes was modulated by Emerson into an American dialectic that he called Fate, Freedom, and Power.

In American poetry, after our mother Emily Dickinson and father Walt Whitman brought the American canon on a par with the British, our great uncles, Wallace Stevens and Dr. Williams, showed us how to make our poems from the products of the American cultural imagination and American speech patterns. Fifty years ago, most critics believed T. S. Eliot and Ezra Pound would be the most influential figures in American letters, but Stevens and Williams produced poetic bodies of distinctly original purpose and surprise, infusing their poetry with the games, fictions, and metaphors that capture and accommodate the plain sense to human need. "A poetry standing 'in its own bare bones,' or poetry so transparent that we should see not the poetry, but what we are meant to see through the poetry," said Eliot, and he dreamed of such architecture in his epic *The Waste Land*. But Eliot and Pound are both suffused with the scaffolding of the nineteenth century, and because their work stands in relation and reaction to the past, they are unable to foster a vision of the future in the chain of readers who would encounter them in the latter part of the twentieth century.

The plain sense of things is always dependent on the understanding of larger, present questions and the recognition of changing custom and authority. So poetry must change, cannot remain naked, but as Stevens said, it should wear "some fictive covering." Metaphor begins to remodel the plain sense of the reader as soon as he begins to think or speak about it; therefore, the reader has primacy, and for the poet, the words of the world are the life of the world. In *The Necessary Angel*, Stevens wrote: "What makes the poet the potent figure that he is, or was, or should be, is that he creates the world to which we turn incessantly, without knowing it, and that he gives to life the supreme fictions without which we are unable to conceive of it."

For Stevens, the French Symbolists were an influence, but only in the sense that he made some of their elements his own. He seems to me most closely related to Paul Valéry, who famously said, "Poetry is to prose as dancing is to walking." Stevens seemed more intent than his predecessors and peers to express *where* the imagination lives and to illustrate its power, but not *how* it lives or why. In this he is like William Blake, an enemy of reason or explication, which destroys the very things it dissects. Pound wanted to "make it new," but Stevens wanted to make it *present*, and in his way, no

American poet is more original or memorable. Consider this, the eighth and last stanza of his most famous poem, "Sunday Morning," published in *Poetry* by Harriet Monroe in 1915:

She hears, upon that water without sound,
A voice that cries, "The tomb in Palestine
Is not the porch of spirits lingering.
It is the grave of Jesus, where he lay."
We live in an old chaos of the sun,
Or old dependency of day and night,
Or island solitude, unsponsored, free,
Of that wide water inescapable.
Deer walk upon our mountains, and the quail
Whistle about us their spontaneous cries:
Sweet berries ripen in the wilderness;
And, in the isolation of the sky,
At evening, casual flocks of pigeons make
Ambiguous undulations as they sink
Downward to darkness, on extended wings.

It seems to me impossible to imagine a more auspicious debut or a more accomplished first collection than *Harmonium*, which appeared in 1923, when Stevens was forty-four years old. His second book, *Ideas of Order*, followed twelve years later. His words do seem a world apart from the routine and retinue of his existence, but in one regard this only serves to prove his belief in the life of the mind and in poetry as "life's redemption." He has fixed the flow of the world with the parallel of his own internal lyrical rhythm and, as such, his poems do not have "to mean, but be," as Archibald MacLeish wrote in his "Ars Poetica."

When I first read Stevens in college, I memorized long swaths of "The Man With the Blue Guitar," and "The Auroras of Autumn." Twenty-five years later, I read Stevens with greater pleasure than before, though I was more willing to immerse myself when I was eighteen and read poetry with the wide-eyed amazement of a Cortez or Magellan, certain I was discovering these vistas for the first time. Distance, time, experience, failure, and recognition are all factored into my appreciation of Stevens now, and I read him as an explorer might read his maps, familiar with the terrain and careful

The Rhythm Method, Razzmatazz, and Memory

not to be seduced by his lush style and signature tone. Both Stevens and Dr. Williams talk about the power of Eliot's early work and how they wanted to resist him as one resists the allure of the circus, an unreal world whose rhythms pull you away from your own reality. The discovery of the work of Blake became my earliest touchstone, particularly the hypnotic throb of the aphorisms in "The Marriage of Heaven and Hell," lines so powerful they made me want to become a poet and find a way into that power—a passageway to such intellectual authority.

The importance of masters to the young poet or freshly-developing writer is essential to his development, as I have said earlier, and how to emerge whole out of the early cocoon of influences is a key question during the beginning writer's struggle for his voice. Many poets find like-minded peers to connect with and share their creative experience. This is probably why so many "schools" of poetry have emerged in the history of literature as specific poets banded together and helped one another unravel similar problems. But in his personal and creative life, Stevens had little to do with other writers, made very little correspondence, and never presented himself as a literary figure to his business associates at the Hartford Accident and Indemnity Company. Stevens remarked, "Reading one's friends' books is a good deal like kissing their wives, I suppose; the less said about it, the better." Nevertheless, his poetry is filled with exciting pronouncements and unexpected flourishes and, regardless of his hermetic nature, real empathy for the struggles of his fellow man. Take, for example, this final passage from "The Idea of Order at Key West":

> Ramon Fernandez, tell me, if you know,
> Why, when the singing ended and we turned
> Toward the town, tell why the glassy lights,
> The lights in the fishing boats at anchor there,
> As the night descended, tilting in the air,
> Mastered the night and portioned out the sea,
> Fixing emblazoned zones and fiery poles
> Arranging, deepening, enchanting night.
>
> Oh! Blessed rage for order, pale Ramon,
> The maker's rage to order words of the sea,
> Words of the fragrant portals, dimly-starred,

And of ourselves and of our origins,
In ghostlier demarcations, keener sounds.

Stevens spent years "living on the bread of faithful speech," as he wrote at the end of *Notes Toward A Supreme Fiction*. His contemporaries were praised early, but he was feted late, living just long enough to receive his due acclaim. One of his last poems, "The Planet On The Table," stated simply what the master had settled into knowing. Here are the last three stanzas:

His self and the sun were one
And his poems, although makings of his self,
Were no less makings of the sun.

It was not important that they survive.
What mattered was that they should
bear some lineament or character,

Some affluence, if only half-perceived,
In the poverty of their words,
Of the planet of which they were part.

It seems clear to me that although he was ensconced in New England and Florida and never visited Europe, Stevens's flights of mind made his travels less important than the books he traveled through. His belief in the power of the imagination sustained him.

CHAPTER 11

Dynamism and Vibratory Space: What Editors Want

W hat is the line, so beloved and essential to the poet, as necessary to his course as the horizon? We build our houses line upon line; they are containers for our breath, straws from which we sip the ineluctable vibrations of the damned and the divine, the arrow without its quiver that we carry searching for a bow. And the bow is voice, our memory and experience, the pull of the poem whose exact tension varies with its target's distance. And the target, alas, is always moving. It is important to have several arrows for one's bow, since truth has a protean face and shifts repeatedly and we are unable to stand transfixed before any single truth for a protracted length of time. So we fix our sights as best we can, accept our inability to trap our quarry, and move forward, "changing" with it. Wherever the light is touched, everywhere touches back. A poem has to be capable of anything, "a religion without hope," Jean Cocteau called it, and our beautiful accidents occur from searching in the dark, where we are not perceived but received, so that the poem's structures and equations are invisible and seamless, soaking down into the darkness of its reader, unimpeded by analysis.

If anything can be said to be true about the writing of poetry, it is that *process* reigns supreme. In John Keats's letter written in December 1817 and addressed to his brothers George and Thomas, he claimed that "the excellence of every Art is its intensity, capable of making all disagreeables evaporate, from their being in close relationship with Beauty and Truth." He then went on to elucidate his famous concept of Negative Capability, that state of intellect and emotion in which, he said, one "is capable of being in uncertainties, mysteries, doubts, without any irritable reaching after fact and reason." If we were to study the works of those writers affected by this trait, he said, such analysis would "perhaps take us no further than this, that with a great poet the sense of Beauty overcomes every other consideration, or rather obliterates all consideration." I believe Keats was right, but I believe he was talking about music in the poem, which is where a poem's secret beauty is unlocked and its pleasures are loosed into the reader, for better or worse.

> *Only through the great love of the language can the contemporary editor sustain himself and not let his own work slide into obscurity or oblivion.*

Being a poet is hard work. First, the stakes are high because one is by definition dealing constantly with matters of the human spirit and because one is always in competition with the work of all the poets who have come before. Second, the success of the work is always in question, since poetry is largely void of statistical absolutes. You can always balance your checkbook, and you know what your credit rating is, but you will never know when you have written a great poem—one that will live inside its hard-shell coating, primed to satisfy readers for the next hundred years.

A poem is filled with hundreds of choices. As a maker, it is imperative that we can defend our choices for the poem we have created. At each crossroad, did we carefully construct the poem in such a way that it is clear to everyone, and if not, what is wrong with the poem, what step did we miss in the sympathetic construction, the spell we meant to cast? By the time most good poets start to publish their work consistently, they've amassed dozens of reaction slips, in all shapes and sizes. Even great manuscripts have failure rates worse than the best batting percentage of a major league player, and it is difficult on the best days not to quit. But Keats also said that "poetry must come as naturally as leaves to the trees or not at all." If the words keep coming, we owe it to ourselves to hone our axe, to sharpen our perspective and our tools, to make for ourselves the best possible atmosphere for success.

All editing is subjective. When we place ourselves in the hands of an editor, no amount of background, biography, or back-slapping will help him

The Rhythm Method, Razzmatazz, and Memory

decide to publish or reject a poem. There is only the poem in front of him, and it is as naked or sophisticated as the day it was born. The decision an editor makes in those moments is as arbitrary as possible and yet contains a million other factors, dependent upon his mood, the weather, the amount of work, the themes of the issue, conscious and unconscious stylistic bias, his last meal's agreeable digestion, the time that it took to read the poem, his children's piano lesson, the lack of a title, the length of the title, the worth of the first line, the color of the paper stock, the unmitigated gall to send a multi-page biography, the fact that it's another damn sonnet, the fact that it's the perfect damn sonnet, the lack of a shower, bravado, pitch, vocabulary, humility, sweep, vision, humor, shape, rhetoric, form, diction. The action of the editor, however quixotic, is riveted with love. Only through the great love of the language can the contemporary editor sustain himself and not let his own work slide into obscurity or oblivion.

Voltaire said, "The only reward to be expected for the cultivation of literature is contempt if one fails and hatred if one succeeds." What the editor wants is transformation, the right combination "of algebra and fire," to quote Jorge Luis Borges—to be surprised, knocked off center, silenced. The best poems stop us in our tracks, shut us up, make us read the poem again and again, because it has suddenly opened another room in our brain that was hidden to us before. On the path home, a new house that had been obscured by trees or smoke is suddenly visible, having been there all our lives.

THE KEYS TO THE KINGDOM

If you want an editor to publish your work, do your research; know the editor's propensities and the type of work he or she has published in the past. If you have an idea for an essay or book review, run it by the editor first and see if your idea may fit with the agenda of the journal. When submitting new work or simply a query proposal, be direct and to the point. Editors are famously overworked and underpaid; nothing gets returned quicker than a coy letter, or one filled with the philosophies of an unpublished neophyte. Give enough biographical information to be pertinent. If you have purchased a sample copy prior to submitting your work, you not only have begun your research, but are supporting the efforts of the editors you seek to convince. Book reviews and essays should always contain some measure of analysis mixed with conclusive biographical and historical detail. Query interviews with editors, but remember, the best interviews come from being prepared for your conversation with a chosen writer long before you begin the questions. The Internet has shortened the distance between us all, flattened the world, as it were, and most writers appreciate the opportunity to think about written questions, rather than the truncated time allotted for knee-jerk answers to complex inquiries.

I started *Asheville Poetry Review* in 1994 and we have grown—without non-profit status, federal grant monies, or university affiliation—from distribution in three local stores to more than six hundred stores in thirty-five states in America, and six European countries. We have published more than 1,300 writers from twenty-two different countries thus far and now receive more than 8,000 submissions per issue. Since we subsist solely on subscriptions and retail sales, our success has been beyond my wildest expectations.

I had three primary considerations in mind from the outset: first, to never have nor develop any political agenda or preconceived notions; second, to publish as many first-time poets and as many translations from other languages as I could reasonably include; and third, to always run the most vivid and arresting art I could find for the covers, to set us apart from the myriad other magazines perched on the newstands. I have been submitting my own poetry to other editors for their appraisal since I was eighteen years old and have known from firsthand experience the pain of that rejection letter. So I treat prospective contributors the way I would want to be treated myself, and I hope my process bears the quality of tenderness.

CHAPTER 12

Moving Through Time: A Slinky the Size of a Boa Made of Steel

Winston Churchill said, "We make a living by what we get. We make a life by what we give." I have never given one thought to the questions of *Can poetry survive?* or *Does poetry matter?* It is as immutable as my next breath; it sustains, guides, challenges, defeats, distorts, regales, mocks, shocks, and stocks me. My life would be unimaginable without it, and, as a result, I have never pondered its omission or extinction. I have spent, however, most of the last twenty-five years pondering what it is and how to create it. Here are fifteen rules to write by.

FIFTEEN RULES TO WRITE BY

1. Always allow your true nature to be expressed and apply no limitations to your beginning flow. Let come what may, as much as possible. "The road of excess leads to the palace of wisdom."—William Blake

2. Inspiration is fleeting. Technique is eternal.

3. "Compose aloud: poetry is a sound."—Basil Bunting

4. Music is the universal language because it is mathematical. Always know the number of beats in your line and the number of lines that want to be a stanza.

5. Never fall back on cliché, or use any metaphor, simile, or other figure of speech that you have ever seen in print.

6. Never use a long word when a short one will do. Scientific terms are rarely short, but have their purpose if they do not have to be explained. Never explain, never apologize, never withdraw.

7. Examine every sentence for more active verbs. Never use the passive where you can use the active.

8. Never use an abstract concept when a concrete image will do. "No ideas but in things." —William Carlos Williams

9. Fear gerunds, participles, and adjectives that bleed your nouns of energy.

10. Beware the artificial music of prepositional phrases. Remove them when you can.

11. Give a poem the distance to speak clearly, and never send a new poem to be published. Compose in a flood. Edit in a trickle.

12. Cut out every word you possibly can and realize that every line is a muscle in the body of the poem. Be muscular.

13. Less is more. Repeat number 12. Condensation is the final frontier.

14. Admit no impediment. A poem must flow with authority. Remove all obstacles—technical, psychological, or musical.

15. Rhythm loves proximity. Balance all like sounds for greatest impact. Avoid syncopation unless that is your goal. Variance in rhythm creates surface tension, propulsion, and momentum.

P.S. Start the poem with action and leave it in motion.

American poetry was born of two most opposite parents; our family tree is built and nourished on the short, compact rhyming forms of Emily Dickinson, and the long, Old Testament rumbling cadence of Walt Whitman. Dickinson is interior, a mirror whose soul and secret life informed her poems. Whitman is exterior, a window whose expansive, inclusive nature contained multi-tudes and opened new vistas in the history of literature. Reading their poems together makes us aware of the rising tide in American poetry that lifts all boats and styles equally. When Thomas Wentworth Higginson first encoun-tered Dickinson's poetry, Dickinson was thirty-one years old and was writing to Higginson, a professional man of letters, to inquire whether her verses "breathed." She dared bring herself to his attention because she had just read his "Letter to a Young Contributor," practical advice for those wishing to break

The Rhythm Method, Razzmatazz, and Memory

into print, and the lead article in the current issue of *The Atlantic Monthly*. "Charge your style with life," he commented, and went on to declare that the privilege of bringing forth "new genius" was fascinating. His article happened to appear exactly at the moment that Dickinson was ready to seek criticism. She knew him to be a liberal thinker, interested in the status of women, in general, and women writers in particular. Higginson thought her verses were "remarkable though odd ... too delicate—not strong enough to publish." But he asked to see more work, asked her age, her reading, her relationships.

Later, after her death, when her accomplishment was clear, the one who was so "elusive of criticism," in the words of Higginson, had, over the course of thirty-five years, written 1,775 poems unlike anything else in the nineteenth century. The old preacher had been trying to corral a cube with the rules of plane geometry, and Dickinson was not so easily apprehended. She published only eight poems during her lifetime, and she always concealed the wildness of her imagination underneath a mask of mischief or playfulness. After she had sunk into herself, plumbing the depths of her mysterious intellect, she spent all her days rattling around her father's large house in Amherst, punctuating her poems, as she did her recipes, only with dashes, as if her mind was moving too fast to halt, but could momentarily hover. When asked if she knew the work of Whitman, in one of Higginson's early letters to her, she replied, "You speak of Mr. Whitman—I never read his book—but was told that he was disgraceful." Too mystical to employ the body in her poetic endeavors, the only hint of sexual excitement is her periodic flirtations with the subject of death. Our own, our Emily, our white widow, could not have known how easily she sidestepped death's cold advance. "Nature is a haunted house," she wrote, "but art—a house that tries to be haunted." Listen to Dickinson's perfect pitch in her poem "632":

> The Brain—is wider than the Sky—
> For—put them side by side—
> The one the other will contain
> With ease—and You—beside—
>
> The Brain is deeper than the sea—
> For—hold them—Blue to Blue—
> The one the other will absorb—
> As Sponges—Buckets—do—

The Brain is just the weight of God—
For—Heft them—Pound for Pound—
And they will differ—if they do—
As syllable from Sound—

Genius makes its own rules. Whitman's first edition of *Leaves of Grass* appeared in July 1855 and did not have his name on the cover, but it contained a portrait sketch of him. It was printed at the poet's own expense; he also personally set the type for it. A year later, the second edition was published, and it was followed by others, nine in all, each with additional poems, until his death in 1892. The first edition consisted of 795 copies. Until the fifth edition, he did not make a single penny of profit, and from the fifth he earned a whopping twenty-five dollars. To support himself, Whitman was a nurse, a clerk, a carpenter, and a journalist, and he wondered aloud days before his death if his work would live into the next century. His painful self-examination seems almost quaint in hindsight, but Whitman's mission was no less than to change the landscape of American literature, to create a dialogue with America, and to show Americans, in radiant imagery, what was possible for their country. Henry Miller compared Whitman and Johann Wolfgang Goethe, saying:

> In Whitman, the whole American scene comes to life, her past and her future, her birth and her death. Whatever there is of value in America Whitman has expressed, and there is nothing more to be said. The future belongs to the machine, to the robots. He was the poet of the body and the soul, Whitman. The first and the last poet. He is almost undecipherable today, a monument covered with rude hieroglyphics, for which there is no key ... there is no equivalent in the languages of Europe for the spirit which he immortalized. Europe is saturated with art and her soil is full of dead bones and her museums are bursting with plundered treasures ... Goethe was the nearest approach, but Goethe was a stuffed shirt, by comparison. Goethe was a respectable citizen, a pendant, a bore, a universal spirit, but stamped with the German trademark, with the double eagle. The serenity of Goethe, the calm, Olympian attitude, is nothing more than the drowsy stupor of a German bourgeois deity. Goethe is an end of something; Whitman is a beginning.

Poetry is born of a painful awareness, created for an immense minority, and is naturally averse to the swell of conformity from every age. It requires unadorned explosions of expression, channels of air blossoming with sounds, the orchestras of the mind playing as a single instrument, breaths overlapping and interlocked like feathers on a wing, the body in thrall, surrendering to the primitive central force of the imagination. Words change as history changes, and meaning is distorted by the pressure-cookers of governmental and academic controls. But the best poetry is timeless, its symbology fixed and its propulsion strengthened by the tests of time, chipping away the excess until the streamlined spear tip of its message cuts uninterrupted through the air, rhythmically perfected and lethal. You can't be wise and in love at the same time, but the best poems are drunken frenzies, soberly told, controlled mayhem tumbling forward on the weight of its own sonic momentum. Imagine a slinky the size of a boa made of steel. But don't take my word for it; go to the next section and let these words rest for a spell. I'll leave you with these lines from Whitman's *Leaves of Grass*:

> You shall not look through my eyes either, nor take
> things from me.
> You shall listen to all sides and filter them
> from your self.

PART 2

Learning to Observe

RAZZMATAZZ AND SOUL

Seeking the sources of inspiration

If the doors of perception were cleansed everything would
appear to man as it is, infinite.
For man has closed himself up,
til he sees all things thro'
narrow chinks of his cavern.

— WILLIAM BLAKE, *THE MARRIAGE
OF HEAVEN AND HELL*

INTRODUCTION

Learning to Observe:
A Prequel

The contemporary movie studio has always been concerned with making blockbusters, but in today's climate, a real success (after *Jaws* and *Star Wars* and *Rocky*) is to create a franchise spinning sequels and parallel merchandise away from its core appeal, even to the point of filming two or three films at once, such as *The Matrix, Lord of the Rings,* or *Pirates of the Caribbean* (whose original premise was based upon an amusement park ride). Now when a franchise has grown stale, such as the James Bond movies or the *Batman* series or even *Star Wars,* a prequel can be configured, which predates all the other films and re-tells the story in a new and interesting way, speaking to the informed fan with a wry wink and a nod, most of the heavy lifting or character-building built into the narrative already.

Marcel Proust said that "a book is the product of an ego other than the one we display in our habits, society, and our vices," so this prequel is a way of fashioning some preconceptions about the enormous amount of information you are about to receive in this section, leaving my ego and your own at the door. Since this discussion is about observation, the best place for a poet to begin is with the Surrealists.

The Symbolist poets and their precursor, Charles Baudelaire, were very concerned with the process of poetry and how it could be changed. Many of their changes came from their keen and unusual perceptions of the objects around them. Many of those objects were the materials of the city, namely a great city in the center of Europe, around which all the events of the last 150 years have settled and been discussed. Surrealism was born in France, and every proponent of the club made their way, either early or late, to Paris.

This section will discuss not only the concepts of these artists as they made their work and interacted with one another, but we will consider their process. From the early prose poems of Charles Baudelaire to the automatic experiments of Andre Breton and Guillaume Apollinaire, as well as the influence of Pablo Picasso and Salvador Dali on the poetry and perceptions of the movement, we will examine the original ways of seeing that lead to the most pronounced and durable revolution of artistic sensibility since the Renaissance.

How those groundbreaking techniques spread around the globe and settled in America will be a major part of our examination, as well as how the various splinter groups in the United States forged their own alliances and ultimately saw Surrealism become assimilated into our literature, our painting, our advertising, and our cinema. Each of these disciplines have valuable lessons for the poet because Surrealism points out the clearest parallels by virtue of its distortions, just as the funhouse mirror at the carnival gives us a truer vision by blowing perspective to its barely containable extremes. The purpose of art is to become as sedate and unmoveable as the mountain, passing the acquired knowledge free of ego to the next artist in a continuous conduit of newly discovered things. Having a faith in things unseen is one of the dear characteristics of the poet. How to call the invisible world to the surface, in the service of art, is the agenda of this section.

CHAPTER 13

Arranging the Text With Your Eyes

I n the previous section, we focused our attention on recognizing the aspects of language that create rhythm—derived primarily from our practiced ability to listen—and combining that ability with technique. To find "a tree growing inside the ear," as Rainer Maria Rilke said. But just as memory and experience are our primary wellsprings, our ability to see and respond descriptively affects the vision and scope of the poem, its ability to suspend our disbelief and to deepen our understanding. Memorable poems are gateways that engage all the senses; their agility and music propel them into the reader's body, but their transformative power rides upon the willful use of their metaphoric and symbolic imagery, details, and unexpected associations. The poet's ears may write the poem, but his eyes arrange it. Just as sweeping abstractions tell the reader instead of showing them, so too can mere lists of things become tedious—associative, yes, but not emotional.

Between the concrete and abstract are what John Gardner called the "discursive" and "poetic." The discursive mode is the language that you see before you now: the prose of the essay that explains as it communicates, instructs by the piling up of evidentiary strategies and accumulated details. The poetic mode, however, is dependent upon specific images whose symbolic nature varies as the reader changes and, by contrast, does not attempt to explain its strategy (it may not have one) and is not necessarily interested in the facts. "It is the mark of great natural ability," Aristotle wrote, "for the ability to use metaphor well implies a perception of resemblances." The well-made poem is filled with suggestions of reality based upon single piec-

---

es of balanced perception, unbalanced by their comparison to one another. In his *Opus Posthumous*, Wallace Stevens said, "Reality is a cliché/ from which we escape by metaphor." Taking his cue from the French Symbolists, Stevens wanted the poet to extend the possibilities of his origins to belief in an original system of thinking, not mere inspiration or that which refuses to go away. Those images may have emotional resonance for the creator and mean nothing to the reader. The best imagery comes as a surprise for both, passed thoroughly through the rhythm filter and taking away the universal weight upon its flight, symbols evolving in a descriptive wake.

Symbols evolve, or emerge, by blurring the edges of contrasting imagery so that the reader cannot discriminate between what is real or unreal. The poem thus contains its own reality and guideposts that the reader willingly follows. In fact, the poem lets in more of the world through its various comparisons. Explanatory or discursive writing tends to restrict, and even to reduce, the reality by eliminating all possibilities save the one that is being proven. Poetry, through its heightened imagery, always expands the scope of the world, enlarging its realities. When Rilke, in one of his sonnets to Orpheus, compared the mirror to a gateway or opening to another world, his assembled accessories make the possibility not only plausible, but imminent:

> You, spendthrift, still giving yourself away to the empty ballroom—
> When the dark dawn comes, as wide as the forests,
> And the chandelier goes, like a sixteen-point stag
> Through your impossible gateway ...

Comparisons this distinct give a sense of control, illuminating and reassuring the reader at the same time. Our senses give us an instant order that is convincing, even if our reason cannot deduce the cause. There is strength in discovery and pleasure lit by promise when our experiences are expanded by poetry, when the hidden connections between dimensions are unveiled and made to sing. If Federico Garcia Lorca wrote that "coins in mad swarms/ Devour the abandoned children," or Theodore Roethke, in his great sympathy, claimed to see "the lives on a leaf," and continued his inventory of the infintesimal and microscopic "squirmers in bogs/ And bacterial creepers/ Wriggling through wounds/ Like elvers in ponds,/ Their wan mouths kissing the warm sutures," then the reader is transplanted and shaken out of his mundane notions, his conditioned responses to a static-free environment.

His shaken senses may want to move the underground into his common day, knowing that poetry is the supreme leveler and full of forensic proofs, revealing, unpeeling, and detailing the truth.

For the Surrealist, the existence of a hidden world inside this literal world was suggested by the arrival of Sigmund Freud and his theories about the subconscious. The Surrealists hoped to extend all metaphoric associations as far as possible, expanding the possibilities of seeing into unexplored realms. The poem or painting became a new nexus of comparisons, with fresh sources of inspiration and infinite exploration. Images and textures became denser, multilayered, and open to wider, less discriminate definitions.

Animism, personification, and apostrophe in the hands of Surrealists deified almost everything, and stripped the conventional wisdom from things that had long been deified. The animistic belief that natural phenomena are alive and have souls, which is rarely found in its religious form in our culture, is celebrated by the poet and serves to dramatize a drab and listless world, connecting all things in the sweep of these fresh associations. The artist is so empowered by this new way of seeing that he may in his work now address previously unassailable authorities, governments, spirits, or God.

Between the theories of the id and relativity came relative vibratory spaces filled with invigorating new ideas. Painters, poets, and musicians began the process of cross-pollination and consilience. The end result would forever change our preconceived notions of the trajectory of art, which was now infused with political reactions to a world overrun with technology and science and on the verge of either confronting God directly or becoming extinct as a species. As Paul Valéry said, in one of his many quotable moments, "God made everything out of nothing, but the nothingness shows through." As God collapsed, the makers rushed to fill the hole with poetry.

With the rise of Freudian psychology, Darwinian evolution, Albert Einstein's theories of relativity, and the birth of quantum physics, the artist was presented with an entirely new blueprint for the construction of the world. With the recognition of the significance of dreams, the principles of psychoanalysis were not only generalized but popularized.

Freud's *The Interpretation of Dreams*, which appeared in 1900, has come to occupy the same central and important place for abnormal psychology as Charles Darwin's *Origin of Species* did for biology. As Einstein and his cronies harnessed the power of the atom and stretched the space-time continuum by measuring the speed of light, all previous definitions of man's existence and superiority were swept away. The interior of the mind and the exterior of space became limitless and filled with proof of man's fragility. The acclaimed economist Lester Thurow said, "Successful societies create and manage a tension between order and chaos without letting either of them get out of hand." Einstein dropped out of high school at the age of fifteen; renounced his citizenship a year later; lived on the margins socially, economically, and morally; called himself a gypsy; and was viewed as a bohemian. His life was, in some sense, a search for order in disorder, both scientifically and socially.

Memorable poems are gateways that engage all the senses; their agility and music propel them into the reader's body, but their transformative power rides upon the willful use of their metaphoric and symbolic imagery, details, and unexpected associations.

Great creativity requires hard facts, wild imagination, and non-logical leaps forward that are then proven to be right by working backward to known principles. Only the rebellious can do it. Amongst these collisions of technological advancement and the deterioration of the old political dynasties, the artists—long the antennae of the race—began to try and define what was taking place. Though these changes were widespread and affected the populations of every country, the clear center of the evolving mood, where artists seemed most comfortable to assemble and exchange ideas, was Paris.

The Rhythm Method, Razzmatazz, and Memory

CHAPTER 14

Paris Calling:
The Flowers of Evil

The devastation and savagery of World War I brought home, with dizzying sureness, the lethality of man's new capacity and appetite for war, but it also made the world smaller. Charles Lindbergh's triumphant crossing of the Atlantic diminished its vastness, and artists began, for the first time, to correspond and cooperate across cultures and the barriers of language. Beginning with Gertrude Stein and her brother, who arrived in France well before World War I, the story of American writers in Paris during the 1920s and '30s is almost a cliché; the image of the starving artist, wide-eyed in a Parisian cafe, serving his apprenticeship among like-minded individuals is an enduring myth.

Ernest Hemingway, F. Scott Fitzgerald, William Faulkner, Hart Crane, William Carlos Williams, Ezra Pound, Sherwood Anderson, E. E. Cummings, Djuna Barnes, Kay Boyle, Archibald MacLeish, Malcolm Cowley, Laura Riding, Katherine Anne Porter, John Dos Possos, T. S. Eliot, Henry Miller, Glenway Wescott, Langston Hughes, Anais Nin, Harry Crosby, James Farrell, George Oppen, Nathaniel West, and many others either visited Paris or spent an extended amount of time wandering through her streets. Whether these writers brought Paris to bear inside their literary projects or influenced the cross-cultural influx of artists traipsing through the Parisian gatherings does not matter. Like bees having visited the same tangle of honeysuckle, they spread out across their various continents and carried the remnants of their experience within them. What is plain, however, is that the environment was conducive to creative enterprise and sympathetic to the aims of the artist.

The French Academy of Literature has been in existence for well over three hundred years, and so, as an institution, it not only has the effect of removing literature from the realm of the everyday or refuting the idea that literature is disposable, but of elevating the writer as a personage, a figure not of derision or frivolity but an entity of consequence and purpose, to be respected. The subsequent results have not been to create conservative and august authors but, rather, for poets at least, to create a tradition to rebel against. Secure in the fact that literature is a high calling, the poets have set themselves squarely against the figures of authority, whether literary, governmental, or parochial in nature. Beginning with François Villon and François Rabelais, continuing through Jean-Jacques Rousseau, Charles Baudelaire, Arthur Rimbaud, and the cult of the *poete maudit,* and then on into the twentieth century with Guillaume Apollinaire, the Dada movement, the Surrealists, Jean Cocteau, and Jean Genet, the French have systematically and defiantly attacked the accepted notions of their own culture and previous literary philosophies. Indeed, the idea of the literary outlaw—be it Villon, De Sade, Rimbaud, or St. Genet (as Sartre called him)—has become a part of French mythology, the blessed thief operating outside the repressive moral climate of his time.

BAUDELAIRE

One of the most influential books of poetry in any language is Baudelaire's *Les Fleurs du Mal*, or *The Flowers of Evil*. The sensual aspects of Baudelaire's poetry feel modern; they are complex and evocative, even though the book was published in 1857. Baudelaire roamed the luxurious and intoxicating quarters of the world seeking a spiritual payoff. He plunged headlong into "the depths of the unknown in order to find the *New!*" A master of harmonic undertones, the immediacy of his lyrics kindle one association after another, each image creating a chain reaction against the next. There is no vague sentimentality in his work; he is almost rigorous, ordained by "the tragic sense of life."

Disciplined and conscious, Baudelaire never flinches from the hard core of his discoveries. Writing to his mother in July 1857, he declared, "This book, *The Flowers of Evil*, is clothed in cold and sinister beauty, and was created with rage and patience. Besides, the proof of its positive value lies in all the evil that has been said of it. The book infuriates people. People refuse me everything: power of invention, and even a knowledge of French. I despise all these imbeciles, for I know that this volume, with its defects and its qualities, will make its way into the minds of the literary public beside the best work of Victor Hugo, Theophile, Gautier, and even of Byron."

Baudelaire's vigilant ambivalence is always at play in his poems, the mixture of love and hate, the sublime and the banal, the radiant loves and repulsions are always being fused inside the poet, and his conflicts create a powerful tension. When *The Flowers of Evil* was condemned by a French court and several individual poems banned and excised from the text, Baudelaire protested vigorously, writing to the judge who oversaw his case: "No one, any more than I, could imagine that a book characterized by such ardent and eloquent spirituality as *The Flowers of Evil* could be the object of proceedings, or rather the cause of a misunderstanding. I do not feel guilty at all. I am, on the contrary, very proud of having written a book that inspires only fear and horror of evil." Here is one example of his famous dualism, stanzas three and four from his poem "The Venal Muse," translated by Arthur Symons:

> You must, so as to gain your bread, day after day,
> Like a young chorister makes the censer sway,
> Chant the Te Deums wherein no God was seen,
>
> Or, fasting mountebank, expose your charms and after,
> Hide your soaked tears that do not hide your laughter
> From the common herd's exclamatory spleen.

"Damned Women," one of the poems banned from his book, was a study of lesbian love between Hippolyte and Delphina, who are damned because they "flee the infinite they bear within themselves," the prize that Baudelaire sought over all others—a grasp of the infinite contained in this world, fusing the spiritual and the sensual inside the formal boundaries of his vision, the world his poems sought to reconcile. But Baudelaire was also driving home the powerful implosive effects of repression, how repressed or hidden impulses—be they artistic or sexual, religious or political—cause the deterioration of the psyche or imagination, essentially tearing down the body from within. In "Death of the Artists," he began:

> How many times must I shake my stupid shins
> Before I kiss your hideous visage, Caricature?
> To hit the mark, O mystical quadrature,
> How many, O quiver, lose of my javelins?

The sense of being ignored, or worse—"we lose our soul in subtle plots to save our sins"—makes the artist mad, and in his madness he mirrors the sickness of the society that has formed him. The twin destructive forces of inadequacy and omniscience are strewn throughout the landscapes of Baudelaire and indeed, in his wake, throughout the accomplishments of all the Symbolist poets that followed him. In this manner, they anticipate Sigmund Freud and his theories of the unconscious, his definitive models sympathetically outlining their plight.

FREUD AND THE INNER IMAGINATION

Both the hysteria and the byproducts that it produced were seen by Freud and his colleagues as evidence of deeper mental instability and were, in effect, the body's way of alerting others that it was in need of help. When Freud said, "Let us trace the hysterical vagaries to their source in personal, intimate, emotionalized situations, and there in turn to whatever motivations may lie behind them," his voyage was launched. He named his three ships of discovery, much like Columbus before him, with phrases that were close to his heart. First, *determinism*—the symptoms of mental distress were not haphazard or meaningless, they had a cause, a psychic cause. Second, the origin of the symptoms operated invisibly, hidden from the patient in the *subconscious*, which to the Romantics and Baudelaire would pose as the inner imagination, the artists' propulsion. Third, the reason for *suppression*, by the artist or the society at large, was that the reality was loaded with unpleasant memories, conflicting emotions or definitions that played havoc with any preconceived sense of normalcy or peace of mind.

Freud believed there were "two orders of thinking." The neurotic repressed the unpleasant, but the dreamer, under similar stress, expressed the pleasant. Dreams are romance in the wake of desire, from which fairy tales and myths are concocted. Dreaming as romance is an ancient and universal concept; we are all inveterate dreamers. But Freud believed that two principles guide our mental procedures awake or asleep. First, the pleasure principle directs our body's urges; when unconstrained, we wish and daydream, the lottery or jackpot always in sniffing distance. But there is also the reality principle, to which we must adjust in this rigid, codified, censored, time-driven world of work and schedules and responsibilities. When released, our minds naturally

The Rhythm Method, Razzmatazz, and Memory

drift as we stroll and muse, but during office hours we are bent on the errand at hand, keeping our minds on the job and the clock, giving our minds away to the bidder who pays for and controls our time.

Thus, the question from the psychiatrist to the patient, "Tell me some of your dreams," becomes laden with potentiality, the underground stream loaded with ore, symbolism straight from the source. Metaphor, simile, analogy, and words themselves are variously symbolic. Minds sharing experiences and emotions, traditions and environment, will naturally develop similar symbols, though, as Freud acknowledged, most symbols are individual; each dreamer uses a dictionary of his own. "Free association" is required to determine the clue or motive of the symbol as it arises in the individual's mind.

Carl Jung became the psychologist of symbolism *par excellence*; seeing was a byproduct for the embodiment of the minds' predilections, charting the method and mood of freer mental movement and possibilities. Jung believed the study of the subconscious world led us to discover the brain's deeper obscurities and mystical, cross-cultural properties, which Joseph Campell later elaborated on and advanced through his travels and writings.

Artistic achievement could be viewed through this prism as a compensatory activity, a recourse to fantasy in an escape from the too-rigid demands of the reality principle. By extension then, poetry could enforce the principle of living or completing in fantasy what is denied or imperfect in reality. It projects a psychology of the artist latent in every man. Therefore, according to Joseph Jastrow, "there is a psychoanalyst in every artist, which will find expression alike in creation and criticism." The poet labors in a sick society to realize dreams or to mirror reality; art arises in the type of media favorable to subconscious assimilation.

THE POETRY OF OPPOSITION

Baudelaire, in his "duel with the beautiful," was the first great poet of rigid opposition, of juxtaposition to the extreme. The first title of *The Flowers of Evil* was *Limbos*, then *The Lesbians*, before settling on the delicious and controversial final image. His incredible duality was formed at an early age. Born in Paris in 1821, Baudelaire was the son of a father sixty years old and a mother aged twenty-six. His father died when the boy was six years old and the mother married again within a year. Her husband was a rising young officer named Aupick, destined under Napoleon III to become a general, a senator, and a French ambassador to Spain. (There is much in this biography for a Freudian to remark upon.) Like Hamlet, Baudelaire was deeply wounded by his mother's quick and unseemly second marriage and did not take kindly to his stepfather's entreaties to military service. Indeed, during the June Revolution of 1848, Baudelaire mounted the barricades and joined the revolutionaries who vowed to shoot General Aupick, who personified the bourgeois attitudes that Baudelaire detested—careerism, materialism, and smug provincialism.

> *Poetry could enforce the principle of living or completing in fantasy what is denied or imperfect in reality.*

Not only was he a world-class poet but an art critic and translator as well; his translations of Edgar Allan Poe and Thomas de Quincey were highly influential. But by 1860, Baudelaire's reckless experiments with alcohol and opium, amid years of implacable debauchery, brought him into physical distress. He had contracted syphilis early on and suffered his first stroke that year. His body disintegrated as he suffered one mental crisis after another. In 1864, he survived a second stroke and was paralyzed, but he drifted in agony for three more years, mentally hopeless and physically devastated. He died on August 31, 1867, at the age of forty-six. It is hard to overstate the impact he had on the generation that followed him. A young Arthur Rimbaud wrote to a friend in May 1871 that he had been reading Baudelaire and exclaimed, "He is the first seer, king of poets, a real God!" Indeed, it was Rimbaud who became Baudelaire's spiritual heir and most accomplished practitioner of the form that haunted Baudelaire's later output, the prose poem.

In the preface to his *Prose-Poems*, Baudelaire wrote that he had dreamt of the "miracle of a poetic prose, musical without rhythm and rhyme, flexible enough and harsh enough to take the mould of the lyric impulses of the soul, the variations in mood and dreams of the poetic temperament, the agitations of the conscience." Baudelaire did not invent the form, if it can be called that; the ownership of the first published "poems in prose" belonged to Louis Bertrand, whose collection using the form, *Gaspard de la nuit*, or *Gaspard of the Night*, appeared in 1842. But it was Baudelaire who gave the structure its status, whose obvious enthusiasm for the prose poem assured its practice among other poets who followed his example, who made the real model, the one most admired, and it was Baudelaire's importance that made the prose poem a genre of writing still practiced by ever-growing numbers of poets today. It may turn out to be one of the most conspicuous examples of French influence upon Western literature.

What hastened the development of the form for Baudelaire was his love of life's ever-changing duality and clash of opposites. According to Suzanne Bernard, in her book *Le poeme en prose de Baudelaire a nos jours,* "The prose poem, not only in its form, but in its essence, is based on the union of opposites: prose and poetry, freedom and rigor, destructive anarchy and organizing art." For a poet interested in tearing down preconceived ideas about literature, the prose poem is ready-made for that battle. There are still conflicting ideas about its governing principles, but it does allow the writer to operate outside of recognized boundaries, to create a parallel or alternative universe, re-creating the world.

The prose poem's first and perhaps most prominent feature is its unity and unique concentration. "Everything inside it," said Bernard, "works aesthetically, everything contributes to the overall impression, everything is indissolubly tied together in a tightly unified set of relations." It is rare for a prose poem to contain memorable or flash-point lines that stick in the reader's mind. Its entire purpose is for each line to cohere, bonded entirely to the lines that follow and precede it. Thus, there is never the feeling in a successful prose poem of lines being forced into position or shoe-horned into the structure for dramatic effect.

Also, the sense of narrative flow must be maintained without a particular sense of time. Not time as in rhythm—rhythm is essential to all successful writing—but time in terms of the particularized sequence of events. The prose poet may leap brutally from one idea to the other—or neglect transitional phrases altogether. In fact, after Rimbaud's work and that of the Surrealists to follow, the more disconnected or discontinuous the writer's universe, the better to deny the existence of the real, failed one. This timelessness is achieved by the absence of repetition, where time is set by repeated observations of the same idea, or by the juxtaposition of images from several vantage points, each vision allowing for a vanishing set of resemblances. The prose poem wants to hang in the air, suspended from gravity or time or meaning, like a hummingbird belonging to two dimensions at once, its machinery whirring invisibly at breakneck speed. And, like the hummingbird,

---

the prose poem wilts in captivity, unable to be pinned down by analysis or trapped inside an abiding series of definitions.

For poets of confrontation like Baudelaire and Rimbaud, the prose poem is most successful if the subject matter is most implausible, ambivalent even, with the contraries or dualities at play. Lines like this from Baudelaire's "The Old Clown" do not wish to be reconciled: "Everywhere joy, money-making, debauchery; everywhere the assurance of tomorrow's daily bread; everywhere frenetic outbursts of vitality. Here absolute misery, and a misery made all the more horrible by being tricked out in comic rags ..." Entire texts are constructed around perfect symmetries: "The Double Room" consists of nineteen paragraphs—nine for the dream, nine for the reality, and one paragrah that separates them and begins, "But ..." Likewise in "Venus and the Motley Fool," we find three paragraphs devoted to joy, three to suffering, and a seventh in the middle that says: "Yet, in the midst of all this universal joy I caught sight of a grief-stricken soul."

The effect of piling one contrast upon the other creates an unexpected regularity and the contradictions begin to disappear. Like the amazing aphorisms in William Blake's *The Marriage of Heaven and Hell*, the effect on the reader is to disorient him, to lose sight of the programmed idea and embrace the incongruities of rival notions, crumbling the high moral ground beneath the reader's feet.

CHAPTER 15

Verlaine and Rimbaud: The Time of the Assassins

It's not hard to see how Charles Baudelaire's Parisian spleen and melancholy reality would appeal to Arthur Rimbaud, one of the great prodigies in the history of poetry, whose entire literary output would take place between the ages of sixteen and twenty-one. Born in 1854 in Charleville, a French town near the Belgian border, Rimbaud began to compose poems at age eight. By thirteen, he wrote a letter in Latin hexameters to the imperial prince. A little over two years later, during 1870, his talent blossomed into twenty-two poems that resembled nothing else written in the history of French letters.

The son of an infantry captain who'd abandoned the family and a mother who had spent her entire life on a farm dictating a strict and authoritarian Catholicism to her children, Rimbaud quarreled ceaselessly with his mother and school officials. He ran away to Paris a month after graduation, traveling by train, only to be shuffled into Mazas Prison at the end of the trip because he had not purchased a full ticket. Later, on foot, he roamed around Belgium like a vagabond, returning home on the edge of starvation.

His inner turmoil, religious in nature, struggled with impending adulthood as well and was easily reflected in the French political climate. The Franco-Prussian War erupted and after France's quick and devastating defeat, revolutionary sentiment rose among the rural populace. Rimbaud, upon his return to Paris, served with the people's army during the popular uprising known as the Paris Commune, but he lost faith in that cause as well and returned to his mother's farm in Charleville, where he wrote his

---

most famous lyric poem, "The Drunken Boat." It is better to read the poem in its entirety to feel the superior flow of narrative energy—and to get a fix on its speed, precision, and layered imagery—but here are stanzas 12–13 from Louise Varese's still-unmatched translations:

> And, yes, on Floridas beyond belief I've fetched,
> Where flowers and eyes of panthers mingle in confusion,
> Panthers with human skin, rainbows like bridles stretched
> Controlling glaucous herds beneath the sea's horizon.

> I've seen fermenting marshes like huge lobster-traps
> Where in the rushes rots a whole Leviathon,
> Or in the midst of calm the water's face collapse
> And cataracts pour in from all the distant span.

Many of these lines were composed on the young poet's journeys on foot across France and Belgium, observing and recording the surrounding landscapes, sometimes delirious from hunger, sometimes from drink or fear in jumbled combinations. But the poet's experience is steady when filtered through his poetry. Here are stanzas 18–21 from "The Drunken Boat":

> I, lost boat in the hair of estuaries caught,
> Hurled by the cyclone to a birdless apogee,
> I, whom the Monitors and Hansamen had thought
> Not worth the fishing up—a carcase drunk with sea;

> Free, smoking, touched with mists of violet above,
> I, who the lurid heavens breached like some rare wall
> Which boasts—confection that the goodly poets love—
> Lichens of sunlight on a mucoid azure pall;

> Who, with electric moons bedaubed, sped on my way,
> A plank gone wild, black hippocamps my retinue,
> When in July, beneath the cudgels of the day
> Down fell the heavens and the craters of the blue;

> I, trembling at the mutter, fifty leagues from me,
> Of Rutting Behemoths, the turbid Maelstrom's threats,
> Spinning a motionless and blue eternity
> I long for Europe, land of ancient parapets.

The Rhythm Method, Razzmatazz, and Memory

This longing for Europe was a longing for Paris, for freedom, for creative recognition. Encouraged to write to the poet Paul Verlaine, Rimbaud was delighted by an invitation to visit him and his wife, Mathilde. Verlaine, having read "The Drunken Boat," could not have ascertained it was written by a precocious, brilliant, rude, and dangerous man-child of seventeen. Thus were events set in motion that nearly destroyed both men.

Many stories, poems, songs, and even movies have documented their strange and sordid thirteen-month relationship, which culminated with Rimbaud being shot by Verlaine and the older poet sentenced to two years in a Belgian prison. During their troubled and intense love affair, Verlaine would intermittently leave his wife and her respectable family for extended periods of time, participating enthusiastically in drunken trysts with Rimbaud and financing trips abroad for the both of them where they wrote, took opium, and drank absinthe in huge quantities.

The poet, Rimbaud asserted, must become a visionary and possess truth in body and soul by an "immense and reasoned derangement of the senses." In 1871, he took Baudelaire's cue and began to compose the prose poems that would comprise *Les Illuminations*, while he and Verlaine holed up in London. As their relationship unraveled and began to turn violent, Verlaine longed to salvage his marriage one last time and left his young charge alone and penniless on a London dock. Rimbaud began to write *A Season In Hell* upon Verlaine's departure and finished it a year later after returning to Charleville and his beleaguered mother. This passage is taken from "Alchemy of the Word," again translated by Varese:

I dreamed crusades, unrecorded voyages of
discovery, republics without a history, religious wars
hushed up, revolutions of customs, the displacement
of races and continents: I believed in sorcery of
every sort.
I invented the color of vowels—A black, E white,
I red, O blue, U green.—I regulated form and
the movement on every consonant, and with instinctive
rhythms I prided myself on inventing a poetic
language accessible some day to all the senses.
I reserved all rights of translation.

> At first it was an experiment. I wrote
> silences. I wrote the night. I recorded the
> inexpressible. I fixed frenzies in their flight.

Having written most of *Illuminations* and *A Season In Hell*, Rimbaud followed Verlaine to Brussels, where he was staying with his wife and her mother. Soon the relationship between the poets resumed and the wife returned to Paris, determined to divorce her husband at last. Verlaine also resumed his bouts of wild drunkenness, interspersed with bouts of depression and acute religious fervor. Disgusted, discouraged, and flush with the outline for his masterpiece, Rimbaud tried to leave Verlaine, and the latter, having purchased a pistol with which to kill himself that morning, shot Rimbaud through the wrist instead.

The Symbolist's poem was characterized by its malignant sexual reductions coupled with an overwrought sense of music, mysticism, and mortality.

Sentenced to two years in prison, Verlaine was forced to take stock of his life. He embraced his latent Catholicism while in prison and published a book of religious poems, *Sagesse*, upon his release. Verlaine and Rimbaud did not see each other again, except for a short reunion in Stuttgart, Germany, where their erotic episode led Verlaine to momentarily forget his newfound religious convictions. But this time their passion for each other quickly dissipated and they headed their separate ways. For Verlaine this meant a bohemian life of dissolution and poverty. Already an absinthe addict for at least a dozen years, Verlaine flitted from one cafe or drinking session to another, helpless to break the cycle of destruction. He did, however, continue to write and publish his poetry.

Of the group known as the Symbolists, including Baudelaire, Rimbaud, Stéphane Mallarmé, and Paul Valéry, Verlaine was the one to receive the most recognition for his work in his lifetime, and despite his remedial and even criminal behavior, he was elected "Prince of Poets" by the review *La Plume* shortly before his death in 1894. Penniless and alone, Verlaine's last years were a downward spiral of fits and starts, drunkenness and despairing confessions leading to a sporadic embrace of his faith and positive literary outputs between monumental dances with his "green fairy," absinthe.

In his life, Verlaine published eighteen books, and his work has an immediacy, lucidity and warmth at its best. Many modern musicians, especially the French composers Claude Debussy, Maurice Ravel, Yves-Alain Favre, and Reynaldo Hahn, have set Verlaine's lyrics to music. He hoped to "take rhetoric and wring its neck," seeking the nuances between the surface sounds of his words, to find not only the tangible associations between images, but the hidden life. His poems evoke rather than describe; he wants to identify and confound the separate senses of scent, sound, and color; and he was in large part responsible for Rimbaud's experiments in syntax and structure, where he created vowels assigned as colors and then symbolically arrayed them throughout the poem.

Of the many attempts to define the essence of Symbolism, Verlaine's publication of a series of essays on Tristan Corbiere, Rimbaud, and Mallarmé was the most influential among his colleagues, labeling the aforementioned fellows as *poetes maudits*, accursed poets who found genius an extreme liability that isolated them from their contemporaries and helped to foster their hermetic and idiosyncratic styles of writing. He invoked Arthur Schopenhauer, the philosopher of pessimism, who held that art was a temporary refuge from the world of blind and willful strife. The Symbolist's poem was thus characterized by its malignant sexual reductions coupled with an overwrought sense of music, mysticism, and mortality. The death's head is everywhere apparent and inescapable.

Verlaine remained loyal to the work of his young lover, publishing his *Illuminations* in a volume together with *A Season In Hell* in 1892 (a year after Rimbaud's death) and Rimbaud's *Poesies*, completed in 1893, both with prefaces written by Verlaine. His belief in the genius of his "sacred monster" never abated. Besides some sporadic work on additional prose poems, Rimbaud turned his back on literature when he and Verlaine parted that final time in Stuttgart. Rimbaud was nineteen years old, and his literary fame was already assured among the vanguard of Parisian poets. He spent the next eighteen years in a frantic attempt to earn money, traveling to places where no white man had been seen before. In 1891, he died from cancer in a hospital in Marseilles with his mother and sister at his side. He was thirty-seven years old and already a legend in French literary circles, where his poems had been circulating and argued over during his long exile.

The major accomplishment of *A Season In Hell* is clear, but the *Illumina-tions* have aged the best. They are the culmination of Baudelaire's dream of a poetry without verse, contrary to what has come before. But, unlike Baude-laire, Rimbaud's structures do not contain obvious metaphors; the similes are not interested in varying degrees of similarity and seem totally unmo-tivated to create comparisons, even obvious ones. Over and over, the world of these compositions is ruled by incoherence; there is music, but no totality of rhythmic structure. There are concrete images, but they are compared to and animated by abstractions. Optical illusions are discussed as clear reali-ties. All governing principles of reality are inverted like the fingers of a glove. They hold together through the arabesque of the consonants and vowels, the gestures of the sentences toward a sense of melody, like fish nudging through water toward a light. Long and short phrases are balanced against one another, the way smaller rocks are used as ballast between the larger rocks in a wall; the consonants become the grit, the vowels breath and color.

The effect allows the underside of the world to be revealed; logical pre-sumptions are suspended. Rimbaud has a penchant for setting extreme posi-tions, then whirling dervish-like away from one back toward the other with-in the same structure, sometimes using universal quantifiers like an erotic politician: "All their characters were reflected in my face," he wrote in "War," or "I have the blue-white eye of my Gallic ancestors," in "Bad Blood." His po-ems were built from trances, stupors, deliriums, seeking "an alchemy of the world." They are splattered with exclamation marks, howls, and insults and screams. From "Morning of Drunkenness," hear the histrionic voice, which narrows into a face with slits for eyes, face to face with the End:

> O MY GOOD! O my Beautiful! Atrocious
> fanfare where I never falter. Rack of enchantments! Hurrah
> for the unbelievable work and for the marvelous body, for the
> first time! It began in the midst of children's laughter, with their
> laughter it will end. This poison will stay in all our veins even
> when, the fanfares shifting, we shall return to the old inharmony.
> O now let us, who are so worthy of these tortures! redeem that
> superhuman promise made to our body and our soul created:
> that promise, that madness! Elegance, science, violence! They
> have promised us to bury in darkness the tree of good and evil,

to deport tyrannic respectabilities so that we may bring hither our very pure love. It began with a certain disgust—and it ends—unable instantly to grasp this eternity,—it ends with a riot of perfumes.

Laughter of children, discretion of slaves, austerity of virgins, loathing of faces and objects here, holy be all of you in memory of this vigil. It began with every sort of boorishness, behold, it ends with angels of flame and of ice!

Little drunken vigil, holy! if only because of the mask you have bestowed on us. We pronounce you, method! We shall not forget that yesterday you glorified each one of our ages. We have faith in the poison. We know how to give our whole life every day.

The time of the Assassins is here.

The early vision of the Surrealists is transmitted through this mystical portal: "A breath opens operaesque breaches in the walls"; "Magic flowers droned"; "The comedy drips on the grass platforms"; "There is a swamp with a nest of white beasts"; and this conclusion from "Metropolitan": "The morning when with Her you struggled among those bursts of snow, those green lips, those blocks of ice, black banners and blue beams, and those purple perfumes of the polar sun—Your strength." Reality was too thorny for Rimbaud's great personality, but the city was where he found his comfort, no matter how many times he returned to Mama's farm in Charleville to recover from his excesses. Though he had spent the majority of his time in Paris, a dozen of the prose poems reflect a certain number of visual, cultural, and linguistic references to London. What Verlaine essentially found in London was a city favorable for his sentimental ramblings, but Rimbaud roamed through the various neighborhoods and extracted the elements of an incomplete aesthetic, one whose variety and juxtaposition reflected the many races and voices brushing and bumping past one another on that seething metropolitan boilerplate.

Urban space in Paris had helped Baudelaire discover the bizarre new face of the modern world, and he based *Spleen de Paris* on his contact with the city's shuffling together of the ephemeral and the eternal, the banal and the transcendent. Rimbaud, though less precise, carries the modern tone forward in his verse itself. London is more incomprehensible than Paris, especially to a rural French teenager, and where Verlaine describes and Baudelaire elucidates, Rimbaud hallucinates. From the familiar vantage points, he extracts—almost like a Sufi mystic released from his worshipful moorings—an authentic trajectory of unmistakable visions. He hoped to find the perfect formula that would deliver the world's secrets into his hands.

As I have stated, Rimbaud's method is to veer among extremes but also to ratchet up and down his dynamic on the page by the use of smaller phrases balanced against longer sentences, outbursts accompanied by explication or descriptive language, drawing the reader to his anguished breast through the use of mimesis. Inside the prose poem dichotomy, all rules disappear. When the poet enacts his "rational derangement of the sense," his real purpose is to try and control the hallucination, to systematically unbridle the intelligence in a search for the unknown. The poetry that arrives in this marvelous country would no longer keep pace with reality; "it will precede it." In his essay on Surrealism, "The Last Snapshot of the European Intelligentsia," Walter Benjamin links the occult with the intellect of the visionary artist: "We penetrate the mystery only to the degree that we recognize it in the everyday world, by virtue of a dialectical optic that perceives the everyday as impenetrable, the impenetrable as everyday ... the reader, the thinker, the loiterer, the flaneur are types of illuminati just as much as the opium-eater, the dreamer, the ecstatic. And more profane. Not to mention the most terrible drug—ourselves—which we take in solitude."

CHAPTER 16

The Prose Poem: A Union of Opposites

I n his last twelve or thirteen tortured years of existence, Charles Baudelaire labored over fifty or so prose poems. From age nineteen to twenty-one, Arthur Rimbaud's last attempts at a literary production consisted of the prose poems in *Les Illuminations*. Many significant poets of the twentieth century have subsequently found the prose poem useful in their various missions and projects: Edgar Allan Poe, Max Jacob, James Joyce, Oscar Wilde, Amy Lowell, Gertrude Stein, T. S. Eliot, Carl Sandburg, and Williams Carlos Williams all practiced the form. Williams's book *Kora in Hell* was patterned after Rimbaud's *A Season In Hell*. Among more recent poets to take up the prose poem are Karl Shapiro, Anne Sexton, Robert Bly, James Wright, Charles Simic, Michael Benedikt, Robert Hass, Rosemarie Waldroup, W. S. Merwin, David Ignatow, C. D. Wright, and Russell Edson (who writes exclusively in prose poetry and is probably the most accomplished of the American poets). Jorge Luis Borges's exquisite collection *Dreamtigers* also leaps to mind, as well as Kenneth Patchen's experiments of the 1950s and Stephen Berg's memoir parables, *Shaving*. So prevalent is the form that almost every poet of the last thirty years has probably taken a stab at it.

But even though more than one journal is devoted solely to its practice, reams of critical studies are devoted to its analysis and importance, and a few very good anthologies have gathered them up, offering useful surveys and an abstract census showcasing its proliferation, the prose poem is still a renegade form, not taken seriously by everyone. Charles Simic has written, "the prose poem has the unusual distinction of being regarded with suspi-

---

cion not only by the usual haters of poetry, but also by many poets themselves." Its main characteristics are the lack of line breaks—usually a tough hurdle for the lyric poet to leap over—and a nearly invisible narrative flow built almost (but not always) entirely around clusters or layers of images. But all other normal characteristics of poetic language are present, rhythm and narrative progression being foremost among the "musical" principles, but internal rhymes, assonance, consonance, what have you, also conspire to keep the poem a poem and not a short story.

> *The prose poem feels closer to our dreams than other forms because the technical devices that poets usually employ are hidden or nonexistent, so the poem is dislodged in time, having crossed the threshold of immediacy seemingly without artifice.*

The most overarching truism about the prose poem is that it has no real set of governing principles and is thus free to be transmogrified by the poets as they wish. This makes the form a very attractive way to experiment, or to improvise, and it also feels closer to the subconscious, which does not usually manifest itself in purely lyrical ways. This also gives many successful prose poems their warm, organic, somewhat "automatic" dreamlike feel. The prose poem is usually built around a central object or conceit and revolves around it, issuing sparks by its various contacts and permutations. Or it may be coolly analytical, avoiding the subject altogether, creating a surface tension by its near misses.

Since the primary themes under advisement for this section are the art of seeing, observation, and recognition of the true triggers of inspiration—be they painting or cinema (which is painting by numbers in order to tell a story)—the deep image-filled texture of the prose poem seems an appropriate form to contemplate. I have noticed that many stage directions or screenplays, when properly balanced, read like prose poems. Prose poems can represent nuggets or distillations of a scene, directions toward the scene's enactment, the glimpse of something coming, the sense of events reaching critical mass or sadly interrupted, and can find boundaries forming but unfinished. The prose poem can be a particle, a clue, a fragment (but clearly drawn), an arrowhead but not the arrow. "A jeweler's art," Norman Mailer called it.

The Rhythm Method, Razzmatazz, and Memory

One of the prose poem's most consistent characteristics is that, even with the number of poets using the form increasing exponentially, it continues to elude definition and morphs according to the whims and talents of its composer. Charles Simic's book *The World Doesn't End* was awarded the Pulitzer Prize and was entirely comprised of prose poems. The title poem for Henry Taylor's 1986 Pulitzer Prize-winning collection, *The Flying Change*, is in two parts, one prose and one rhymed and metered.

Most folks think of prose being separated by paragraphs, poetry structured in stanzas. "Paragraph" originally meant a graph outside the main graph. In other words, it was a mark that manuscript copiers in the Middle Ages used to indicate a break in the text. So the indention in a paragraph denotes a new idea or the shift in action or locale. For the contemporary prose poet, the indention may come anywhere, but its importance varies on the weight of the negative space it follows, just as the decision by a poet to justify each margin strictly left and right to create a silo of words or a column that the words are subsequently poured into becomes a statement about the flexibility of language or, alas, its opposite.

The prose poem feels closer to our dreams than other forms because the technical devices that poets usually employ are hidden or nonexistent, so the poem is dislodged in time, having crossed the threshold of immediacy seemingly without artifice. The voice feels direct, almost conversational like a memoir or diary entry, and is therefore not without prejudice or authoritarian bias. If the key element of verse is the line, then the key element of prose might be syntax, and pace seems not as important as tone. Could this discovery by the French be the real fulcrum between the traditional and the experimental and its birth be the first breath of modern poetry?

T. S. Eliot, whose masterpiece *The Waste Land* sometimes reads like prose, asserted in his 1917 essay "Reflections on *Vers Libre*" that "*Vers Libre* does not exist ... and the so-called *Vers Libre* which if good is anything but free, it can better be defended under some other label." What keeps memorable free verse from being free is its constant vacillation between adherence to, and departure from, rhyme and regular meter. "It is this contrast between fixity and flux ... which is the very life of verse," Eliot declared, "the division between conservative (or traditional) verse and *vers libre* does not exist, for there is only good verse, bad verse, and chaos." Eliot went one step further when he labeled Walt Whitman as a great prose writer. Karl Shapiro was driven crazy by this when he wrote his essay "Is Poetry an American Art?" In it, he published Whitman's own notion about the obliteration of traditional form and the notion of prose poetry. This is Whitman pushing for "a heaven of prose" and issuing a call to arms for poets who were looking backward for their models:

> In my opinion the time has arrived to essentially break down the barriers of form between prose and poetry. I say the latter is henceforth to win and maintain its character regardless of rhyme, and the measurement rules of iambic, spondee, dactyl, etc., and that even if rhyme and those measurements continue to furnish the medium for inferior writing and themes (especially for persiflage and the comic, as there seems henceforward, to the perfect taste, something inevitably comic in rhyme, merely in itself, and anyhow), the truest and greatest poetry (while subtly and necessarily always rhythmic, and distinguishable easily enough), can never again, in the English language be expressed in arbitrary and rhyming meter, any more than the greatest eloquence, or the truest power and passion. While admitting that the venerable and heavenly forms of chiming versification have in their time play'd great and fitting parts—that the pensive complaint, the ballads, wars, amours, legends of Europe, etc., have, many of them, been inevitably render'd in rhyming verse—that there may have been very illustrious poets whose shapes the mantle of such verse has beautifully and appropriately envelopt—and though the mantle has fallen, with perhaps added beauty, on some of our own age—it is, notwithstanding, certain to me, that the day of such conventional rhyme is ended. In America, at any rate, and as a medium of highest aesthetic practical or spiritual expression, present or future, it palpably fails, and must fail, to serve. The Muse of the Prairies, of California, Canada, Texas, and of the peaks of Colorado, dismissing the literary, as well as social etiquette of oversea feudalism and caste, joyfully enlarging, adapting itself to comprehend the size of the whole people, with the free play, emotions, pride, passions, experiences, that belong to them, body and soul—to the general globe, and all its relations in astronomy, as the savants portray them to us—to the modern, the busy Nineteenth century (as grandly poetic

The Rhythm Method, Razzmatazz, and Memory

as any, only different) with steamships, railroads, factories, electric telegraphs, cylinder presses—to the thought of the solidarity of nations, the brotherhood and sisterhood of the entire earth— to the dignity and heroism of the practical labor of farms, factories, foundries, workshops, mines, or on shipboard, or on lakes and rivers—resumes that other medium of expression, more flexible, more eligible—soars to the freer, vast, diviner heaven of prose ...

It is possible that there was, in the resounding wake of the Romantic movement, a flicker of universal innovation sweeping from Europe that called for a new aesthetic, a collapse of the old world order. Whitman felt this himself and became our first truly great and universally recognized bard of America, a world poet. England had Shakespeare; Germany, Goethe; Russia, Pushkin; Italy, Dante; and so on. But Whitman felt the American sense of manifest destiny and the need to make it new and distinctly our own. Shapiro wondered in his essay whether Americans would ever embrace their poets and if poetry is antithetical to the American ideal. But in his great struggle as a poet and critic, Shapiro began to reject the distinctions between poetry and prose; he explained, there is only "greater or less heat." The prose poem gave him an opportunity for the expression of what he called (borrowing from Whitman again) "cosmic consciousness," a sense of the unity of all life.

What E. O. Wilson has called consilience, Shapiro has identified as man on the verge of a "tremendous synthesis ... between modern science, the ancient psychologies of the past, and what we call poetry or art." Whitman, D. H. Lawrence, Rainer Maria Rilke, Rimbaud, Henry Miller, and Carl Jung were all searching for the same thing, the development of a unified, overarching consciousness that was grander than governments and individual philosophies. Here is an example of a prose poem that Shapiro wrote in 1964 called "Lower the Standard: That's My Motto":

Lower the standard: that's my motto. Somebody is always putting the food out of reach. We're tired of falling off ladders. Who says a child can't paint? A pro is somebody who does it for money. Lower the standards. Let's all play poetry. Down with ideals, flags, convention buttons, morals, the scrambled eggs on the admiral's hat. I'm talking sense. Lower the standards. Sabotage the stylistic approach. Let weeds grow in the subdivision. Putty up the incisions in the library facade, those names that frighten grade-school teachers, those names whose U's are cut like V's. Burn the *Syntopicon* and *The Harvard Classics*. Lower the standard on classics, battleships, Russian ballet, national anthems (but they're low enough). Break through to the bottom. Be natural as an American abroad who knows no language, not even American. Keelhaul the poets in the vestry chairs. Renovate the Abbey of cold-storage dreamers. Get off the Culture Wagon. Learn how to walk the way you want. Slump your shoulders, stick your belly out, arms all over the table. How many generations will this take? Don't think about it, just make a start. (You have made a start.) Don't break anything you can step around, *but don't pick it up.* The law of gravity is the law of art. You first, poetry second, the good, the beautiful, the true come last. As the lad said: We must love one another or die.

Shapiro believed that a revolution of the senses was taking place, which did not recognize borders but made artists kinsmen, traveling and listening, tuned to the international wavelength. A true warrior for peace, he made rousing speeches in defense of the Henry Miller's *Tropic of Cancer*, which was banned as obscene in the United States. "Everything we are taught is false," Shapiro said. He believed new poets and new forms were called for with the branding of American multiculturalism, that the polyglot tongue and patchwork sensibility of the immigrant would combine to create a unique and unmistakably American art form. "The good poet's language is always at the periphery of the existent languages of his own tongue," he wrote in his essay "The Critic In Spite Of Himself." "From the vulgar dialects to the King's English, language is his element and he moves through it in every dimension, apart from the dictionary meanings and the semantics of words. The poet uses language plastically."

Robert Bly said that "prose is the natural speech of democratic language. We are all secretly longing for prose." In 1744, Giambattista Vico laid out three stages of culture, moving from the gods to the heroes to the ordinary people—from the sacred culture, as in Egypt, to the aristocratic culture, as in the Renaissance, to the democratic. In the sacred phase, all words are

The Rhythm Method, Razzmatazz, and Memory

signs, and the natural form is a sacred chant. In high Greece and Renaissance England, kings, queens, heroic types, the class system, metrical poetry, and complicated syntax are the rule. In the third phase, the horizontal phase, meter, syntax, and classes all go away, and the natural form is prose. Vico called it "epistolatory or vulgar which serves the common use of life." The key, said Bly, "is to keep the high spirits, the subtlety, and the verbal brilliance of the two earlier phases while letting the sentence itself—not the foot or the line—be the primary unit."

Necessary equipment for the creator of the prose poem should include an especially keen ear for rhythm, for the rhythm of human speech in particular, as prose simulates conversational language. Rhymes, half-rhymes, internal rhymes, and a broad sense of humor inform most successful prose poems. Many contemporary poets only become humorous or cool in prose or find a wry detachment that the lyric poem does not afford them. Russell Edson said he wanted to create a "prose that is a cast-iron aeroplane that can actually fly, mainly because the pilot doesn't seem to care if it does or not. Nevertheless, this heavier-than-air prose monstrosity, this cast-iron toy will be seen to be floating over the trees." If we agree that the prose poem is a transgressive medium, then the "shamelessly hybrid modalities" ought to empower their author to make striking theoretical and even politically subversive leaps.

But generic border-crossing is by no means the central virtue of the prose poet. Edson's poems read like parables, and his staunch refusal to waver stylistically, or write in a style that engages in active dialogue with the styles of his contemporaries, makes a resounding statement. Refusal to engage can become a calculated form of engagement, like a hunger strike or a trade embargo. The humor of recognition, when the poems are humorous, becomes the sad realization tinged with regret at one's own foolishness, the rational word bouncing off the absurdity of the poem's situation or the situation rides on the series of absurdities, girding the reader for the unexpected, which he then finds everywhere. Consider these three examples of Edson's quirky and faintly surrealistic style, two from his 1976 volume *The Intuitive Journey and Other Works* and one from *What a Man Can See*, published by The Jargon Society:

THE FALL

There was a man who found two leaves and came indoors holding them out saying to his parents that he was a tree.

To which they said then go into the yard and do not grow in the living-room as your roots may ruin the carpet.

He said I was fooling I am not a tree and he dropped his leaves.

But his parents said look it is fall.

THE AUTOMOBILE

A man had just married an automobile.

But I mean to say, said his father, that the automobile is not a person be cause it is something different.

For instance, compare it to your mother. Do you see how it is different from your mother? Somehow it seems wider, doesn't it? And besides, your mother wears her hair differently.
You ought to try to find something in the world that looks like mother.

I have mother, isn't that enough of a thing that looks like mother? Do I have to gather more mothers?
They are old ladies who do not in the least excite any wish to procreate, said the son.

But you cannot procreate with an automobile, said father.

The son shows father an ignition key. See, here is a special penis which does with the automobile as the man with the woman; and the automobile gives birth to a place far from this place, dropping its puppy miles as it goes.

Does that make me a grandfather? said father.

That makes you where you are when I am far away, said the son.

Father and mother watch an automobile with a *just married* sign on it growing smaller in the road.

COUNTING SHEEP

A scientist has a test tube full of sheep. He wonders if he should try to shrink a pasture for them.

They are like grains of rice.

He wonders if it is possible to shrink something out of existence.

He wonders if the sheep are aware of their tininess, if they have any sense of scale? Perhaps they just think the test tube is a glass barn ...

He wonders what he should do with them; they certainly have less meat and wool than ordinary sheep. Has he reduced their commercial value?

He wonders if they could be used as a substitute for rice, a sort of wooly rice ...?

He wonders if he just shouldn't rub them into a red paste between his fingers?

He wonders if they're breeding, or if any of them have died.

He puts them under a microscope and falls asleep counting them ...

Edson said he often works from first lines, using the remainder of the poem as a logical counterpoint to that first move. As a strategy, Edson's line-by-line development moves in the opposite direction of the Surrealists, who used irrational language to scorn rational thought. Edson's poems can take on the nonsense inside them because the language is so rational. He makes something out of nothing, pulling a fully realized story from an odd recollection of sequenced events, the sense of the events only apparent in their seeming evolution. His fables are absurd, but like life they arrive where they should at the end, as if by appointment or self-fulfilling prophecy. "We ask not necessarily to understand," Edson said, "in fact most cases we'd rather not, we ask only to believe ... Art makes us believe what we cannot understand."

Much of what cannot be understood, especially in poetry, is not impossibly hidden behind true reality, but an implied or counterfeit reality. For the Symbolists, the transient objective world was not true reality, but a reflection of the invisible absolute. "To name is to destroy," said Stéphane Mallarmé, "to suggest is to create!" Though Mallarmé's work was initially met with hostility for its difficulty and obscurity, his experimental music and intricate theories of literature eventually made him an influence on generations of Western writers. According to his theories, nothing lies beyond reality, but within this nothingness lies the essence of perfect forms and it is the task of the poet to reveal and crystallize these seemingly transparent or invisible essences. His poetry is prized for its condensation, highly focused imagery, and unorthodox syntax. Each poem is built around a central symbol, idea, or metaphor and relies on a host of subordinate images that develop and expose the validity of the core symbol.

Mallarmé went beyond Baudelaire in stressing the sacred incantations in the poem, using the juxtaposition of musical effects to persuade and sublimate the reader, to invoke the object little by little, bringing to light a state of the soul through a series of unravelings. "The childishness of literature up to now," he stated in 1891, "has been to believe, for instance, that choosing a certain number of precious stones and writing down their names on a piece of paper, even very precisely, was to make precious stones. Well, no! Poetry being an art of creation, one must draw from the soul of man states, glowing lights, of such absolute purity that, well sung and well lighted, they become the jewels of man: that is what is meant by symbol; that is what is meant by creation, and the word poetry here finds its meaning: it is, in sum, the only possible human creation. And if, in truth, the precious stones with which one adorns oneself do not convey a state of the soul, one has no right to wear them ..." This technique, however vague, was championed by the Symbolists as "pure poetry," and Mallarmé's patchwork of sonic intentions is sometimes believed to be the theoretical underpinnings of Cubism. It would take the emergence of Apollinaire and the collapse of Dada to make this accomplishment clear.

The Rhythm Method, Razzmatazz, and Memory

CHAPTER 17

After the War: Remaking the World

Paris at the turn of the twentieth century was the center of the world both for artists and aspiring despots of every stripe and persuasion. After being the flash point for two World Wars and a geographical shift in international, political, and cultural dynamics, that title now belongs to New York City. But if you were an artist in 1900, Paris was the place to be, the petri dish for every hothouse artistic theory imaginable. Three buddies of varying backgrounds, talents, and renown were, along with the indomitable Gertrude Stein and her revolving salon, at the center of this incredible artistic rotisserie. It may actually have been their differences that attracted Guillaume Apollinaire, Pablo Picasso, and Max Jacob to each other. Though he was the larger man and the more out-sized personality, Wilhelm Wladimir Alexandre Apollinaire de Kostrowitzky possessed a name only one third the size of Pablo Diego Jose Francisco de Paulo Juan Nepomnceno Maria de los Redemios Crispin Crispiano Santisima Trinidad Ruiz y Picasso. Fittingly, Picasso took his first and last names and flushed the rest, with the Alpha and Omega of art poised just beyond his fingertips for most of the twentieth century. No middle ground was ever going to be enough to satisfy the appetite and curiosity of the little minotaur. Max Jacob, whose name consisted of two first names pushing together in a nonchalant manner, was torn by his mad homosexual love for Picasso and devotion to his painting.

"Stick to poetry," said Picasso, and Jacob seems to have taken the Spaniard's advice. In exchange, Jacob repaid Picasso many times by taking him in, helping him to learn French by reading him the poems of Paul Verlaine

---

over and over, and most importantly, introducing him to the many artists, writers, dealers, and models ensconsed in the Boulevard Voltaire. Jacob, addicted to ether, alcohol, astrology, and the occult, would read palms, staring intently through his monocle and wryly commenting on the person's sexual peccadilloes or lack thereof. For a rural Catalan painter of nineteen, the twenty-five-year-old Jacob must have seemed like an alien from outer space, but he would remain Picasso's friend through one of the most extraordinary periods of creativity in the history of art.

In 1901, Picasso was destitute, living wherever he could, bouncing from Barcelona to Paris, and painting, painting, painting. From 1904 until 1912, Picasso would move from his Blue Period through the Rose Period and on to the explorations with African art and masks that would result in *Les Demoiselles d'Avignon* and change twentieth century art for good. By 1908, he had entered Cubism, and his collaborations with Georges Braque on collage and the geometric experiments that ensued would ensure his international celebrity and prestige. This Picasso would go on to become the wealthiest and most prolific painter of all time and stand astride the art world of the twentieth century like a colossus. But that would be later; for our purposes here, let's return to the first meeting of our three principals in an English-style pub in the winter of 1904, Jacob and Picasso listening to Apollinaire pontificate on the future of art to a dozen bright-eyed Parisian youths. The three men drank the rest of the night, smoked what opium they had, and would continue as friends, rivals, peers, and apologists until the war commenced—the war that would change everyone and everything in its path.

APOLLINAIRE

Guillaume Apollinaire was born in Rome on August 26, 1880, to a Polish mother and an unknown father. His famous cosmopolitan manner and poetic objectivity were brought to bear early by the circumstances of his upbringing and the over-arching influence of Olga, his mother. Olga, also known as Angelica, was a courtesan and a *traineuse,* which is to say she took her cut of the money spent by high rollers and itinerant gamblers from the casinos or nightclubs that employed her. Apollinaire was thus brought up in Monte Carlo with a mother of ill repute and the influence of various "uncles," some of whom were very wealthy and allowed the boy to partake of their libraries

The Rhythm Method, Razzmatazz, and Memory

and learning, while Angelica constantly reminded him that he was descended from Napoleon and the other nobles of a dim past and beat him if he kept what she considered to be sordid and unworthy company.

This was the background for the man who would become the center of intellectual life in pre-war Paris, a man who Francis Carco would describe as being perfectly capable of consuming two full meals in quick succession: "a gourmand, huge in size, yet somehow appetizing to look at, who would crush between his jaws the bones they served him, would suck on them, becoming smeared with grease, and in the course of relating some story about a painter, would fart into his seat cushions without the least concern for his reputation. What had he to fear? He was like some hilarious god." It was true that Apollinaire had traveled through Europe much more extensively than any of his peers, and as a consequence, his poems are never content to speak of France alone; there is a keen sense of the universal with bits of brilliantly conceived imagery, prophecies, and conversations he has overheard on his travels.

John Richardson, in his *Life of Picasso*, wrote that because they were "reassured by the whiff of brimstone and brilliance they detected in each other, Picasso and Apollinaire became the best of friends ..." Until he died, fourteen years after they met, Apollinaire would be a constant solace and a constant goad to Picasso. Apollinaire opened up Picasso's imagination to a vast new range of intellectual stimuli: to new concepts of black humor, to the pagan past, and the wilder shores of sex. Apollinaire, who was already obsessed with the works of the Marquis de Sade ("the freest spirit that ever existed," he wrote), had no difficulty converting Picasso to the cult of the Divine Marquis's definition of art as "the perpetual immoral subversion of the existing order."

PICASSO

Picasso is such a rare combination of contradictory impulses, that the one constant in his life is easy to see against the jumbled backdrop of appetites. He worked, tireless and totally consumed by the problems and riddles that his art presented, almost until the day he died. As a poet, I have been refreshed and influenced by Picasso's ability to transform himself as a maker, to eternally raise the bar as his discoveries mounted and his accomplishment was in plain sight. Never content to settle, Picasso remained in love with forms and, like a restless ghost, moved to inhabit as many forms as possible, moving from vessel to vessel with a Herculean impatience to know more, to see inside himself the invisible creations that yearned for shape. Picasso has often been called shamanic in his arresting and charismatic tendency to forecast where art may yet proceed. I spent the better part of a decade trying to pin him down in a poem after seeing his giant *Bust of Sylvette* on the New York University campus. I eventually settled on a first-person account, using many quotes directly attributed to him by André Malraux. So some of these lines belong to Picasso, some belong to Malraux through a French filter, some are in my own peculiar Appalachian interpretation, but all I hope give a sense of channeling the wild bull whose purpose is singular, and that purpose was always to create. Here is Picasso in the first four stanzas of my poem "The Painter As Mantis Sings the Blues," from the Iris Press collection *The Lost Sea*, which was published in 2000:

I came stillborn into this world.
Don Salvador blew cigar smoke
into my little pinched nostrils.
Terrified angels flushed out of my eyes
like Apaches charging on white mustangs,
screaming *Wake up, nino, wake up*.
My father took me in his cape and wrapped me
in its folds. I was always hungry.
I learned to walk by pushing a tin
of biscuits. I learned to paint
by watching my father sketch

dining room pictures, partridges and rabbits,
pigeons and lilies. By the age of thirteen,
my birds and bulls came alive.
Disciples see more clearly than masters.
So my father gave over to me. Twenty years later,
as the war spilled out, his death created an avalanche.
First him, then Eva, then Braque and Derain.
Apollinaire, nervous, his head exploding
like a clover leaf, was never the same.
The Tao of history is combat and the urge
to destroy is not a creative urge.

The Rhythm Method, Razzmatazz, and Memory

I told Brassai, you're a born draftsman.
You own a gold mine and exploit
only the salt, with this photography
business full of haloes and cosmetic fog.
But he found the world more fraught
with genius than himself and chased
his own tail through Paris for decades.
What bullshit, a peeping Tom blowing
magnesium bombs all through the night,
with Goethe as a guide, posing prostitutes
side by side like potatoes.

Painting is the oldest profession,
best practiced by old men. I remember watching
Goya's fingers in his eighties, trembling as he painted
his last torture scenes, roped to the mountain,
swinging above the ice-fields of his last days,
the chutes, trapdoors, partitions and tunnels,
the hidden places where Death lies waiting.
Painting is praying, and while the street preachers
rub their Bibles and pull their hair
denouncing all sinners, the places we paint
become churches. Why not risk everything?

Picasso took the same violent liberties in his approach to the canvas that he employed in his competitive interpersonal relatinships. But he was *always* working, indeed he was painting the day before he died. Here are the last four stanzas of "The Painter as Mantis Sings the Blues":

Nature has to exist so that it may be raped.
I am against everything, everything unknown
is an enemy and if we give spirits a form,
we become free. The mules and cockroaches
do not imitate life, they work as life does,
always on the verge of departure.
Painting makes me do just what it wants me to.
Like Rembrandt who is a tropical forest,
with all the bamboo uprooted and trampled
by elephants. That's how painting erupts,

out of widow's weeds, out of pet shops.
Painting is a very large plow carving its duty
across the terrain of the dispossessed,
a real hodgepodge, like the platypus
or the squirrel that do not know
where they come from or what they are.
I feel and do not decide.
One slaughter follows after another,
processions of totem poles laughing like bear traps.
I do not seek, I find camouflaged

acrobatic flowers bristling with razor blades,
a sunset spreading the confused shadows
of windmills, an owl with the head of a man
cocked beneath a three-cornered hat.
The soul of painting is tension
and perpetual enchantment, to turn
a block of wood into a bird, a toy car
is a baboon's head driving the hunched
shoulders forward. The cat eats the bird.
Picasso eats the cat. Painting eats Picasso.

They just keep coming up, like mismatched cousins,
order and adventure, math and mayhem,
like the scorpion and the owl
hunting among the dusty wild cactus
and rosemary of the Catalan desert,
where all the caves are like doorways
to the interior of the Shadow.
Sometimes when the forms are swarming,
when one form swims over into another form
like sex, the voice of God says do this,
do that, but God is confused and Picasso is not.

Blaise Cendrars, and the other poets who came into Picasso's orbit, believed him to possess a literary aptitude, which he employed in his strategies, a sense of the narrative of life which made his paintings pulse with extraordinary energy, elegance, perversity, tenderness, and mystery. All those
who encountered the Spaniard remarked on his fearsome stare, "the look"

The Rhythm Method, Razzmatazz, and Memory

that pierced through any personal artifice. Here are Cendrars's thoughts, from his *Selected Writings*:

> ... I do not say that Picasso creates literature (as did Gustave Moreau), but I do claim that he has been the first to introduce into painting certain techniques considered, until now, exclusively literary. Neither study nor copy of reality. True absorption. Contemplation. Magnetism and intuition. Here is the first liberated painter. He creates. He has that mysterious sense of metaphysical correspondences and is in possession of the secret cipher of the world. He evokes, he transposes. He strips bare enigmatically. He insists. He points with his finger. He never blinks for he has the transfigured eyes of faith. He affirms life. He adores. Dazzled. Nor is there in him any scientific analysis, any Protestant theory, any preconceived lies; but only the eternal religion of the catholic senses and that overwhelming truth of the heart. For he loves. And everything that comes from his hand is alive, always ...

THE CIRCUS OF THE MODERN WORLD

After the Symbolists, the Impressionists, and a vast migration of bohemian culture to Paris, the path was clear and the culture ripe for experimentation. Between the magical practices of Jacob and the magical writing of Apollinaire, who was single-handedly defining Cubism as Picasso and Georges Braque created it, the priceless energy of the magic they encountered was not squandered. The collapse of logic lends magic the refuse it needs to germinate. Among the various artists moving in and around our three protagonists during this period are Andre Salmon, Blaise Cendrars, Pierre Reverdy, Jean Cocteau, Erik Satie, Marc Chagall, and Marcel Duchamp. What an astounding array of talents and voices, and in the center is the tireless Apollinaire, a hub in this wheel of influences, writing poems, stories, articles, erotica, columns for the daily newspapers, and the defining essays and reviews for the art and movements in his orbit.

His first collection of poetry was *L'enchanteur Pourrissant* (1909), but *Alcools* (1913) established his reputation. Influenced in part by the Symbolists, the poems veer back and forth in time, juxtaposing the old and new, combining traditional poetic forms with modern imagery. These can range from graceful love lyrics to bolder experimental visions, from rhyme to free verse to "shape" poems. Apollinaire is a poet for all of Europe, like Goethe, but this romanticism has been shattered and reshaped by the world of trains, planes, and automobiles and by the shifting forms of the artistic personalities that surrounded him. Here are the first fourteen lines of his most famous poem "Zone," which opens *Alcools* and is translated for us by Samuel Beckett:

In the end you are weary of this ancient world
This morning the bridges are bleating Eiffel Tower oh herd
Weary of living in Roman antiquity and Greek
Here even the motor-cars look antique,
Religion alone has stayed young religion
Has stayed simple like the hangars at Port Aviation

You alone in Europe Christianity are not ancient
The most modern European is you Pope Pius X
And you whom the windows watch shame restrains
From entering a church this morning and confessing your sins
You read the handbills the catalogues the singing posters
So much for poetry this morning and the prose is in the papers
Special editions full of crimes
Celebrities and other attractions for 25 centimes

During his Rose Period, with its clowns and jugglers and monkeys and harlequins, Picasso found a potent metaphor for the mystery and missing magic of the modern life unfolding before him. The circus contained the buried realities and evasions of logic that seemed to be the residue of the urban lifestyle. In this thinking, Apollinaire matched his friend step for step. In May of 1905, six months after he had met Picasso, Apollinaire wrote the following in *La Plume*: "It has been said ... Picasso's work shows a precocious disillusionment. In my opinion, the contrary is true. Everything he sees enchants him and it seems to me he uses his incontestable talent in the service of an imagination that mingles delight and horror, abjection and delicacy ... One feels that his slender acrobats, glowing in their rags, are true sons of the people: versatile, cunning, dextrous, poverty-stricken, and lying." The idea of the circus troupe as metaphor for the modern condition began to seep into Apollinaire's poetry as well. In this lithe, dreamlike poem,

The Rhythm Method, Razzmatazz, and Memory

"Saltimbaques," translated by Donald Revell, we see Apollinaire considering the resourcefulness of a life lived in motion:

In flatlands the acrobats
Escape through the gardens
Through drunken hotel exits
Through churchless towns

The children guide them
Others follow in a dream
When the acrobats call them
Even the orchards surrender

The acrobats have all the equipment
Tambourines barbells golden hoops
And a wise bear and a sagacious monkey
To collect the money as they go

Apollinaire is the gateway from the nineteenth century into the modern age, and as such, he could not remain unaffected by the war that engulfed Europe. Indeed, he was, from the outset of his literary career, surrounded by revolutions of one sort or the other and each of these artistic revolutions claimed him as a forefather or interpreter, be it Modernism, Cubism, Orphism, Dada, Surrealism, or Dualism. Apollinaire helped to introduce the new century to itself. He sought French citizenship and enlisted in the infantry. In March 1916, he was seriously wounded in the head by a piece of shrapnel and underwent two skull operations in Paris. He wrote the first Surrealist play, *The Breast of Tiresias*, while he was recovering, and coined the word "Surrealism" in the program notes for Jean Cocteau and Eric Satie's ballet *Parade*, which was first performed in May 1917. Still weak from his injuries, Apollinaire died of influenza in the Spanish flu pandemic of 1918.

As the tireless promoter of artists and their various works, Apollinaire was the figure around whom many of the best and most important poets gathered. Cendrars, whose work had influenced a young Apollinaire and who befriended Henry Miller during his impoverished sojourn in Paris, tried to capture Apollinaire's cosmopolitan spirit and his enormous influence on the poets to follow in this homage entitled "In Honor of Guillaume Apollinaire," written in Paris in November 1918:

IN HONOR OF GUILLAUME APOLLINAIRE

The bread is rising

France

Paris

A whole generation

I am speaking to the poets who were present

Friends

Apollinaire is not dead

You followed an empty hearse

Apollinaire is a sorcerer

It was he smiling in the silk folds of flags at the windows

He was amusing himself throwing flowers and wreaths at you

While you were following his hearse

Then he bought a little tricolor rosette

I saw him that same evening demonstrating along the boule-
vards

He was straddling the hood of an American truck and brand-
ishing an enormous international flag flying like an air-
plane

LONG LIVE FRANCE

Time passes

The years slide away like clouds

The soldiers are back again

In their home

In their country

And there's a new generation rising

The dream of TIRESIAS' BREASTS is realized!

Little Frenchmen, half English, half Negro, Half Russian,
some Belgian, Italian Annamite, Czech,

One with a Canadian accent, another with Hindu eyes

Teeth face bones joints curve gait smile

They all have something foreign about them and yet are
really from among us

In their midst, Apollinaire, like that statue of the Nile, the
father of waters, stretched out with children everywhere

The Rhythm Method, Razzmatazz, and Memory

flowing from him
From between his feet, under his armpits, in his beard,
They look like their father and are different
And they all speak the language of Apollinaire

Cendrars, Reverdy, and Jacob are the three most associated with Cubism and its uses of collage and animism. Jacob loved to make people laugh and was frequently the center of the party. He was a singer, pianist, and actor as well as a poet, and his most enduring work is contained in his 1917 collection of prose poems, *The Dice Cup*, where the language is continually erupting into puns and parodies and various satirical elements. Nothing is ever as it appears to be, and metamorphosis occurs with lightning swiftness, unexpectedly entering the poems without foreshadowing. In the beginning, Jacob was an unceasing sidekick to Picasso and lived three doors away from the painter for the better part of a decade. For most of his life, Jacob was addicted to opium and lived in extreme poverty, working at all manner of jobs to sustain himself. Born a Jew, he converted to Catholicism in 1915 and moved six years later to a small village outside Paris, which was close to a Benedictine church where he worshipped. It was there that he was apprehended by the Nazis in February 1944 and died the following month in the concentration camp at Drancy.

Reverdy, a provincial farm boy whose father raised grapes and whose grandfather was a sculptor, arrived in Paris on October 10, 1910. Almost immediately, he found himself among the artists and poets of the Bateau-Lavoir and was befriended by Jacob, Juan Gris, Picasso, Braque, and Apollinaire, who became his mentor. Inspired by the Cubist doctrine and disenchanted with the idealism of the Symbolist school, Reverdy's first book, *Cale Seche* (*Dry Dock*), chose the most direct objects in order to effect a return to the physical world. Apollinaire and the Cubists viewed their arts as one based upon an intellectual reality (like playing three-dimensional chess) as opposed to a more traditional objective reality and perspective.

Many of Reverdy's poems undertook to seek the independence of its objects from fixed notions of physical reality and separated the authentic, pure semantic properties of words from arbitrary or preordained conventions. The influence of Stéphane Mallarmé can be found in *Poemes en Prose* (1915) and *La Guitare Endormie* (*The Guitar Asleep*, 1919). Many of these poems were quiet spectators peeping through windows and down stairwells where the most common objects—lamps, pipes, mirrors, chairs, and street-lights—dominate the landscape.

It was during the heady, unsure days of my senior year in college that I first encountered Reverdy and was transfixed by the vividness and constant emotional pitch of his lines. Trying to pin the narrator in a Reverdy poem is akin to catching light with a fishnet. The voice of the anti-hero moves like a wraith across his opaque surfaces. An accumulation of fragments is synthesized inside a proliferation of sensual data, and as a result, the poems feel as if they are perpetually searching, unlike any other poems I have ever read. Compare Reverdy's, "The Poets" and "The Traveler and His Shadow," both translated by Mary Ann Caws:

THE POETS

His head took shelter fearfully under the lamp shade. He is green, his eyes red. There is a musician perfectly still. He is asleep: his severed hands play the violin to help him forget his misery.

A staircase leading nowhere climbs round the house. Nor are there any doors or windows. On the roof shadows can be seen shifting about and tumbling into emptiness. One by one they fall, unharmed. Quickly they move back up the stairs and start again, eternally charmed by the violinist still playing, his hands not listening.

THE TRAVELER AND HIS SHADOW

It was so hot that he shed his clothes piece by piece along the road. He left them hanging on the shrubs. And when he was naked, he was already nearing the town. An immense shame came over him and kept him from entering. He was naked, and how could he help being stared at?

Then he went round the town and entered by the opposite gate. He had taken the place of his shadow which, going first, protected him.

The Rhythm Method, Razzmatazz, and Memory

The narrator waits on the inside of a Reverdy poem, sitting in the center and singing one instant, but feel for him and he is mist, climbing a trellis of flowers toward the sky. Mystical, multilayered, and forever joyful, it's as if the poems are emptied of bombast and then re-filled with the reader, surprised to find himself trapped inside the hollow of perfect stillness. Donald Revell said, "Reverdy was an author of prolific reticence whose published novels, notebooks, and volumes of poetry mount an enormous drama from which he turns aside, almost a little sadly, as though he could not find a place for himself in his own words." Early on, Reverdy was identified as the poet whose aims best captured or reflected the plasticity of Cubism, but he believed the very term was ridiculous.

Arriving at the end of Modernism, not wholly comfortable with his adoption by the rabid Surrealist circle of Breton, and too independent to dwell long in the salons of Picasso and Cocteau, Reverdy was an outsider who could belong to any club. In 1917, Reverdy founded the literary review *Nord-Sud* (*North-South*). Its title was inspired by the subway line that connected the two major artistic communities, Montmartre and Montparnasse. As editor-in-chief, Reverdy looked upon the review as an opportunity to represent two directions in poetry: the generation of 1914 and that of the post-World War avant-garde. The former artistic group, led by Apollinaire and supported by the Cubists, contributed their faith in the progress of the new century, while at the same time recognizing their presymbolist heritage, the thematic traditions of Baudelaire, Mallarmé, and Rimbaud, all of whom were to ultimately influence Reverdy. The latter poetic generation sought by their collaboration to announce new trends in poetry, first Dada, founded by Tristan Tzara, and then Surrealism, at that time a barely recognizable aesthetic under the aegis of Andre Breton. Yet, *Nord-Sud* was more than just an introduction to new directions in poetry; it provided Reverdy with a means of expression for many of his first aesthetic ideas, such as this one in the March 1918 edition: "The image is a pure creation of the mind. It cannot be born from a comparison but from a juxtaposition of two more or less distant realities. The more the relationship between the two juxtaposed realities is both distant and true, the stronger the image will be, the greater its emotional power and poetic reality."

Again, the next chapter of Reverdy's life would be initiated by Jacob. Although Reverdy and Jacob often quarreled, Reverdy was impressed by

Jacob's religious fervor and evangelism, and as a result, he and his wife converted to Catholicism in 1921. Five years later, Reverdy moved to the monastery of Solesmes with his wife, but by the end of his second year there, he had completely lost his faith. Instead of a higher spiritual state, Reverdy experienced bitter resentment toward the church; religion as an institution was irreversibly tainted by human interpretation:"Man's great anxiety," he wrote, "does not derive from death. Religions have greatly contributed in creating and aggravating it, religions with their sinister promises of good and evil, in any case, an eternal life in fire or honey."

Although bitterly disillusioned, Reverdy continued his self-appointed exile. Withdrawn from the mainstream of Paris, his work received decreasing notice, a situation which further aggravated his depression. His relationships with Jacob, Cocteau, and Picasso deteriorated. The Greek poet Odysseas Elytis said upon meeting Reverdy what first impressed him was "his constantly clenched teeth." Reverdy, whose age and generational placement caused him additional consternation, cried out in a French café, pointing toward a motley band of Parisian youths:"Not one of them knows me, not one!" Seclusion as a theme is investigated over and over in his poems, seeking the shadows when the spotlight was in view. But the poems—whose influence has been evidenced by translators as diverse as Samuel Beckett, John Ashbery, and Kenneth Rexroth—however beguiling and insecure, always contain a measure of humanism in its rarest form, a love of the world so pervasive that the reader cannot resist. Reverdy stayed in Solesmes until his death in 1960. Here is "Memory," which has been translated by several poets, but Patricia Terry does the honors for us:

MEMORY

Scarcely a minute
        And I've come back
Having grasped nothing of all that passed
A point
        The larger sky
        And at the last moment
    The lantern going by
        The footstep overheard
    Of all that's in motion someone comes to a stop

They let go of the world
           And everything in it
The dancing lights
           And the spreading shadow
There's more space
           If you look ahead
Inside a cage a living animal leaped
With an identical gesture of breast and arms
A woman laughed
           Throwing back her head
And someone happening by mistook us one for the other
All three of us were strangers
And formed already
           A world full of hope

CHAPTER 18

Destruction, Derision, Dada

The West Indian poet Derek Walcott has written, "For every poet it is always morning in the world. History and elemental awe are always our early beginning, because the fate of poetry is to fall in love with the world, in spite of history." By 1914 in France, history had pulled the forces of destruction into a noose and tightened them in a circle around western Europe. Among Fauvism, Symbolism, Cubism, Dadaism, Surrealism, Simultanism, Orphism, and Futurism, one must add Nationalism, the real cause of the first World War, a war of machines which consequently produced the first air forces, the first chemical warfare, the introduction of vast tank batteries, and the devastating realities of trench war strategy. City-sized trenches of men, force-fed their governments' jingoistic spin, were lashed into fronts that produced casualties the like of which the world had never seen. Never before had men rained fire down upon innocent civilians; never before had the whole world mobilized one nation against the other, each nation's economy focused on the mass production of armaments. The western front between France and Germany became a stalemated killing ground without a single truly decisive battle having been fought. The United States' entrance into the maelstrom in 1917 tipped the balance for the Allies, but the various inadequacies of treaties settled upon at the war's conclusion probably set the stage for the next monstrous war that followed two decades later.

Out of this destruction and moral ambiguity, many artists found themselves unable to define a strategy or find solace in their work. Vaslav Nijinsky famously told his audience, "I will dance for you now this war which

---

The Rhythm Method, Razzmatazz, and Memory

destroys us all." He promptly danced himself into exhaustion and collapsed. His mental state never fully recovered and he, like Antonia Artaud, one of the greatest twentieth-century French writers, spent most of the rest of his life institutionalized. Dada, more mood than movement, was the intellectual foreplay necessary for Surrealism to consummate itself in the European cultural reaction to the first World War. The ugly underbelly of technology was first exposed in the tremendous body counts created by the war machines of the competing countries, and mankind was forced to reflect upon its clear capacity for self-immolation. Dada's founders saw through the hypocritical nationalism and humanistic bromides espoused by the governments of western Europe, whose irrational, capitalistic ambitions had created the atmosphere for war in the first place.

One of Dada's many (and shifting) mottos was their intention to "sow world peace." The Dada artist saw his work as a necessary armament or shield against the general public numbness to the chaos and savagery perpetrated by the governments that represented them. Dada, then, was an anti-art movement that emerged out of the ashes of Germany, a decided effort by artists to change the way art was presented and/or appreciated by an uncivilized world. Dada had no formal definition or system, but its adherents shared an ethic of nihilism and absurdity. The word Dada itself, which denotes both "hobby horse" and "father," was arrived at by accident and endured because of its suitably nonsensical connotations.

As Dada moved out of Zürich, the revolt was characterized by its attacks on civilized or bourgeois sensibilities, making negative symbols out of the icons of the old, dead culture. The senseless barbarity of the war had destroyed all previous visions of hell or logic, and the hypocritical men who had conducted these deathly orchestras became fair game for the artist, despite the dangers this strategy might create under certain oppressive political conditions. Hugo Ball, one of the founders of Dada, wrote these words in his diary in 1917: "A thousand-year-old culture disintegrates. There are no columns and no supports, no foundations anymore. They have all been blown up ... the meaning of the world has disappeared."

The Dada artist attacked the notion of art itself, transforming his rage into a subversive doubt, filled with parody, caustic humor, and black self-contradictions. "The true Dadaists are against Dada," wrote Tristan Tzara in one of his manifestos. The point was never to take anything too seriously—

especially yourself or your own creations. Tzara's recipe for writing a Dada poem was to "Take a newspaper. Take a pair of scissors. Select an article as long as you want your poem to be. Cut out the article. Then carefully cut out each of the words that form this article and put them in a bag. Shake gently. Then take out each scrap, one after the other. Conscientiously copy them in the order they left the bag. The poem will resemble you. And there you are, an infinitely original writer, with a charming sensibility, beyond the understanding of the vulgar." Thus, Tzara had adapted the Cubist idea of collage and forged a new literary aesthetic, hoping for a new and striking juxtaposition of images and words.

One famous Hannah Hoch photomontage showed German politicians bathing in the nude, stripping the pomp and ceremonial mystique from their public images, revealing a less-than-heroic posture as they cavorted in their birthday suits. Some Dadaists, like Berliner Raoul Hausmann, used the photomontage method by cutting illustrations and advertisements out of popular magazines. Popular culture, being fair game, was also incorporated into the Dadaists' notion of what art was made from, and a new dialogue was created between the publishers of pop culture and the artists who now defined it.

Tzara moved to Paris in 1919, introducing Dada to the restless Parisian art scene. Here is the second stanza of his poem "Approximate Man," translated by Paul Auster:

> what is this language that whips us as we tumble into the light
> our nerves are whips in the hands of time
> and doubt comes with a single colorless wing
> twisting tightening shriveling inside us
> like the crumpled paper of an unpacked box
> gift from another age to the slithering fish of bitterness

This style, and many of the poems from this period, arrive at a narrative by means of layering and repetition, propelled forward by musical intuition—a process of discovery for both the poet and the reader, not an end unto itself. As Dada spread from Zürich to Paris to New York, Cologne, Hanover, and to some extent, Russia, the artists took any and all materials into their work. The collages of Kurt Schwitters that were created in Hanover were ready-made objects of ordinary, everyday usage and subversive because they were litter, bus tickets, candy wrappers, and other scrap papers.

Man Ray's basic tool was the camera, and he also invented the rayograph by placing objects directly against the photographic paper and quickly exposing them. Ray, who had the good fortune to be friends with the celebrated Parisian artist Marcel Duchamp, could not find work or sustenance in New York. In 1921, he wrote Tzara about spreading Dada to America: "Cher Tzara, Dada cannot live in New York. All New York is Dada, and will not tolerate a rival." Duchamp introduced him to the entire galaxy of Parisian artists in July 1921, and there wasn't a single painter present. Ray began to work for André Breton on the magazine *Litterature* and slowly made the acquaintance of every important personage in France, eventually working his way into high-fashion spreads and the elite of Parisian society. "For me," he said, "there's no difference between dream and reality. I never know if what I'm doing is done when I'm dreaming or when I'm awake. When I took photos, when I was in the dark room, I deliberately dodged all the rules. I mixed the most insane products together. I used film way past its use-by date. I committed heinous crimes against chemistry and photography, and you can't see any of it." Though considered experimental, Ray's work found its way into *Vogue, Harper's Bazaar, Vanity Fair*, and other mainstream publications, helping to form a bridge from Surrealism to the advertising world. Experimentation was rampant; Max Ernst used the technique of grattage (scraping) to transfer frottage (rubbing) from drawing to oil painting. To transfer the image, he laid arbitrary patches of color onto a piece of paper. A clean piece was then rubbed gently on top. When separated, strange grottos, exotic vegetation, and underwater scenes suggested themselves to the imagination. A picture was made by chance.

Poets like Hugo Ball and Tzara staged poetry readings and plays designed to outrage and shock their smug, respectable audiences. Cacophany replaced the lovely lyricism of the late Victorian period, as Dada began to mirror the anarchy and obscenity that were hallmarks of the war-weary citizens. The aristocracy was openly mocked and derided in art and performance; witness Duchamp's famous urinal as public fountain with its obvious socio-political overtones or his mustachioed Mona Lisa, which was probably the first example of graffiti as a viable artistic alternative. By the time Duchamp migrated to New York and returned to Paris, Dada's negative parodies and nihilistic resentment of "old" artistic attitudes was replaced by Breton's Automatism and Surrealism's liberated embrace of Freudian theory.

The collision of disciplines and layered themes demonstrated Surrealism's belief in a future, a way out of chaos through the subconscious imagination, the hopeful idea that beauty lurked inside man's baser impulses. Dada gave the Surrealists permission not only to shock their audience but also the responsibility to replace conventional thinking with broader possibilities. Mockery and debasement were tools of the artist, not merely a destination. Also, the liberation of the body and the body's sexual undercurrents, which had been derided by Dada, were now integral to the motives of Surrealism. Disorderly and indiscriminate subversion was the essence of Dada, but it was usually done with a wink or a shrug, and its lasting value was its belief that art had no boundaries and that the old rules no longer applied.

Photography was as interesting as printing; collage made Cubism possible; puppets were as valuable as sculpture; and performances that merged music, poetry, dance, and design were a staple of Dada. Fusion of the arts, which appealed to all the senses at once, made the commingling and various textures of Surrealistic technique come alive. The concept of Dada lacked sophistication and deployed its energy in all directions, but that freedom gave Surrealists like Salvador Dali and Pablo Picasso room to expand their visions. Though Picasso and Georges Braque had already discovered the art of collage with paper, scissors, and glue, Dadaists like Raoul Hausmann used anything he could get his hands on—wire, wood, metal glass, even hair and bones—to form endlessly mutating works that were streams of his unsettled and undisciplined consciousness.

In many ways, you could call Dada the collapse of hope, but the willingness of artists to continue in the face of such devastating conclusions was utopian. No matter how ugly your materials or how base your subject, beauty could be found waiting in the wings, with humor as the calling card that helps her find her suitor. Subversion in art is usually accompanied by seismic changes in cultural attitudes and societal upheavals. It is not important to pinpoint whether one is the cause or effect of the other, but certainly in the case of Dada, the war and its suppression of artistic instinct and viability created the atmosphere, if not the foundation, for the movements that followed.

CHAPTER 19

A Pope in the Throes of Convulsive Beauty

With religion excised from their lives, the avant-garde artists who would be Surrealists needed a pope to replace the one in Rome. André Breton was that man. Born in Normandy and raised modestly by a local shopkeeper and his wife, Breton's origins don't foreshadow the versatile thinker and writer he was to become. But the budding poet was trained in medicine and, later, psychiatry, falling under the influence of Sigmund Freud, whom he met in Vienna in 1921. Unable to join the army during World War I, Breton worked in the psychiatric wards and made some attempts at Freudian psychoanalysis with the patients he encountered there.

One of these young soldiers named Jacques Vaché, whose anti-social views and rebellious nature had an import on Breton, declared art to be nonsense. His angry response to the senseless slaughter in the trenches on the Western Front became a symbol for the anti-war stances of the artists in the Dada movement. His wartime letters to Breton and others were published after his death by suicide in 1919. This volume, entitled *Letters de Guerre*, was bolstered by four introductory essays written by Breton, who edited the letters and found their publisher. This same year, Breton became disillusioned with the nihilism and negativity of the Dada movement and founded the seminal journal of the new movement. He called it *Litterature*, somewhat piously or satirically depending on your point of view, and with Louis Aragon and Phillipe Soupalt as co-editors, he began to systematically define their rebellion in literary and philosophical terms.

Guillaume Apollinaire coined the term "surrealism" in 1917 to describe a spontaneous verbal creation, one that was beyond, or *sur*, reality. Breton took this observation a step further by viewing Surrealism as a means of revisiting conscious and unconscious realms of experience so completely that the world of dream and fantasy would be joined to the everyday rational world in "an absolute reality, a surreality." Drawing heavily from Freudian theory, Breton saw the unconscious as the wellspring of the imagination. Thus, he defined artistic genius in terms of the artist's ability to access this previously untapped realm. This open channel was not the purveyor of destruction but was antithetical to it; expression was a way of releasing negative energies and turning them into art.

Breton began to formulate his ideas into a manifesto for the group. But first, he needed to shed the old ways of living and thinking. "Leave everything," he said. "Leave Dada. Leave your wife. Leave your mistress. Leave your hopes and fears. Leave your children in the woods. Leave the substance for the shadow. Leave your easy life, leave what you are giving for the future. Set off on the road." Already influenced by Stéphane Mallarmé and Paul Valéry among the Symbolists, and encouraged by their essays on literature, Breton launched his career and his subsequent iron-fisted control of the new movement, with all the cynicism of an elder, disheartened but hopeful.

THE SECRET WAR OF ART

Breton's *Manifesto of Surrealism* was published in 1924; in it he defined Surrealism as "pure psychic automatism, by which an attempt is made to express, either verbally, in writing, or in any other manner, the true functioning of thought, the dictation of thought, in the absence of all control by reason, excluding any aesthetic or moral preoccupation." According to Breton, Surrealists should strive to attain "a mental vantage-point from which life and death, the real and the imaginary, past and future, communicable and incommunicable, high and low, will no longer be perceived as contradictions." Both the by-laws for personal freedom and social liberation would spring from the liberation of the unconscious mind. Thus, the only way to truly cope with a chaotic external reality was to embrace the disorder and transform its fractured imagery for your own artistic purpose. The *Manifesto* was a brilliant call to arms, naming those qualified to fight (even their artistic pre-

The Rhythm Method, Razzmatazz, and Memory

decessors) and giving them the tools to fight with. Among the writers who coalesced around the young firebrand, besides the aforementioned Aragon and Soupault, were Paul Éluard, René Crevel, Michel Leiris, Benjamin Péret, Antonin Artaud, and Robert Desnos. Each would alternately join or leave the movement at various times, as their sanity warranted, or as their relationship with Pope Breton caused their excommunication or canonization.

"The French tradition and the English tradition in this epoch are at opposite poles to each other," wrote the Mexican poet Octavio Paz. "French poetry is more radical, more total. In an absolute and exemplary way it has assumed the heritage of European Romanticism, a romanticism which begins with William Blake and the German Romantics like Novalis, and via Baudelaire and the Symbolists culminating in twentieth-century French poetry, notably Surrealism. It is a poetry where the world becomes writing and language becomes the double of the world." The poetry of Breton and all the Surrealists who followed him created a clearinghouse in their poetry, an environment that could assimilate all the literature that had come before, as well as song lyrics, overheard conversational snatches, and cultural bric-a-brac. The political language that George Orwell so feared was subsumed in the giant cauldron that Surrealism stirred, a soup of contrary positions and images, the pawnshop's gathering of thrown-away ad copy, newsreels, guitar strings, and discarded clocks.

This was an art of what was possible, in the belief that art had its own war to wage, a war that would take back the language from the governments and politicians, an art of the fantastic, the marvelous, in celebration of life and sex and death, all in service of the artist. The borders of nations were of no consequence; the imagination was the United Nation, the storehouse and sublime transfer point uniting the mystical and mundane, superimposing the mythological and the patently human, the convergence of humor and despair, tragedy and comedy fused in a single line, as ambivalent as life itself, fair play brought to bear only in the creation, the freedom to be, do, see, write, or sing whatever the imagination reveals to the writer. Analysis becomes pertinent only after it has been preceded by spontaneous delight.

Poetry this ambitious is asking for a new evaluation of reality and requires a transformation of the world. The tools of the preceding poets—the traditional euphony, lyricism, and elegance of the formal structures—had been reassuring for the poet and his audience. Surrealism tears down all expectation and rejects the philosophy of rigorous formalism. The poet could now make each work an adventure, transcendent in the sense that no previous definition or yardstick would suffice. The poet was now free to choose whatever tools suited him, all at once or none at all.

> *The poet could now make each work an adventure, transcendent in the sense that no previous definition or yardstick would suffice. The poet was now free to choose whatever tools suited him, all at once or none at all.*

Dylan Thomas, who rejected the automatism of the Surrealists, was nonetheless transformed by their ways of seeing. "I am a painstaking, conscientious, involved, and devious craftsman in words," he said in an interview with Henry Treece in London in 1937, "however unsuccessful the result so often appears, and to whatever wrong uses I may apply my technical paraphernalia. I use everything and anything to make my poems work and move in the directions I want them to: old tricks, new tricks, puns, portmanteau-words, paradox, allusion, paranomasia, paragram, catachresis, slang, assonated rhymes, vowel rhymes, sprung rhythm. Poets have got to enjoy themselves sometimes, and the twistings and convolutions of words, the inventions and contrivances, are all part of the joy that is part of the painful, voluntary work."

Breton was keenly aware of Freud's discovery that in dreams, the categories of contradiction and opposition are voided, the unconscious is blind to negation, and dreams evince a particular tendency to join opposites together into a unit or to represent them in a single object, iconic or symbolic of the overall feeling. Unquestionably, dreams distort; the dreaming eye sees astigmatically and out of focus. What seems remote to the reader may seem less so for the poet who seeks to reveal the hidden connections between dreams and the "waking" reality. With or without psychoanalysis, it is plain that typical dreams are concerned with common desires, individually expressed. Most dreams are as individual as the person's experience; he alone can supply the clues.

Yet is has long been realized, even before Freud, that the process of thinking in symbols is natural and inherent in the mental procedure. Man has a symbol-making mind. We both feel and see resemblances, and in words we hear rhythms that please, repulse, or attract. Thinking is imagin-

The Rhythm Method, Razzmatazz, and Memory

ing; the pictorial predates the verbal. The art of communication makes primitive man a sign-maker, his urge to explain makes him a myth-maker and a believer in signs. Myth and fable derive their appeal from the same source. As poor a thing as our dreams may be, even Heraclitus recognized that they are mostly conjured in our own private places. But we still have parallel and comparable dreams of flying or falling or fighting a common foe.

Thus, Breton's war on reason, however original, still finds sympathetic ground because successful poems are formed, even intuitively, into watertight compartments that have moving parts tightly organized and universally recognizable, capable of great energy. Here are the last twelve lines of Breton's "Sunflower" dedicated to Pierre Reverdy and translated by Jean-Pierre Cauvin:

> A farm was prospering in the very heart of Paris
> And its windows looked out on the Milky Way
> But no one lived there yet because of unexpected callers
> Drop-in guests known to be more devoted than ghosts
> A few like that woman seem to be swimming
> And in love there enters some of their substance
> She interiorizes them
> I am the pawn of no sensory power
> And yet the cricket singing in the ashen hair
> One evening near the statue of Etienne Marcel
> Gave me a knowing look
> Andre Breton it said pass on

REVERIE AND THE DIVINE FEMININE PRINCIPLE

In the early 1920s, Breton had taken Arthur Rimbaud's "derangement of the senses" to heart, and many of the early literary "experiments" took place under the influence of hypnotism, drugs, drunkenness, or sleep-deprived trance states of exhaustion or hunger. Breton eventually rejected these "mechanical aids," as he would later reject the automatic mode of writing, understanding that as his work progressed, patience and careful editing also lead to breakthroughs in logic, narrative, and objectivity. It can also be argued that Freud's understanding of psychoanalysis was at loggerheads with the Surrealists' aim. Freud's use of the technique carried with it the intention of curing man's mental and emotional disorders in order to make him capable of functioning "normally" in modern society. For Breton, the anarchic energy of unconscious desire must be liberated in order to shatter the easy continuation of bourgeois life. The process of free association made collage possible, but the Surrealists had other games, such as Exquisite Corpse, where one person would begin a drawing or sentence, cover it, and pass it on to others to be continued and completed. They also developed a literary equivalent to Truth or Dare, or Truth or Consequences, creating hilarious scenarios as each participant upped the level of punishment as "truth" was withheld.

It is no accident that many of the Surrealists' themes were overtly sexual; much of the Freudian method required close examination of sexual tendencies, repression, and manifestation of symbolic desires. Most of the artists had open relationships with their partners, glorifying the chance encounter and the *ménage à trois*, all potential gateways to self-revelation and poetic material. Breton's most famous work, a novel entitled *Nadja*, documents an intense affair and begins with the words, "Who am I?" *Nadja*, published in 1928, is a portrait of Breton and a mad woman, a patient of Pierre Janet. The title refers both to the name of a woman and the beginning of the Russian word for hope. Breton's first-person narrative is supplemented by forty-four photographs of places and objects that inspired the author or were associated with *Nadja*. His poem "Free Union" demonstrates the idea of layered imagery, the overwhelming convergence of emotion and disparate associations. Here are the first fifteen lines, translated by Mary Ann Caws and Patricia Terry:

> My love whose hair is woodfire
> Her thoughts beat lightning
> Her hourglass waist
> An otter in the tiger's jaws my love
> Her mouth a rosette bouquet of the highest
>   magnitude
> The footprints of white mice on the white earth her teeth
> Her tongue rubbed amber and glass
> My love her tongue a sacred host stabbed through
> Her tongue a doll whose eyes close and open
> Her tongue an incredible stone

A child's hand traced each eyelash
Her eyebrows the edge of a swallow's nest
My love her temples slates on a greenhouse roof
And their misted panes
My love whose shoulders are champagne

Much of the interplay of erotic imagery in Breton's work concerns the paradox of the feminine principal activating the masculine, not vice versa. This is wholly reminiscent of Johann Wolfgang Goethe's observation that "the Eternal Feminine is in truth the keystone of the edifice," and the observation by the German theosophist J. W. Ritter that "Man, stranger on earth, is acclimatized here below by woman alone." Breton echoed both men in his assertion that "love and women are the clearest solution to all enigmas." The consummation of desire and orgasmic fulfillment is viewed by the Surrealists as the arrival of logic, convulsive beauty the result of a dialectical process, the precise balance of action and inertia, manifested between spontaneity and chance, "neither dynamic or static." In the conclusion of *Fata Morgana*, Breton wrote:

When the basilisk passed close by without seeing me
Just let him come back I've got my mirror trained on him
Unprescribable human jug is made there to be consummated
In a convulsion ended by a splash of gilded feathers

Breton's theories on art as reverie were constructed on the idea that the source of convulsive beauty lies in its pre-existent form, where the poet must swim upriver to find his anima waiting, to strip from himself the pretense of listening or seeing. Devoid of causality, the poet may, in the words of Mallarmé, "hear in its flesh the diamond crying." Breton had imagined a movement of divine proportions, not a philosophy for art, but for life itself, a pathway toward deeper connection, between men and women, between man and the natural world, between cultures devoid of governmental controls. In his book *Communicating Vessels*, Breton laments the burden of fame as his epoch burns out:

This time I live in, this time alas, runs by and
takes me with it. That crazed and, as it
were, accidental impatience in which it is

caught up spares me nothing. There is today,
    it is true, little room for anyone who would
    haughtily trace in the grass the learned
    arabesque of the suns.

UNDONE BY COMMITTEE

Breton believed, above all, in the reason and reactions of a group. He believed in himself as an organizer of artists, for whom their collective passion would inspire the others outside to passionate rediscovery, the idea that there was a "superiority of impassioned people to people with mere common sense." In the beginning, Breton and Soupault had collaborated, then he with Paul Éluard, then René Char. Each of the members had worked with one another, with varying degrees of success. But the idea of the collective, coupled with an intense need for change, caused the caucus to embrace the ideas of Karl Marx as readily as those of Freud. From the beginning, even after the publication of the first manifesto in 1924, the group established political hierarchies, such as the establishment of the "Bureau of Surrealist Research," headed by Artaud, who had joined the group and who helped organize the journal *La Revolution Surrealiste*.

Many of the new recruits after this initial notoriety were painters, such as Joan Miro, Yves Tanguy, André Masson, and especially Salvador Dali, whose work would, along with René Magritte, Marc Chagall, and Paul Klee, bring Surrealism worldwide notoriety. Pablo Picasso, whom Breton revered, had always remained aloof, too independent to answer to the tenets of a group philosophy. Breton's initial precepts had defined Surrealism in literary and philosophical terms, but he was an art collector himself and had written essays on the work of Giorgio De Chirico, Francis Picabia, Marcel Duchamp, and Max Ernst, whose own experimentation had inspired a generation of Parisian artists.

Many of the original artists named in the first manifesto as inspirations to the movement were painters, such as Francisco de Goya, Hieronymus Bosch, Henri Rousseau, William Blake, Paolo Ucello, Giovanni Piranesi, John Henry Fuseli, and the work of Paul Gaugin in Tahiti, which produced mystical visions of everyday life. The African masks and primitive art that had inspired Picasso and Georges Braque during their Cubism period were also hailed as precursors to automatic reverie and imagery. But as the 1930s came with political upheavals in Russia and Spain, the worry of painters in the movement took a back seat to the embrace of Communism.

From 1929 to 1933, the group published a new review, *Surrealism at the Service of the Revolution*. This desire for political affiliation is also reflected in Breton's *Second Manifesto* of 1929, which turned the group toward socialist concerns while simultaneously demanding the "occultation of Surrealism" against the narrowness of scientific rationalism. Much of the rest of the manifesto is taken up with Breton's self-justifying arguments against those he felt were betraying the spirit of surrealism and who had thus left or been expelled from the group.

Of all the poets associated with the movement, only Benjamin Peret remained faithful to Breton over the long term. Soupault, by nature averse to the notion of any literary organization, lost interest by 1927. Both Artaud and Robert Desnos were excommunicated in 1929—Artaud for opposing Surrealism's cozying-up to Communism, and Desnos for supposedly compromising his integrity by working as a journalist. Aragon, Tzara, and Éluard all joined the Communist Party in the 1930s. Raymond Queneau and Jacques Prévert parted amicably after a brief flirtation. Breton, meanwhile, rejecting the dictatorship of the French Communists, sought a more productive (if short-lived) collaboration with Leon Trotsky, that culminated in their co-written "Manifesto for an Independent Revolutionary Art" in 1938.

From 1927 to 1935, Breton had been a member of the French Communist Party, but he broke away in disgust with Stalinism and the Moscow show trials, one of the reasons he had sought out Trotsky in the first place. When the Nazis occupied France, Breton fled to the United States with Duchamp and Ernst. He held a radio broadcasting job for *Voice of America* in New York and arranged a Surrealist exposition at Yale University in 1942. In fact, along with Dali, the exile of these men to the United States during World War II was a primary catalyst for Surrealism's quick spread into America.

By the early 1940s, Breton, having been right for the better part of twenty years, suddenly began to be wrong. Samuel Johnson once wrote, "All censure of a man's self is oblique praise. It is in order to show how much he can spare." On at least two occasions, Breton got in public fistfights over his increasingly rigid ideas about literature. In 1935, he slapped the Soviet writer Ilya Ehrenburg in the face for the Russian's perceived attacks on Surrealism and was forcibly removed from the Congress. Breton then completely broke with Communism and condemned Stalinism as an aberrant version of Marx's teachings. In 1947, while attending a lecture at the Sorbonne by Tzara, who declared that Surrealism had run its course, Breton stormed the stage and began pummeling his old friend.

It could be argued that this type of passionate commitment to an ideal is sorely missing these days, but it is also clear that Breton could not abide being the founding father of an anachronism or take into account conflicting reminders of Surrealism's adaptability, now that it had morphed into streams and was flowing into other cultures and countries. French and Spanish Surrealism are twins in name only. American Surrealism was and is the red-headed stepchild in literature, with the arts of painting and sculpture more directly amenable to its pervasive effects.

One of the most alluring aspects of Surrealism at the outset was its openness to new concepts. Poets wrote novels, novelists wrote librettas. Photographers made paintings, painters and sculptors made films. The movement's *Central Bureau* of *Surrealist Research* invited the public to share its views, and gave out literature outlining their aims. Pamphlets and fliers were distributed that bore slogans like "If you're not a priest, a general, or an ass, you'll be a Surrealist," "Unbutton your brain as often as your fly," "If you love love, you'll love Surrealism." In the 1930s, Surrealism had spread through most of Europe, with an especially active chapter in Prague. In the 1940s, during World War II, many of its greatest figures decamped for America and Mexico, where the movement began to thrive even after Breton's death in Paris in 1966.

Breton, who battled right to the end, visited many Indian reservations while in the United States, and spent time in the West Indies before returning to France in 1946. He then began to champion primitive art and wrote several more books of poetry and criticism before his death. Afterward, his three-room studio at 42 Rue Fontaine in Paris became a research center, preserved by his third wife, Elisa Claro. His daughter Aube (from his second marriage to Jacqueline Lamba) decided to put his archives on the market in 2003 after the French government refused to purchase his highly valuable personal collection of books, drawings, paintings, sculptures, photographs, and letters. Buried in the *Cimetiere des Batignolles* in Paris, the headnote on his grave marker reads: "I seek the gold of time."

Breton believed that sheer emotion could overcome contradictions, an abstract notion, romantic even, but the Surrealists wanted to create more than art. They considered Surrealism a mode for living—a vastly ambitious one to be sure—hoping, through "lyric behavior," to transform human understanding of art and the world. Consider this passage from *Communicating Vessels*, translated for us by Mary Ann Caws:

> The poet to come will surmount the depressing idea
> of the irreparable divorce between action
> and dream ... From then on the poetic
> operation will be conducted in broad daylight.
> No one will any longer try to pick a quarrel
> with a few people, who in the long run
> will become all people, because of actions
> long considered suspicious by others and
> ambiguous by themselves, actions they pursue
> in order to retain eternity in the moment
> and to fuse the general with the particular
> ... they will already be outside, mingled
> with everyone else in full sunlight, and will
> cast no more complicitous or intimate a
> look than others do at truth itself when
> it comes to shake out, at their dark window,
> its hair streaming with light.

CHAPTER 20

The Destructive
Tendencies of Diamonds
That Won't Stay Coal

The fact that many of the Surrealists' precepts about free love came to influence sexual attitudes the world over in the 1960s and 1970s does not solve the complicated emotional entanglements that such attitudes can create. André Breton's ideas about emotion trumpeting contraries or that the "problem of woman is the most marvelous and disturbing problem in the world," were probably conceived before he met the "mother" of Surrealism, Helena Dmitrievna Deluvina Diakonova, renamed Gala by Paul Éluard. Paris between World Wars was full of beautiful muses and artists' models, many made famous by the painters who immortalized them on canvas. Many others fed themselves by posing for the camera of Man Ray. Pablo Picasso's Fernande Olivier, Eva Gouel, and Dora Maar; Man Ray's Kiki of Montparnasse; Lee Miller, Nusch, Alice Apfel, Meret Oppenheimer, and many more dropped their clothes and their expectations and then became quite famous for their image or their marriages. Some had more staying power than others.

Perhaps the most successful was Gala, who was born in Russia around 1895 of Jewish descent. She met Paul Éluard in 1912, when both were inmates of a Swiss tuberculosis sanitarium. Four years later, still a mere teenager, she traveled alone across several countries in the middle of World War I in order to rejoin her lover, who had been drafted into the French army and was on furlough at his parent's home outside Paris. They married in the winter of 1917, and by the next summer, Gala was pregnant. Baby Cécile was remanded into the care of Paul's mother, and the glittering first couple

The Rhythm Method, Razzmatazz, and Memory

of Surrealism, having both survived TB and the war (which found Paul badly wounded by mustard gas), now set their sights on Paris. There they began to throw themselves into the artistic and social experiments swirling about them. Paul Éluard, the pen name of Eugene Grindel, came from a lower-middle-class family in Saint-Denis and was the son of a bookkeeper, whose wife helped with the household finances by dressmaking. Born in 1895, Éluard had begun to write poems while at the sanitarium, inspired by Walt Whitman's *Leaves of Grass*. His first book of poems was published in 1913 when he was barely eighteen.

With Louis Aragon, and under the considerable influence of Breton, Éluard began to develop into one of the finest lyrical poets in twentieth century French literature. His love poems are especially vivid, and the language is built on very simple syntactical ideas. His sentences are typically short but pointed, and like most Surrealist poetry, his images are multi-layered and full of symbology. The idea of love and love-making is more prescient in Éluard's poetry than any of his contemporaries, and many times the idea of love is compared to the creative process itself, as a way to make sense of the world and to escape it.

One of the more seminal characteristics of Surrealist poetry is its mimesis and love of nature. Many of its early proponents are transplanted country boys let loose in the urban scenery of Paris. Thus, nature becomes idealized beyond the city's borders, and the destruction of nature becomes one of the hallmarks of the diseased society the Surrealists were resisting. In 1925, Éluard published one of the best collections of Surrealist poetry, *Capital of Pain*. The collection sought to wed the inner life of the man to the outer physical landscape—believing the processes mirrored one another—and posited the belief that man might improve himself psychologically and, from this vantage point, improve the world. "Elephants are contagious," Éluard said in a sentence designed to illustrate the power of the unexpected, "and love is man unfinished." Before Gala, before the advent of Surrealism, Éluard had felt the weight of inexpressible sorrow; only through poetry did he consider himself saved. These lines are from his poem "At the Window":

There was a time when I seemed to understand
nothing. My chains floated on the water.
All my desires are born of my dreams. To what

fantastic creatures have I entrusted myself, in what
dolorous and ravishing world has my imagination
enclosed me? I am sure of having been loved in
the most mysterious of domains, my own. The
language of my love does not belong to human
language, my human body does not touch the
flesh of my love. My amorous imagination has
always been constant and high enough so that
nothing could attempt to convince me of error.

In 1930, Éluard published, in collaboration with Breton, *L'Immaculate Conception*, a series of poems in prose, in which they entered into communication with the vegetative life of a fetus and simulated demented states. In it, Éluard wrote, "Of all the ways the sunflower has of loving the light, regret is the loveliest on the sundial. Crossbones, crosswords, volumes and volumes of ignorance and knowledge. The doe, between bounds, likes to look at me. I keep her company in the glade. I fall slowly from the heights, as yet I weigh only what minus a hundred thousand yards will weigh ..." By adding words to line and color, Éluard hoped to abolish the barrier between the "seeing" subject and the "perceived" object. Painting, like poetry, was a true conduit for beauty, because it belonged to both the real and the imaginary at the same time.

Another aspect of Éluard's existence merged contrary aspirations of supposed and concrete whims. During a group holiday of artists in the Austrian Alps, the painter Max Ernst fell in love with Gala, promptly left his wife, Lou, and young son, Jimmy, and went to live with Gala and Éluard. Lou Ernst would be one of the first to describe the Russian enchantress in a letter to a friend after Max had left Lou flat broke with an infant in tow: "she is a slithering, glittering creature with dark falling hair, vaguely oriental and luminant black eyes and small delicate bones, who had to remind one of a panther. This almost silent, avaricious woman, who, having failed to entice her husband into an affair with me in order to get Ernst, finally decided to keep both men, with Éluard's loving consent." In actuality, Éluard's loving consent had surfaced in other affairs preceding this one, most notably with another painter, Giorgio de Chirico. "You don't know what it is like to be married to a Russian woman," Éluard had written to Aragon. Thus began the two-year *ménage à trois* of Gala, Éluard, and Ernst, which Éluard described

The Rhythm Method, Razzmatazz, and Memory

in *Investigating Sex*, a series of Surrealist colloquies on the sexual habits and peccadilloes of the artists in the movement. The mystical and smoky Gala was at this time most famous for the nude photos of her circulating among the artists, her unfailingly accurate tarot readings, and her "eyes that could pierce through walls," according to Éluard.

Finally, after many splits, reconciliations, and public dramas, Éluard took off on a trip by himself around the world. Éluard, who partially supported the household by dealing art, was surprised to find Gala and Ernst waiting for him in Saigon. Gala had sold Éluard's entire art collection to pay for their tickets. No record remains of this unexpected reunion, but when the Éluards returned to Paris, they were not accompanied by Ernst. He returned to his wife, and Éluard and Gala settled down for a brief moment of domestic bliss. Neither of them would be prepared for what came next. Neither they nor their Surrealistic colleagues could have forseen the arrival of Surrealism's most famous practitioner, whose canvases would define the movement and carry its message around the globe in ways none of their literary enterprises could possibly have imagined.

DALÍ IN CATALONIA: A GIANT CYPRESS KNOT OF PARANOIA

Whereas the Surrealists had spent the better part of a decade delineating the doctrine whereby one might enter the club, one artist had already become Surrealist in the extreme exigency of his behavior and in the comet-like combustibility of his rapidly expanding brainpan. Salvador Dalí was sprung on Paris fully formed as an artist, already capable of assimilating enormous chunks of artistic strategies and intentions, with a flawless technique at the disposal of his sharply discerning intellect.

Dalí was born in 1904 in Figueras, a small town in the northern part of Catalonia, Spain. His father was the state notary, a very dictatorial man who understood from the beginning that his son was born to be an artist. Beautiful as a child, Dalí was temperamental and difficult, imposing his will on his parents, who doted on him. Even as an adolescent, he began to adopt the attributes of the artist-dandy to enhance his image—wearing odd clothing in bizarre colors, letting his hair and sideburns grow long (the precursor to that crazy flying mustache), and striding about using a cane with a pommel. He began painting in earnest when he was eight years old.

However spoiled the boy was, his upbringing also engendered many morbid fantasies and psychosexual behaviors. He was named after a brother who died before he was born and whose photograph flew like a flag over his parents' bed. Dalí set out to prove his own genius, not the wish fulfillment of disappointed parents. "I am the living one," he told them. It has been suggested by Francine Prose and others that Dalí was molested by an eccentric schoolmaster, that he had an affair with his younger sister Ana Maria, and that, as an older boy, he continued to sleep naked with his mother, possibly to console her for being neglected by her husband, who was allegedly sleeping with his wife's younger sister, whom he married after Dalí's mother died at an early age.

Though Breton had claimed Sigmund Freud as one of the primary architects for the psychological structures and techniques that informed Surrealism's mining of the subconscious, Dalí took the Freudian precepts a step further. Salvador Dalí was a giant cypress knot of paranoia, repressed sexuality, and scatalogical roots tangled together in a method he called "critical paranoia." According to this theory, one should cultivate genuine delusion, as in a clinical paranoid state, while remaining residually aware at the back of one's mind that the control of reason and will had been deliberately suspended. He claimed that this method should be used not only in artistic and poetic creation but also in the affairs of daily life. His paintings employed a meticulous academic technique that was contradicted by the unreal dream space he depicted and the strangely hallucinogenic characters of his Catalonian seascapes and desert settings. He described his pictures as "hand-painted dream photographs," and indeed his paintings look like the nightmares or terror-blotted states that every person has experienced during sleep or daydream or drug-induced hallucinations.

Dalí endowed Surrealism, as Breton was to write, "with a weapon of the first caliber," and through this method, he invited Surrealists to systematize confusion and to utilize the first irrational material that their minds confronted. Dalí, an acolyte of Raphael, was a mixture of the classic and the baroque, transcending an impotent subjectivity with an ostensible mobility to form objects of apparent order from compositions that, on the surface, are exploding with ideas of anarchy and even madness. Photographer, writer, and leading Dalí expert Robert Descharnes has called him "an uninterrupted series of fireworks."

In 1922, Dalí moved to the students' residence at the San Fernando School of Fine Arts in Madrid. There, he met the artists Luis Buñuel and Federico Garcia Lorca with whom he became great friends and collaborators, and in the case of Lorca, their collaborations occasionally included a foray into sexual realms as well. In his book *Revolutionnaires sans Revolution*, Andre Thirion described the young Dalí: "In spite of his stay at the Academy of Fine Arts in Madrid, Dalí gave the erroneous impression of having scarcely been cut off from his mother's apron strings. He wore a thin mustache like that of the movie star Adolphe Menjou. He was slender, timid, and phlegmatic, but well mannered. His inexhaustible eloquence was enhanced by the comic effects of his natural humor and Spanish accent, but he knew how to keep quiet and did so for long periods, curled up in an armchair, observant and serious. His prodigious intelligence enabled him to topple no matter what intellectual structure by bringing into play comical enormities at which he was the only one that did not laugh." Dalí was immediately disappointed with the instruction he received at the Academy. The young painter had already assimilated Impressionism, Fauvism, and Pontillism, and through Juan Gris, Georges Seurat, and the Italian metaphysical school, he had begun to demonstrate remarkable facility for the Cubists, sometimes mixing multiple styles within the same canvas. Throughout his teenage years, he had attended night school to perfect his drawing skills. Picasso compared his mind to an outboard motor continuously running.

Much of Dalí's impact is predicated on the precision of his technique. In contrast to other painters, particularly the Surrealists in whose works the backgrounds and landscapes are imaginary, Dalí had codified and systematically accumulated the cliffs, deserts, oceans, towns, and skies of his childhood Spain and given them the realism and intimacy of a room. To view Dalí is to walk along the coastline of Catalonia, accompanied by the most original and terrifying figures in twentieth-century art.

Dalí was suspended from the Academy for a year for inciting the other students to riot against a new professor whom he considered to be mediocre. After a year of intense work, he returned to school in Madrid only to be expelled for good, shortly before the final exams, because he stated that no one on the faculty was competent enough to judge his work.

Shortly thereafter, he had his first one-man show at the Dalmau Gallery in Barcelona (which received a warm reception). His relationship with Lorca deepened after the young poet spent the summer of 1925 with the Dalí family. Their relationship was commemorated by Lorca's "Ode to Salvador Dalí," which was written in loose Alexandrine stanzas that strained to explain what he was seeing in Dalí's paintings and the feelings these paintings and their creator engendered in him. Here are stanzas eighteen and nineteen:

> You love matter defined and exact
> where a mushroom cannot raise its fent.
> You love architecture which constructs in absentia
> and you take the flag as a simple joke.
>
> The steel compass recited its short elastic verse.
> The sphere already contradicts unknown islands.
> The straight line expresses its vertical effort
> and the wise crystals sing their geometries.

Though it has been a matter of some dispute, primarily owing to Dalí's inconsistent accounts, the sexual relationship between the two reached its zenith in that first summer. Some biographers have suggested that Dalí's horror of being touched prohibited any sexual contact, but Dalí is on record as having said, "I felt he was a great poet and that I did owe him a tiny bit of the divine Dalí's asshole." When Lorca had heard that Dalí had fallen in love with Gala Éluard, he is said to have exclaimed, "It's impossible! He can only get an erection when someone sticks a finger up his anus!" It does seem probable that some type of intimacy took place, even though Dalí wrote in *Les Passions selon Dalí:* "When Lorca tried to seduce me, I refused with horror." Dalí also told Carlton Lake that he had never consummated his love with Gala, even though they had been together for decades: "I prefer to remain pure," he sniffed, "and save my sexuality for my work."

This was certainly not the case at the beginning of 1927, when Dalí spent his first week in Paris, "marked," he said, "by three important visits: Versaille, The Musée Grévin, and Picasso." Later, he admitted that he and Joan Miró had made a tour of the most famous brothels in the French capital and that the stairway of the Chabanais had produced the deepest impression of mystery upon him. It was during this trip that he met the Surrealists Paul Éluard and René Magritte for the first time, and they agreed to pay him a visit in Cadaques the next summer. It was a fateful decision for everyone involved.

The Rhythm Method, Razzmatazz, and Memory

THE ARTIST EMERGES FROM A CAVERN OF LIES

Dalí's second trip to Paris did not go exactly as planned. Though he had collaborated with Luis Buñuel on Surrealism's first film, entitled *Un Chien Andalou*, and attracted the attention of several significant artists and gallery owners, Dalí did not rule Paris "like a Caesar," and he had not succeeded "in finding a woman, elegant or not elegant, who would agree to lend herself to my erotic fantasies." Most importantly, however, the Surrealists had seized his imagination, and from this merger, his mature work burst forth in full flower: *Honey is Sweeter Than Blood*; *Illumined Pleasures*; *Portrait of Paul Éluard*; *The Enigma of Desire: My Mother, My Mother, My Mother*; and especially *The Great Masturbator* were paintings of a singular talent whose combination of technique and intellect would produce images that came to define Surrealism for the rest of the world, especially in America.

One piece of the puzzle leading to Dalí's world dominance and complete transformation was still missing. She came strutting into place in the summer of 1929, on the arm of Paul Éluard and accompanied by René and Georgette Magritte and Luis Buñuel. Gala Éluard was already becoming Dalí's advocate, whispering in the ear of Camille Goemans, the Parisian art dealer that would give him his first French commissions, that the young Catalonian was a world-class talent and his painting *The Lugubrious Game* (so named by Paul Éluard) was just the beginning of his output. Indeed, Goemans decided to head to Spain that summer with the rest of the group, to drop in on their young charge to see what he was doing and to plan an exhibition of his work. Gala had already learned that the most popular labor-saving device in Paris was a husband with money. Salvador Dalí would become that money tree, perpetually in blossom for the next fifty years.

From his memoir, *The Secret Life of Salvador Dalí*, Dalí describes his preparation to meet the group for a planned day at the beach: "I tried on my sister's earrings several times. I liked them on myself but decided they would be a nuisance for the swim. Nevertheless I put on my pearl necklace and took my finest shirt and cut it irregularly at the bottom, making it so short that it did not reach my navel. I began to tear it artfully: one hole, baring my left shoulder, another the black hairs on my chest, and a large square tear on the left side exposing my nipple that was nearly black." Dalí then decided to wear his sporty swim trunks inside out so as to exhibit the shit stains on the cotton lining. The painter was clearly in an existential panic, merely twenty-five years old and feeling that he was facing a jury of older artists who would decide once and for all if he would be admitted to their exclusive Parisian club.

So, on the morning of this most important day, Dalí was exhibiting a character trait that would help make him such an eccentric figure in the media. (Some notorious examples include carrying a long-molded loaf of bread through the streets while leading an ocelot on a leash, arriving at an art opening in a Rolls Royce filled with cauliflower, and giving a lecture in London in a deep-sea diver's suit and almost suffocating.) As Dalí prepared himself to meet his friends, he continued to find just the right combination to express himself. "What could I do about my swimming costume?" he wrote. "I decided to shave the hair under my arms. I went and got some laundry bluing, mixed it with some powder, and dyed my armpits with this. The effect was very fine for a moment, but immediately my sweat caused this makeup to run ... then I had a new idea, I took my Gillette and began to shave again, pressing harder so as to make myself bleed. In a few seconds my armpits were all bloody ... My transformation appeared to me more and more desirable, and each moment I fell more in love with my appearance. Adroitly I stuck a fiery-red geranium behind my ear ... I should have liked some kind of perfume, but I had only *Eau de Cologne*, which made me sick to my stomach. I would therefore have to invent something else for this. I began to boil some water in which I dissolved some fish glue. While waiting for this to boil, I ran out in back of the house where I know several sacks of goat manure had been delivered. Back in my studio, I threw a handful of this manure, and then another, into the dissolved glue. I let the whole thing jell, and when it was cold I took a fragment of the paste that I had made and rubbed my whole body with it."

At that moment, Gala passed by his window and Dalí was struck by her bare back, so like an adolescent in size. Her back, according to Dalí, "served as an infinitely svelte hyphen between the willful, energetic and proud leanness of her torso and her very delicate buttocks." He was smitten and frantically began to wash the stinking paste off his body and throw away his "fashionable" trunks, though he retained the pearl necklace and the red geranium. Somehow this giggling, paranoid, wildly talented, immature Spaniard—with his feeling of being an outsider—seduced, or was seduced by, the lioness Gala within a few days.

When Paul Éluard returned to Paris, leaving his wife and daughter with Dalí in Cadaques, he believed he was returning to prepare his family's new flat on the Rue Becquerel. He would respond to Gala's absence by writing her long pornographic letters of great detail and full of gossip, travel, politics, and his ever-burgeoning sexual longing for her. Thus, their pattern was almost immediately set; Éluard's letters followed by short reunions where they would have sex and then go back to their subsequent partners and more letters. Their passion for one another seems never to have abated, and this connection became deeper than their common feelings for their daughter, Cécile. It is little wonder that Éluard's love poems are some of the most beautiful lyrics by the Surrealists. Here is a relatively mild offering, called "Marine," from *Derniers Poemes d'Amour*, translated by Marilyn Kallet:

I look at you and the sun grows
Soon it will cover our day
Wake up heart and color first
Dissolve night's sorrow

I look at you everything is bare
Outside the boats are in low tide
Everything must be said in a few words
The sea is cold without love

It is the beginning of the world
The waves are going to rock the sky
You rock yourself in your sheets
You pull sleep toward you

Wake up so that I may follow your tracks
I have a body to wait to follow you
From the doors of dawn to the doors of shadow
A body to spend my life loving you

A heart to dream outside your sleep.

Éluard eventually recovered enough to re-marry Nusch, a gorgeous model who was a favorite of both Man Ray and Picasso. During World War II, Éluard served in the French army and in the Communist resistance, publishing poems under such pseudonyms as Jean du Hault and Maurice Hervent. To avoid the Gestapo, he and Nusch constantly changed addresses and were protected by a network of friends and artists. Éluard's most famous poems during these years, "Liberty" and "Rendez-vous Allemand," were spread throughout France. After the war, Éluard retained his commitment to Communist causes the world over and eventually died of a heart attack in 1952.

Many years of Éluard's life were filled with episodes trying to reconcile Cécile and her mercurial mother. Cécile, who sold many of the Dalí paintings in her possession in order to survive the second World War, never believed that her mother loved her and was estranged from Gala for long periods of time. After Éluard's death, the two women never spoke again. Éluard's deep feelings for his "sex gypsy" were consistent throughout his life, even during the Occupation. He composed more than seventy books, inspiring poets and filmmakers (Jean-Luc Godard's *Alphaville* was inspired by Éluard's *Capital of Pain*) with his direct, highly symbolic imagery. One of his last poems is entitled "Even When We Sleep" and shows his remarkable optimism and belief in the power of nature and the visionary effects of love, the cause of man's most lasting joy. Here is the small poem, again translated by Kallet:

Even when we sleep we watch over one another
And this love heavier than the ripe fruit of a lake
Without laughter without tears has lasted forever
Day after day night after us.

The joint enterprise of Gala-Dalí emerged from the Spanish cliffs with a hydra-headed spirit of artistic capitalism. First, Dalí set out to conquer the Surrealists with his exhibition at the Goemans Gallery in Paris. The show included all the paintings completed while Dalí had languished in Spain after Gala's departure; they were like nothing the Surrealists had seen or attempted. They did have aspects of de Chirico and Bosch, but the backgrounds, with infinitely receding planes and haunting perspectives of light and shadow, were new and bizarre, marked by a fresh level of technical brilliance and a frenzied courage to communicate the artist's foreboding dreamscapes. They were sprung from a world of terror with a Freudian sureness that their symbolism was important, even prophetic.

In his foreword to the exhibition catalog, Breton placed his hopes for the future of Surrealism in Dalí's eager hands. Breton wrote that this was perhaps "the first time that the mental windows have been opened wide ... We feel ourselves sliding toward the trapdoor of an evil sky." Frightened and excited by the presence of Dalí's art, Breton called it "the most hallucinatory we have yet seen ... a veritable menace. Completely new beings, visibly

The Rhythm Method, Razzmatazz, and Memory

well-intentioned, have started on the march." Breton understood the break-through that Dalí represented, and the old concept of reality that the Sur-realists detested could now be brought down, with the full Freudian arsenal in the hands of a painter whose technique was impeccable. Both Breton and Éluard contributed essays to Dalí's book *La Femme Visible*, which was largely put together from Dalí's diary entries and rambling notes on his method. Gala had provided the editorial direction and proposed the involve-ment of her ex-husband and Breton, who happily obliged, declaring Dalí the artist most capable to liberate man from "his cavern of lies," that "miserable expedient that calls itself reality."

During the Goemans exhibit, all the paintings were sold for six to twelve thousand francs, and several were purchased by the Viscount and Viscount-ess Charles and Marie-Laure de Noailles, who would become Dalí's first pa-trons. They agreed to finance his next collaboration with Buñuel, the movie *L'Age d'Or*. This movie brought Surrealism into the general consciousness of the French populace, creating riots and a rupture in the friends' long re-lationship. The Spaniard had arrived, however, and soon he and Gala took their newfound financial security and headed out of Paris back to Spain and the tiny seaside city of Port Lligat. There, they purchased a piece of land and a house that they constantly expanded for the next four decades in their determined samurai march from Port Lligat to Paris and New York and back again. For the most part, they remained in Spain except for promotion-al or financial sojourns to France and the United States. Two events caused them to break their cycle: the Spanish Civil War and the second World War.

AVIDA DOLLARS

This capitalization on his fame and Dalí's subsequently ambivalent political viewpoints finally popped the top of his Surrealist bedfellows. Whereas the program of Dada had been both simple and direct—to wipe out all the old standards of value, including the family, the class system, politics, religion, and the established governmental levers of control, both the police and the army—Surrealism was more optimistic and aimed its precepts specifically at social improvement. Surrealism had inherited all the old targets, but the Sur-realists, with their roots in Freud, believed in the redemptive power of sex and love, and many of its main protagonists eventually joined the Communist Party and embraced the purer aspects of its pointed socialism. Breton's "passionate quest for liberty" believed in the triumph of desire over constraint and the elimination of all conventional modes of thought.

But from the very beginning, the unity of the Surrealist movement had been shaken by the divergent aims and motivations of its many strong-willed members. Dalí's greatest strengths—his unpredictable intellect and independence—soon created a schism between himself and the others. Even before he became a member of the group, they were trying to modify, if not dictate, the content of his paintings. In 1934, he had been called to account for what seemed to some members an unacceptably ambivalent attitude toward Adolf Hitler. In his explanation, Dalí went to great pains to separate the aesthetic from the political in his feelings for the Führer. What fascinated him, he claimed, was the soft, plump flesh he felt every time he began to paint Hitler in his tight-fitting military tunic. Dalí was also accused of racism for some of his Latin-supremacy theories, which according to art critic and curator Carlton Lake, "may have been nothing more than a combination of his paranoic-critical method and his extreme Spanish pride." But Dalí's enormous commercial success and his well-publicized allegiance to General Franco (whose forces had earlier executed Dalí's former best friend, the great Lorca) forced Breton and the others to expel Dalí from the group. Though Dalí's aristocratic, right-wing sympathies alienated him from Picasso and Miró, as well as the Surrealists, he still waited out the Spanish Civil War abroad, away from the reach of any fickle dictators.

In January 1934, the group summoned Dalí to a meeting in Breton's studio. Dalí arrived wearing several sweaters and a muffler-scarf, supposedly suffering from the flu. During Breton's indictment he remained silent, keeping a thermometer in his mouth, with which he periodically checked his tem-

> *Just as the poetry of Baudelaire, Rimbaud, and Apollinaire had anointed the use of juxtaposed and contradictory themes, Dalí's contending imagery is based on seemingly opposed images thrust against one another in the same frame, highlighting their similarities and moving the yard marker of reality for the participating audience.*

The Rhythm Method, Razzmatazz, and Memory

perature. Then, when asked to respond, he took off his wool sweaters one by one and said that since he was trying to describe dreams, he did not have the right (according to Surrealist thought) to exercise any conscious control over their content. Was it his fault, he said, if he dreamed of Hitler or Jean-François Millet's *Angélus* or William Tell? When Dalí came to the passage where he said, "Therefore, according to me, Hitler has four balls and six foreskins," Breton shouted vehemently, "How much longer are you going to continue to bore us with this damn nonsense about Hitler?" Dalí replied, "Since all night long I dream of sodomizing you, I have the right to paint my dream."

Following the meeting, needless to say, Dalí was notified of his expulsion from the group. Breton coined a brilliant anagram for Dalí's name: *Avida Dollars*, which more or less translates to "eager for dollars." Dalí shot back in his *Le Jounral d-ungenie*, "The only difference between me and the Surrealists is that I am a Surrealist. I took Surrealism literally, neglected neither the blood nor the excrements on which its advocates fed their diatribes. In the same way that I had applied myself to becoming a perfect atheist by reading my father's books, I was such a conscientious student of Surrealism that I rapidly became the only integral Surrealist."

THE SPANISH TWIN TOWERS: INVENTING THE MONSTERS

However unsettled his membership in "the club," Dalí continued to speak on behalf of Surrealism all over the world and to paint canvases with political overtones, including *Autumn Cannibalism, Soft Construction With Boiled Beans: Premonition of Civil War, Spain, Six Apparitions of Lenin On A Piano, The Visage of War*, and *The Inventions of the Monsters*. His 1956 painting *Metamorphosis of Hitler's Face Into A Landscape In The Moonlight To The Accompaniment Of Toselli's Serenade* is still stunning when first viewed, as the all-too-familiar visage of Hitler is transformed into a boat floating on a pond at night, the aspects of the horizontal second image buried in the vertical Führer's nose and mustache. Just as the poetry of Charles Baudelaire, Arthur Rimbaud, and Guillaume Apollinaire had anointed the use of juxtaposed and contradictory themes, Dalí's contending imagery is based on seemingly opposed images thrust against one another in the same frame, highlighting their similarities and moving the yard marker of reality for the participating audience.

It is Dalí's equal obsessions with Johannes Vermeer and John-Louis-Ernest Meissonier (both possessors of a flawless style that was the last word in retrograde academic circles) that helped his plunging distortions of classical perspective feel different from any other artist of his time. Reaching back to the nineteenth century, realism was Dalí's most inspired strategy, and to couple this with the receding horizons of the cliffs and beaches of his childhood made his work feel completely recognizable and weirdly disordered, more dreamlike and controversial even than the frightening artistic experiments of Picasso. One never feels that they have lived in a world that Picasso makes, but Dalí's paintings are wholly inhabitable, memorable for their equal parts of familiarity and shared emotional crisis. His *Sentimental Colloquy (Study For A Ballet)* from 1944 shows scores of bearded okolotal figures balancing rocks on their heads as they bicycle away from each other on an unmarked track, with wedding trains dragging behind each rider. They are riding their bicycles around a broken piano filling with water from a spring in a cracked wall. The veils and seeming immobility of the riders makes you feel as if the skeletons are caught in spider webs by their heads and moments away from being jerked simultaneously from their bikes.

Dalí reaches us at our most basic human level; Picasso attacks our most primitive and primordial impulses—his African masks are almost absurd in their mockery of human beings. While Dalí hopes to enter a kind of delirium while keeping a part of the mind alert to the imperatives of the rational world, Picasso is a conduit, an alchemist whose open channel to forces of good and evil is messy and comical. Dalí is an astute manipulator of all schools of art, but Picasso stands alone, a rock around which all schools must flow. Dalí's mind is such that it lands swanlike on every artistic body of water, scooping some in its respite and is thus transformed into a human. Picasso arises from the swamp of art as a beast with human characteristics; his subsequent absence in the landscape causes the swamp to dry up. Dalí needed God and craved the acceptance of a father, even as he poisoned him. Picasso is the father, full of poison, giving quarter to none.

In Dalí's greatest work, there are extensions of El Greco, Diego Velasquez, and Francisco de Goya. "A painter in the classical tradition," Dalí said, "is one who paints things as they are. The greatness of Velasquez lies in his not changing anything. His personages are exactly the way they looked. The proportions aren't arranged, any more than in Praxiteles or Vermeer. There

The Rhythm Method, Razzmatazz, and Memory

is no deformation at all ..." Dalí aspired to continue the tradition but changes whatever suits his convenience. Picasso, who considered Henri Matisse to be the greatest painter of his time, believed tradition was an illusion and his responsibility as an artist was to destroy illusions, creating permanence through the force of will. Marc Chagall once said, "What a genius that Picasso; it's a pity he doesn't paint." Religion was not pertinent to Picasso except as an adversary. Dalí's later religious paintings are some of his best. His *Christ of St. John of the Cross*, from 1951, seems a warm-up to his *Crucifixion (Corpus Hypercubicus)* painted in 1954, but both pictures owe their power to Francisco de Zurbarán's and Velasquez's stark chiaroscuro lighting.

After World War II, Dalí began to try and reconcile his twin passions of physics and religion, which led to the paintings mentioned above, as well as *The Temptation of St. Anthony, The Madonna at Port Lligat, The Ecumenical Council*, and *The Discovery of America by Christopher Columbus*. This return to mysticism and religious themes, along with Gala's never-ending plots for publicity stunts, seemed to hurt Dalí's critical reputation, but neither his technique nor the machinations of his insatiably curious mind ever wavered. Father Bruno, editor-in-chief of *Carmelite Studies*, wrote: "In a tape-recorded conversation in 1956 made with his consent, Salvador Dalí told me that nothing stimulated him more than the idea of an angel. Dalí wanted to paint heaven, to penetrate the celestial vaults in order to communicate with God. God is an elusive idea for him, impossible to make concrete. Dalí, being essentially Catalonian, needs to touch forms, which is also true of angels. While very young, he told me he created a picture about angels, and if he has turned for some time toward the Assumption of the Virgin, it is, he declares, because she rose into heaven through the sheer strength of the angels. And Dalí would like to know the secret of this elevation ..."

Dalí went on to imagine that protons and neutrons are angelic elements, "residues of substances," he said, and this idea led him to the phenomenal dot paintings of the late 1950s and '60s, large-scale intricate fields of enlarged Benday dots, those minute circles of ink that make up a newspaper or magazine photograph, a kissing cousin to the pixel on a computer screen. The Hitler metamorphosis I mentioned earlier emerged from this technique, as did *Portrait of My Dead Brother*, an imaginary face, with no resemblance to the painter, floating above a desert plain where the dots mutate into a bird emerging from his forehead and ranks of soldiers at his chin. Images of struggle and flight, they match Dalí's effort to come to terms with a ghostly brother whose name he was given. Then there is *The Sistine Madonna,* in which a detail of Raphael's *Sistine Madonna* is made to appear within a massive close-up of a human ear—the ear of Pope John XXIII, no less— much enlarged from a magazine photo.

This technique gave way in the late 1960s to two last masterpieces, painted in combinations of tendencies: Surrealism, "quintessential pompierism," pontillism, action painting, tachisme, geometric abstraction, pop, op, and psychedelic art. The first, Dalí called the most ambitious painting he had ever attempted; *Tuna Fishing* was conceived from a photograph on his father's desk. The terrifying imagery in this picture depicts an orgy of violence perpetrated by young beautiful fishermen on the tuna. "All births are preceded by a marvelous spurting of blood," said Dalí, and *Tuna Fishing* shows the "superaesthetic force of modern biology." Dalí was of the belief that the limitations of the universe—its contractions, explosions, and collisions as the tiny particles of the universe, photons and neutrons, came together—was the true nature of the known world and the source of its formidable power and energy.

The convergence of this energy into a single point was the subject of his last paintings, especially *The Hallucinogenic Toreador,* where the Venus de Milo is repeated several times from different angles in such a way that the shadows form the features of a toreador, whose coat of lights is made up of the corpuscles obtained through the multiplication of dots and flies, mingled with the deteriorating head of a dying bull. In the bottom right corner, a fly—in sequence with tiny Venus de Milos beneath it—flies directly at the head of a small boy (the same size) who is dressed in a sailor's suit, carrying a hoop and a block of wood. The boy stares down the suspended fly in the pose of a toreador as well, each image somehow continually replicated in space. The architecture of the bullfight arena is a mixture of Palladian structures seen in Italy and the porticoes of old Greek theatres. It is an astonishing series of images, made more valuable upon repeated viewings. By this time, Gala had largely disappeared from Dalí's paintings, but her presence in his life was omniscient as ever.

CHAPTER 21

The Invasion of America

Pablo Picasso lent Salvador Dalí five hundred dollars to get he and Gala to America for the first time. Dalí spent the voyage huddled in his cabin, tying his canvases to his clothing with strings as if to buoy him on the choppy water. On land and safely beyond the disapproving eyes of the European Surrealists, the Dalís took America by storm, supported and steered socially by Caresse Crosby, Coco Chanel, Elsa Schiaparelli, and others. Dalí's paintings selling by the score from Julian Levy's Gallery and his face plastered on the cover of *Time* magazine, it was hardly a surprise that American Surrealism in the 1930s was dominated by Dalí's influence.

Dalí's regular trips to New York, during which his outrageous statements and behavior were duly reported by the press, only increased his popularity. In 1937, *Art News* stated: "To most Americans, Dalí represents Surrealism in all its horror and fascination." The article in *Time* magazine (accompanied by Dalí's photograph by Man Ray on the cover) declared that "Surrealism would never have attracted its present attention in the U.S. were it not for a handsome thirty-two-year-old Catalan with a soft voice and a clipped cinematic actor's mustache." In January 1932, New York art dealer Julian Levy featured Dalí's *Persistence of Memory* in the second comprehensive exhibition of Surrealism in America. Levy had recently acquired the painting from the artist's Parisian art dealer, Pierre Colle, for the trade price of 250 dollars, and Dalí's image of limp watches hanging from barren trees covered with ants made headlines throughout America. An accomplished publicist, Levy made it his personal mission to promote Dalí, making himself more wealthy in the

---

process. He screened Dalí and Luis Buñuel's film *Un Chien Andalou* at his gallery on November 17, 1932, in the presence of Carl Van Vechten, Mr. and Mrs. Nelson Rockefeller, and George Gershwin. The late 1930s found the Dalís shuttling between western Europe and the United States as the Spanish Civil War raged in his homeland. But Gala had another card up her sleeve as the war dragged on, snatching a patron to support the Dalí publicity machine, greasing the skids with consistent financial lubrication. What the sex gypsy did not count on was an awakening of Dalí's libido in the process.

The Dalís were taken with the eccentric, wealthy, bisexual British poet Edward James (also a godson of King Edward VII), who later claimed to have been Dalí's lover and to have bought off Gala with jewelry after she discovered that Dalí had deceived her in order to spend the night with him. He subsequently reported that Dalí encouraged his voracious wife to take lovers, because the prospect excited Dalí. Gala had arranged a contract with James that would pay Dalí a monthly stipend and give James the option of purchasing all the work Dalí produced for three years, from 1936–39. Although Gala reneged on the contract, the James collection remains the first and best collection of Dalí paintings and drawings assembled before the second World War.

SOCIAL SURREALISM: THE AMERICAN MONGREL

From the time of the Armory Show in New York City in 1913—when Alfred Stieglitz brought the controversial work of Paul Cézanne, Picasso, Georges Braque, and Marcel Duchamp to American audiences for the first time (and where one critic called Duchamp's *Nude Descending a Staircase* "an explosion in a shingle factory")—to Robert Rauschenberg's combines in the 1950s and '60s, to Jean-Michel Basquiat's primitive street paintings in the '80s, Americans have gotten their artistic directions from New York and resisted them in the hinterland just as surely, before the assimilation into the national consciousness and general acceptance set in. Or at least until the next big thing rolled past and the cycle repeated itself. The permanence of the arts has always been the work of a minority.

In 1934, when Peter Blume's painting *South of Scranton* was awarded first prize at the Carnegie International in Pittsburgh, conservative reviewers called the work "pictorial gibberish," with one cartoonist dubbing it "South of Dixmont," after the famous mental hospital. A Dalí painting was included in the exhibition and awarded an honorable mention, but since his melting watches had attained pop culture status, limp objects became a staple of Surrealist paintings all over America. Whether is was Jan Matulka's *Surrealist Landscape*, James Guy's *Venus On Sixth Avenue*, or O. Louis Gugliemi's *Mental Geography* (whose Golden Gate Bridge sways to and fro while its mutinous cables spring precipitously to the forefront, unraveling in the process like a gigantic crippled harp), all of these artists were forging ahead with materials they had found in the Surrealist camp. Dalí's main followers were known as Social Surrealists, and the thrust of their work was predominantly political, plumbing the repertoire of Surrealist images and techniques to convey social commentary and evoke the atrocities of war. In the America of the 1930s, the economic crises led many artists to become political activists, and like their European counterparts who were involved with the Communist Party, American artists joined left-wing organizations such as the John Reed Clubs (1929–1935), the Artists' Union (1933–1943), and the American Artists' Congress (1936–1940).

This loosely knit group included Blume, Gugliemi, Guy, Walter Quirt, David Smith, and the Spanish-born Federico Castellon, a consummate draftsman whose eerie paintings borrowed many of their features from Dalí and Miró. Armed with their fantasies and a new way of expressing them, these artists took a stand on many of the important issues of the day: widespread unemployment, the aggressive reactionary response of capitalist enterprise to the working class and their unions, and the rising totalitarianism and warfare in Europe. Unlike Dalí, whose landscapes and partial images remained ambiguous and open to interpretation, the Americans were more direct.

Guy's oil painting *Police (Public Servants)*, with its darkly ironic title, envisions a nightmare scenario where the police are shown as fascist villains committing atrocities against the citizens they are meant to protect. The central protagonist, fashioned after Sherlock Holmes, is a detective dividing the landscape into two halves. In the left half, his right hand is holding a man by the back of his head while another officer subdues him in the shadow of the penitentiary, which is built conspicuously like a factory. His left hand is in the right half of the painting gesturing for graft, while in the foreground a serial killer is carving up the body of a nude woman in a bizarre autopsy-like ritual, and a thug is abducting a little blonde girl. The police at the foot of the mountain in the distance are attacking the striking workers, and atop the mountain, the KKK in full regalia are lynching a black man with a rope thrown over the remaining branch of a dead tree. Sherlock Holmes is wearing a sandwich board with a black handprint centered on it, like the symbol of a secret organization that the detective has no qualms about promoting in the open. The multiplicity of contiguous events is reminiscent of fifteenth-century Italian religious paintings, with their depiction of successive scenes within the same landscape. The Americans shared the Surrealists' disregard for spatial and temporal logic, making highly stylized portrayals of the suffering populace inside elaborately staged unions of rural and urban dreamscapes.

One of the most famous icons of anti-fascism in America is Blume's *The Eternal City*, which depicts modern Rome with the ruins of the Forum, the Colosseum, the Catacombs, and a votive shrine with an effigy of Christ as the Man of Sorrows. Benito Mussolini, a modern Caesar ruling with the tacit support of Pope Pius XI, is lampooned as the scowling green head of a jack-in-the-box popping out of the ancient subterranean remains, like the papier-mâché leader of a crumbling civilization. The confrontation between soldiers and common people in the background was a reference to the struggle of workers against the military, called upon to crush union strikes and rebellions.

Later, as the war overshadowed social concerns at home, the artists began to focus on the evils of the second World War. Smith's fifteen *Medals for Dishonor* were inspired by the German war medallions he had seen in the British Museum in 1936. One of his medals, *Bombing of Civilian Populations,* was, like Picasso's *Guernica*, a response to the bombing of defenseless civilians. In the frame, Smith substitutes bombs for babies; here, storks are portrayed as dive-bombing planes, the babies are on the bombs, the bombs fall in the highchairs, and the surrounding earth is torn and cracked, its buildings shattered. In the center, standing atop a Greek pillar, is a female disfigured, with an atomic baby being formed in her womb.

Other artists considered war's dissolution of Mother Earth even more distressing for the future of the human race. Lucien Labandt's *Shampoo at Moss Beach* and Alexandre Hogue's *Erosion No.2—Mother Earth Laid Bare* were mimetic portraits of a poisoned environment, as was Herbert Ferber's sculpture *Apocalyptic Rider*, which resembles a scorpion almost escaped from the clutches of a killer taffy tree. A tripod balanced on three points, the insectlike figure has astonishing fluidity and menace. If smoke were given physical form, it would morph into this lethality.

Social Surrealism ended in the early 1940s, as the purging of Russian intellectuals in the Moscow trials of 1936–38, the 1939 Nazi-Soviet pact, and the 1940 Soviet invasion of Finland led to the increasing disillusionment of left-wing intellectuals and artists in America. As America joined the war, it appeared almost unseemly for artists to criticize social life in the United States, and so the Social Surrealists moved toward more abstract and poetic forms of expression. The confrontational tendencies of their earlier work were replaced by a heightened lyricism. Gradually, by the early '50s, a sentimental and elegiac mood took hold, transforming the artists' imagery and converting their paintings into splashes, drips, swirls, and colors devoid of recognizable subject matter. Abstract Expressionism bumped the Surrealists off the top tier and became the American style par excellence.

IN THE ARENA CREATING INFINITIES

For abstract artists, Surrealism provided a way to imbue non-representational forms with psychological meaning. When Surrealism was mixed with the influences of Wassily Kandinsky and Joan Miró, Abstract Expressionism became the potent end result. The Modernist American painters who were working at the turn of the twentieth century were very influenced by Kandinsky's tract *Concerning the Spiritual In Art* (1912), as well as his incredibly energetic paintings, such as *Sea Battle*, in which a ship in the center of the frame is assailed by every conceivable shape and color, barely holding its position as the weight of the colors push into its unsteady form and slashes of surf and light resembling lances stab outward with no apparent purpose. The twin themes of balance and violence make Kandinsky's work unforgettable, and his importance as the primary founder of abstract art is secure.

Since both of Kandinsky's parents played piano, he was encouraged to read and play music from an early age. Because abstraction was derived from visionary, intuitive sources, it is not surprising that Kandinsky saw his painting as an extension of his musical training. "Color is the keyboard," he said, "the eyes are the harmonies, the soul is the piano with many strings, the artist is the hand that plays, touching one key then another to cause vibration in the soul." Kandinsky, along with other early American Modernists such as Morgan Russell and Arthur Dove, was intrigued (like the poets Arthur Rimbaud and Stéphane Mallarmé before them) with the idea of "synesthesia," the idea that colors could equate with sounds. Russell was also a musician, and he hoped to develop an orchestral, abstract, emotional art that he called "synchronism," a Greek term meaning simply "with color." He hoped to create paintings that would convey "color rhythms" and unfold "like a piece of music, within a span of time."

Arthur Dove and Marsden Hartley were Americans who explored the mystical idea of the landscape in representational plants and animals, built from solid unreal forms symbolizing the elemental forces of change in the universe. Georgia O'Keefe also saw abstraction as a powerful tool to strip away the insecure and confused emotions surrounding the natural world. She and the other abstract landscape painters reduced the world to individual forms they could control, a challenge to the disorder and disintegration of the spreading urban and technologically savvy American consciousness. Against this post-war backdrop, the new American painting became dominated by the plastic automatic techniques of the original Surrealists but was imbued with a refreshing confidence. Though the main currents of the Surrealist themes were chaos, confusion, individual anguish, and powerlessness, the geometric ideas of abstraction had a liberating, percussive power. There was, among these artists, a discipline and control, a joy even, after the turmoil of the Great Depression and the triumph of the second World War, building work that was at once spontaneous and rational, mathematic and wildly colorful.

"The source of my painting is the unconscious," Jackson Pollock declared, and there was no Abstract Expressionist of whom this was more clearly true. His work, along with Robert Motherwell, Mark Rothko, Willem de Kooning, and Arshile Gorky, revealed emotions and conflicts close to the surface and delivered a choked, blurting urgency. The energy in the work of these artists was relentless, and the pullulating, thickly scrawled nests of totemic images didn't so much illustrate myth as invoke its presence. Pollock learned to pour his canvases, adjusting his need to what he wished to say. In his left hand he held a half-full can of paint and then he tilted it; the thinned paint trickled out like honey from the can while in his other hand was a hardened brush or stick, mixing the paint and adding turpentine. Dipping the stick, he waved it canvas-bound, but just above its plane. "Memories arrested in space," he called it, so that "energy and motion are made visible." Each of the subsequent pictures are small infinities without borders, completely intuitive in nature. "I am nature," Pollock said, and he coaxed his acutely sensitive structures from the forms he felt within the world but were not obvious, the way trees or streams fork or bifurcate, showing the order that existed in the midst of chaos, the smaller patterns inside the world that define nature's larger, more powerful movements. Pollock believed that the job of the artist was to reveal these unseen, but intimately felt, connections. Pollock called his studio "the arena," and he trusted contact, painting by immersion, to be swallowed by the process and emerge.

Pollock explained his process in the first and only issue of *Possibilities*, edited by Robert Motherwell and Harold Rosenberg: "My painting does not come from the easel ... I prefer to tack the unstretched canvas to the hard wall or the floor ... On the floor I am more at ease. I feel nearer, more a part of the painting, since this way I can walk around it, work from the four sides and literally be *in* the painting. This is akin to the method of the Indian sand painters of the west ... When I am *in* my painting, I'm not aware of what I'm doing. It is only after a sort of 'get acquainted' period that I see what I've been about. I have no fears about making changes, destroying the image, etc., because the painting has a life of its own. I try to let it come through."

Miró often said that forms took reality for him as he worked. "Rather than setting out to paint something," he said, "I begin painting and as I paint, the picture begins to assert itself, or suggest itself under my brush." This ability to wait, to surrender to the painting's deliverance, was a Surrealist idea, allowing the spirit of the art to pass through the conduit of the artist's body—"the brooding of the hand" on the canvas, as Saul Steinberg called it.

De Kooning's nearly all-black abstraction of the late 1940s tapped a collective post-war mood of existential despair. Anxious and foreboding, these paintings prefigured the black paintings of late Pollock creations, as well as Rothko's *Chapel* murals and Motherwell's *Elegies to the Spanish Republic*. "Light reversed itself," wrote Rafael Alberti, "and black was born." Each of these artists tried to find the notes for a song of the abyss, the black future staring back from a nuclear argument, the ultimate nihilism of humankind. De Kooning emerged from the abyss to paint the formidable masterpiece *Excavation*, in 1950, where countless human bodies are tangled in his canvas, jostling for position; each of the jagged movements are flying at breakneck speed against one another, charging and skidding through the dense pigment. Robert Hughes called him "the most libidinal painter America has produced."

Like Gorky's organic prehensile and polymorphous imagery, de Kooning's paintings make sex seem ominous as well as joyful. For Gorky, the world was boundlessly suggestive, drenched in the fertile shapes of seedpods, stamens, and voluptuous insect wings; the rich plumes of his paintings swarm against one another in an almost diabolical frenzy, where the illusion of depth really is depth. For Pollock and Gorky, their climbing, scribbled, humming tribes of images make love and war at once, depending on the viewpoint of the onlooker. Their map to action was the action itself, whereas de Kooning seems to systematically attack all the space of the painting in order to balance it, thus satisfying his urgent mathematical obsession to tip the world into a glass and view it from all sides simultaneously.

Rauschenberg's *Combines* took this idea one step further and blithely exploded all remaining assumptions about what a work of art was supposed to be by making it into a container for everything. A Rauschenberg *Combine* could happily include slapdash washes of paint, old shirts, discarded socks and cans, newspaper clippings, or even a stuffed angora goat with a tire around its middle. Born in Port Arthur, Texas, Rauschenberg arrived in New York by way of Black Mountain College in North Carolina, the training ground of the 1950s avant-garde, where he had befriended the composer John Cage. Cage's rhythmic ideas about chance and randomness fascinated the painter, who began scavenging the streets of New York for junk to incorporate into his works, such as *Satellite,* in which a stuffed pheasant presides atop a canvas patchworked with fabric and running splotches of paint, almost as if an expensive curtain or collage had been shit upon.

Collage had been invented by the Cubists, perfected by Kurt Schwitters, and practiced by Surrealists, Beats, and post-modern artists of every stripe, but Rauschenberg built his works on a larger scale and gave them that industrial strength name: *Combines.* His most famous work, *Monogram,* could exist in any material, anywhere, for any purpose, and find any destination suitable and still astound as a clear work of art. The aforementioned golden angora goat is standing atop a painting, ringed snugly around its middle by a rubber tire, a clear logo for the male libido, a sexual fetish masquerading as a guardian of the abstract world. These kinds of artists say yes to everything, the possibilities for art interwoven with art objects that contain every possible thing. Poetry in America was about to turn the same corner.

CHAPTER 22

The Automatic World: Surrealism's Manifest Destiny

Though American Surrealism had been manifested mainly among the painters under the sway of Salvador Dalí in the 1930s, it took the arrival of André Breton himself to bring the poets into the fold. He arrived in New York in August 1941 and spent most of the next five years working as an announcer for *Voice of America* radio and collaborating with old and new friends, such as Marcel Duchamp, Max Ernst, André Masson, Roberto Matta, and Yves Tanguy. In December 1942, he gave a series of lectures at Yale University on the status of Surrealism between the two World Wars and met his future wife, Elisa Bindhoff. He would also meet a sixteen-year-old student named Phillip Lamantia, who would become a latter-day member of the movement and the first openly surreal poet on the American scene. Before his death on March 7, 2005, Lamantia created a body of work that reflected the intensity and original ambitions of the French pioneers.

Born in San Francisco in 1927 to Sicilian immigrants, Lamantia's father was a produce broker in the old Embarcadero district. Phillip began writing poems in elementary school and was inspired by the paintings of Joan Miró and Dalí that he found at the San Francisco Museum of Art. After being expelled for "intellectual delinquency" at age sixteen, he dropped out of high school and moved to New York City, where he lived for several years and was befriended by Breton and other exiled artists, such as the painters Ernst and Tanguy. Lamantia called André Breton, "contrary to rumor and innuendo, one of the most civilized men I ever met." At their first meeting, Breton introduced the young man to Tanguy, "who of all the visual artists, was most important to me," Lamantia recalled, "as early on I was influenced very much by painters and musicians. But then, in the 1940s and early '50s, it was really about the music! I was hanging out with musicians, jazz musicians mostly. The terminology referring to 'hipsters' was about those people hanging out with musicians and wanting to be musicians."

From the outset, Surrealist thinking centered around the hermeneutic idea of seeking the sacred through artistic endeavors, "the incurable mania of wanting to make the unknown known," as Breton had phrased it. In this search for "the marvelous," a new morality must be substituted for the prevailing morality or the old ordered manner of the status quo. "It is the oracle, the things I say," Arthur Rimbaud exclaimed. Lamantia believed his work should shed the business of "the damned sciences" and proclaim the total surprise of "the automatic world." His poems, especially early on, move quietly from one incendiary image to the next, as if they are telling a story or trying to describe this world to alien invaders.

> Rainbow guns are dancing
> in front of the movie queens
> Everyone is laughing
> flying dying
> never knowing when to rest
> never knowing when to eat
>
> And the fountains come falling
> out of her thistle-covered breasts
> and the dogs are happy
> and the clowns are knifing
> and the ballerinas are eating stone
>
> from Selected Poems

The brushing together of music and art helped the Surrealist poets to collaborate certainly, but it also gave the poets tools with which to break down preconceived visual notions that had existed in poetry for hundreds of years. The pastoral love poem is a different shimmering animal in the hands of a young Surrealist. Consider this piece, "I Am Coming," written by the young Lamantia, and notice also the song-like qualities, almost narrative in nature:

The Rhythm Method, Razzmatazz, and Memory

I am following her to the wavering moon
to a bridge by the long waterfront
to valleys of beautiful arson
to flowers dead in a mirror of love

to men eating wild minutes from a clock
to hands playing in celestial pockets
and to that dark room beside a castle
of youthful voices singing to the moon.

When the sun comes up she will live at a sky
covered with sparrow's blood
and wrapped in robes of lost decay.

But I am coming to the moon,
and she will be there in a musical night,
in a night of burning laughter
burning like a road of my brain
pouring its arm into the lunar lake.

In 1946, at the age of nineteen, Lamantia's first book, *Erotic Poems*, was published by Bern Porter Books in Berkeley, California, followed by two collections, *Narcotica* and *Ekstasis*, published in 1959 by Averhohn Press. During the 1950s he lived off and on with native peoples in the United States and Mexico, also participating in the peyote-eating rituals of the Washo Indians in Nevada and experimenting with opiates in Morocco and Europe. From these initiations, Lamantia's work developed a compulsive, almost trance-like, violent tone. Fascinated by suicides and their viewpoint, Lamantia's new poems sprayed across the page. Here's his "Trance Ports":

The gods are vomiting
I am entering earth
I am walled in light
I am where the song
is shot into my eyes
O hypodermic light!

"As humans," Lamantia said, "we're constantly looking outward for evidence of the sacred. I'm now convinced, however, that the universe is within us! There's no need to go into outer space to find out about the secrets of the universe. In earliest childhood all knowledge is inborn, I believe, and it's all retrievable!" He believed that each individual artist seeks "the golden fleece" on their own. In "Still Poem," he is exploring the connections between the conscious and unconscious worlds, looking for the bridges that Edgar Allan Poe spoke of in his essay "Between Waking and Sleeping," and now the poet is caught in constant flight, seeking "the luminous darkness of God." Here are the first twelve lines of "Still Poem 9":

> This is this distance between me and what I see
> everywhere immanence of the presence of God
> no more ekstasis
> a cool head
> watch watch watch
> I'm here
> He's over there ... It's an ocean ...
> sometimes I can't think of it, I fail, fall
> there IS this look of love
> there IS the tower of David
> there IS the throne of wisdom
> there IS the silent look of love

LOOSENING THE BREATH OF AMERICAN POETRY

It is clear that Lamantia, like the bearer of fire, passed Surrealism to the Beat poets who congregated in San Francisco in the 1950s and early '60s. In a tribute to Lamantia in the March 2005 issue of *The San Francisco Chronicle*, the Beat poet Lawrence Ferlinghetti said, "In the 1950s, Philip was writing a stream-of-consciousness Surrealist poetry and had a huge influence on Allen Ginsberg. Before that, Ginsberg was writing rather conventional poetry. It was Philip that turned him on to Surrealist writing." Lamantia and Ginsberg first met when both were in their early twenties. Lamantia shared books like *The Temple of Man* and Denis de Rougemont's *Love in the Western World* with Ginsberg, familiarizing him with places like the Great Temple at Luxor where sacred texts existed from 1800 B.C., where inside these writings doorways to the other world shined forth, possibilities for the presence of the divine. From these lost corridors came proof of the existence of alternate worlds, which for Ginsberg was the Holy Grail, a belief in love so pervasive that it could encompass all ranges of human experience. Lamantia's own poetry became more and more hopeful as he grew, and anything was fair game for his mind, cut away from its childish attachment to logical reality and set loose in a sea of associations. From *Bed of Sphinxes*, here is a late poem by Lamantia entitled "Ex Cathedra":

To weave garter belts with chaos and snakes, the nun's toenail of
crimson phallus, her breast of alligator, her tail, crow's buttocks.
Steel pricks of the ciborium dovetail her white pantaloons—
snake oil on a eucharistic tongue.

In crystal movies: an owl's path beneath slumbers of the woods
that died to bolster the miserable stations of the cross, instead of
Bugs Bunny laminating the hedgerows through the pews, stench
gathers power in censers of the debasing perfumes.

Time of frostbites laid over crumbs of bile-soaked christies, famines
roasted with divinity, allah jacks up his "prisons within prisons,"
the flayed kaaba-stone pitched to the solar gobbling machine.

After the Great Dusting, this Pope exhibits his toes in carnivals sure
to spring up in sideshows of enigma, hot flints of the anti-christ,
my brother, in lesions of the darkening space,

Revolution the Star in the West springs the play of foam on the
rocks below ...

Field mice from the mouths of "the hell sermon," I hop off the head
of the oldest nun with a fragment of the reforgeable brassy
metallic cross; this priest whipping Sister Matilda with guts
spilled from the monstrance his tongue laps up at her feet. Oh,
junkyards of eternity fester in leads of clock time, but
Humankind invents the bomb I hurl to *The Box of Infanticides*,
Black-hearted children flee gehenna, pissing through mountains
of priestly corpses, those burnt hams in the tree of winds.

Schools of fish move in the night, plagues of scripture blown to smithereens.

Secret rooms fly open absolutely by stealth.

The star card bestows the charm of new rivers, this word tomorrow, Andromeda, and with you, Amor.

With the skull splendors of the imperium romanum, the alchemical pope skewers a host of puffers on the backside of saints.

Cardinals butcher in the market day for clerics.

Inside the chalice of battered gums, the vengeance of witches, salmons to spawn the invisible eruption in the street of the Five Rats.

Talismanic, the marigold's not a wing-feather less!

From the stone bubbles of Mother Angelica a herd of corpses rides to the spider compass of my bones: the blood of swans lace my handcuffs floating the altars, the inebriate sickle quick to slice those melting emeralds inlaid with scripted shit the great unknown rages to fruition on the flanks of Carthage.

The absolute pulverization of all the churches will be the grace of love's freedom!

On that day black holes of thought radiate the wind's lost world, this death that is not death: that day is magic is love.

Ginsberg took this dose of Surrealism, along with a profound borrowing from the well of Whitman and the prophetic voice of William Blake's Old Testament, and forged a document that would become the most famous American poem since T. S. Eliot's *The Waste Land*, which was published in 1922. *Howl* is a panoramic vision of the dark side of the complacent Eisenhower years; it discovered for American literature an anti-community of waifs and strays, dope addicts and homosexual drifters. Ginsberg's poetry offered an alternative to the tightly organized, well-mannered poetry written under the influence of the New Criticism. It was emotionally explosive, unashamedly preoccupied, and metrically expansive, with a prosaic, almost orchestral sweep in its long, loping lines. The Surrealist idea of automatism was taken to its longest, most radical and logical extreme in the poetry of Ginsberg, who stretched this idea to include the dithyrambic line in his employment of poetry that might read as a jazz solo was composed, spontaneously and seriously, with all focused intuition but wholly without thoughtful second-guessing.

The dithyrambic tradition is best expressed in the six poetical books of the Old Testament (Job, Psalms, Proverbs, Ecclesiastes, Song of Solomon, and Lamentations) and the prophetic books of Blake, such as *The Marriage of Heaven and Hell, Milton,* and *Jerusalem,* as well as Eliot's *The Waste Land* (there is also a dithyrambic chorus in *Murder In The Cathedral*), Ezra Pound's *Cantos,* and Hart Crane's *The Bridge.* Ginsberg's *Howl* is a contemporary dithyramb, as is the poetry of Yevgeny Yevtushenko, the long poems of Diane Wakoski, and much of the poetry of that second-generation Beat gal Anne Waldman. There are also a great many dithyrambic prose writers and novelists: Herman Melville, Fyodor Dostoyevsky, Friedrich Nietzsche, Louis-Ferdinand Céline, Henry Miller, and the two novelists who influenced Ginsberg more than any other poet, even Whitman: Jack Kerouac and the inimitable William Burroughs. The critic Helen Vendler wrote in 1986 that "Allen Ginsberg is responsible for loosening the breath of American poetry."

It took a little time, after the hubub died down, for people to realize that *Howl* was not merely a written equivalent of Cage's "musical noise," but the poem had opened language so wide and made it so hungry that, according to poet Paul Zweig, "nothing was safe any longer from poetry." Ginsberg's voice in *Howl, Kaddish,* and *Planet News* is omnivorous and practices radical inclusion, putting a parenthesis around the will, while the contents of the psyche pour forth, unjudged. The poetry of *Howl* clarifies the poet's primary intention by its spontaneous combinations; it is an act of love. The Surrealists, especially Breton and Éluard, argued that love was the essential revolutionary act. Love was the opposite of reason because reason selects and judges, while love embraces. Ginsberg loves not only noble images but all the crippled children limping out of his psyche, the abortions and the nightmares and the hobos and the mad, restive intellectuals whose minds and ideas are dismissed by society. Even Ginsberg's rage against the political hypocrisy of America is a form of patriotic generosity, embracing the best principles of a country that despises him.

Published in October 1956 by City Lights, a small San Francisco bookstore founded by Ferlinghetti, *Howl and Other Poems* was the fourth volume in the Pocket Poets Series. It had a black and white cover and cost only seventy-five cents. By the time the book's signature poem "Howl" was printed, it had gone through as many as eighteen recorded drafts, the first of which was called "Strophes," in recognition of the poem's opening series of refrains. (So much for "first thought, best thought.") In this age of inflation and digital printing costs, you can still pick up one of the million copies of the book in print for a dollar or so in any used bookstore. It is a modest bomb, somberly dressed and portable. When Ginsberg asked William Carlos Williams to write a brief introduction to the book, the older poet agreed and concluded his remarks with a memorable warning: "Hold back the edges of your gowns, Ladies, we are going through hell." Here's an excerpt from the first part of "Howl":

> I saw the best minds of my generation destroyed by madness, starving
>   hysterical naked,
> dragging themselves through the negro streets at dawn looking for an
>   angry fix.
> angelheaded hipsters burning for the ancient heavenly connection to
>   the starry dynamo in the machinery of night,
> who poverty and tatters and hollow-eyed and high sat up smoking in
>   the supernatural darkness of cold-water flats floating across
> the tops of cities contemplating jazz,
> who bared their brains to Heaven under the El and saw Moham-
>   medan angels staggering on tenement roofs illuminated,
> who passed through universities with radiant cool eyes hallucinating
>   Arkansas and Blake-light tragedy among the scholars of war,
> who were expelled from the academies for crazy & publishing obscene
>   odes on the windows of the skull

"Howl" builds its intense effects by the piling on of layer after layer of imagery and a desperate looping swirl of emotional verbs. In this small sample of the poem, you can find the verbs *destroyed, starving, dragging, burning, smoking, floating, staggering,* and *hallucinating.* An abundance of gerunds to be sure, but the poet is attempting an epic delivery of repeated phrases, a mantra of despair that begs its countrymen to awaken and recognize the crucial losses hidden from public view. It is also a chronicle of Beat incidents,

---

and may be read as a historical artifact, a long unscrolling of the events that lead each of the primary protagonists to this meeting of the minds, a Valhalla of intellectual debasement and suffering reaching a critical mass in the voice of the narrator, a contemporary observer wrapped in the cadences of an Old Testament prophet. "The only poetic tradition," said Ginsberg, "is the voice out of the burning bush. The rest is trash and will be consumed."

That's a simple answer to a more complex problem; namely, how to sustain not only the long line but also the repetition of the long dithyrambic line over the course of several pages. It achieves its success partially through musical effects, such as the electrical charge of the chant, best practiced by Buddhist monks but available to everyone by the process of syncopating their breath, allowing the inevitable onrush of oxygen and exhalation to charge and stimulate the body, opening it to the flash and rise of clustered sound, equipoised between breaths. Blake and Whitman changed poetry from a very fixed and classical form to an open form inviting everyone to participate. To merge that invitation with the wild unyielding experimentation of bebop in the 1940s, jazz musicians attempting to cram every conceivable and inconceivable idea into the crosshairs of their instrument, then to add insult and degradation and humiliation for being not only poor but marginalized as Jew and homosexual, what other being could have written this poem, this shriek, this plea, this *Howl*?

Alongside his semiotic layering of imagery and effluvia, the cumulative effect of the repetitions, perfectly standard in religious literature and in the call and response of the minister to his flock, Ginsberg also stamped each section of the poem with a vocal anchor. There are four words or phrases that tie each section together, giving the lines a remembered destination. In the first section, the repeated word that introduces each strophe is *who*. In the second, *Moloch*, the impenetrable industrial wall and spiritually bankrupt boogeyman. In the third, it's *I'm with you in Rockland*, a direct humanizing phrase dedicated to the marginally insane visionaries collapsed in asylums the world over. In the fourth (labeled a "footnote"), the word *holy* is repeated, an unerring assertion that all life has value and that the poem has risen above the initial laundry list of incidents to transcendent ecstasy, a two-beat register of percussive redemption: *HOLY! HOLY! HOLY! HOLY! Where Everything is holy! Everyman's an angel!* The poem is simultaneously mournful, a streaked symphony cataloguing destruction after destruction, and exuberant, even celebratory, insisting that

---

each of these connections is life-affirming, even necessary to a culture awash in capitalism and mislead by its worship of false idols, smug in its isolation and imperialism, dangerous to its own children. *Howl* is filled with the type of *agape* that knows no boundaries, what Williams called "unwordly love, that has no hope of the world, and cannot change the world to its delight."

> *Ginsberg and the Beats did not eradicate the old formal structures or the influence of the New Criticism, but they mortally wounded it, slipping and sliding and crowing in the trail of its blood.*

"The trouble with conventional form," Ginsberg wrote, "is it's too symmetrical, geometrical, numbered, and pre-fixed—unlike my own mind which has no beginning and end, nor fixed measure of thought other than its own cornerless mystery—to transcribe the latter in a form most nearly representing its actual 'occurrence' is my 'method'—which requires the skill of freedom of composition and which will lead poetry to the expression of the highest moments of the mindbody—mystical illumination—and its deepest emotion (through tears—love's all)." Ginsberg's best work is built on uneasy improvisations, slowly building in rhythm that proceeds intuitively and gathers intensity as it swells. Ginsberg and the Beats did not eradicate the old formal structures or the influence of the New Criticism, but they mortally wounded it, slipping and sliding and crowing in the trail of its blood.

Other poets in the Beat tradition, such as Bob Kaufman and Ferlinghetti, were also greatly influenced by the Surrealists and particularly by the inventiveness of the jazz musicians they admired. (We will discuss both writers in that musical context in the next section of this book.) All of these writers, whose sensibilities were marked by inventiveness and rebellion, took their cues from the French Surrealist tradition, leaping into the dreamy associations and unconventional techniques like children into a newfound swimming hole. Breton's original dream, his apostasy and projection, was to see his movement attain universal significance. In the *Second Manifesto* he wrote:

> The hordes of literally frenzied words that Dada and Surrealism acted to set free ... will enter slowly but surely into the small moronic towns of literature as it is still taught ... People try not to notice that the logical mechanism of the sentence has shown itself to be increasingly incapable of triggering in man the emotional shock which gives real value

The Rhythm Method, Razzmatazz, and Memory

to his life. On the other hand, the products of that spontaneous or more spontaneous, direct or more direct activity, such as those offered increasingly by surrealism in the form of books, paintings and films, and which at first shocked him into a stupor, he now seeks out and now more or less timidly asks that they transform his way of feeling.

Breton believed that a time would come when troops of poets would learn to master the techniques of spontaneous language in community training centers and that everyone would heed the call to poetry, its crystalline mystery available to anyone who wished to surrender to its life-affirming properties. In America, with the proliferation of writing programs and with poetry groups dispensing generous advice and friendship seemingly sprouting up on very street corner, Breton's dream seems to have found a fertile ground.

As the 1960s dawned, Surrealism in America split into two distinct camps. The last vestiges of the French influence found its way among the New York poets, poised on the edge of the burgeoning art scene. But the apotheosis of American Surrealism took its marching orders from Spain and Latin America, with poets like Federico Garcia Lorca, César Vallejo, Rafael Alberti, and especially Pablo Neruda leading the charge. In this mutation, the intellectual distance and abstract imagery of the French conceptual design was replaced by an explosive and nature-based torrent of earthy Whitman-esque emotion and lyricism. The poems of the Spanish Surrealist masters were more human, with black soil under their fingernails and exotic birds emerging from their hair. The long muscles of the Mississippi and the Amazon filled out their bodies; the heights of primitive cliffs and the endless waists of trees fastened their feet to their love of their people and their country.

These poets were not cosmopolitan citizens basking in the multicultural institutions of European opulence or decadence. These poets looked to the West, were from the countryside that caved in on the poor subjects of fresh dictatorships, and were beloved, widely read, able to assimilate. Misery was not their catchword; they did not feel that bitterness informed them like Holderlin or Rimbaud, perpetually wandering or suicidal, on the verge of madness. They stood in opposition to corruption and became proud of their right to practice happiness, in full daylight, not read by intense minorities or urban intellectuals but embraced by soccer stadiums full of admiring countrymen. Their verses were memorized by the children and their books were passed from hand to hand like baskets of fruit. Their verses were tuned with great care but filled with emotional exuberance.

The French Surrealists were haunted by suicide and, like Baudelaire, they longed to be "anywhere out of this world." The French society deserved to be torn down, in their estimation, and a new world erected, free from the continual locus of repressions and class-based stupidity. Breton's methods and outlook were irrevocably altered in the Latin consciousness. It became a medicine that American poets easily and greedily digested. The Beat poets were the first, alongside Lamantia, to become a flash point for the new level of consciousness. Indeed, they were looking—like Breton, Dalí, Rimbaud, and Baudelaire before them—for ways to take down the old scaffolding for the expectation of art in a post World War, military industrial America.

Presented with a new technique, the Beats changed their outlook and, consequently, the old ways of seeing inside the poem itself; the old formal structures were surprisingly easy to bring down. To see the invisible, you have to attempt the impossible, or by seeing it, you become confident that what was deemed impossible becomes plausible. Jean Cocteau said that the poet is "an invisible man, but a painter always paints his own portrait." I believe he meant that poems move *through* poets, and paintings were *compelled* by painters. So for the artist, all habits are bad, and change must come not only from book to book, but line by line, for what is most important is the life of the line. A line is in danger of dying all along. "But how to sustain a long line in poetry (lest it lapse into prosaic)?" Ginsberg asked. "It's natural inspiration of the moment that keeps it moving, disparate things put down together, short-hand notations of visual imagery, juxtapositions of hydrogen jukebox—abstract haikus sustain the mystery and put iron poetry back in line. Mind is shapely, art is shapely. Meaning mind practiced in spontaneity invents forms in its own image and gets to last thoughts." Those who first listen to a poet finally become his muses. So to change, or be willing to change our ways of listening or seeing, add electricity to the line as it is created, word by word, sound by sound, meaning and thrust implicit throughout. I want every poem I write to be different than the last one, every structure to have its own peculiar life.

John Ashbery and his compatriots in New York took the cultivation of reasonable absurdity and the aims of Surrealism to be one and the same. The Surrealists believed that where sense broke down, "the marvelous" began. Absurdity and fractured meanings did not portray the emptiness of conventional lives. They were excursions into a domain of lyrical reality. Love him or hate him, Ashbery is one of the few poets of the last fifty years to achieve a voice that is utterly new and inimitable, a mongrel voice equal parts elegant, absurd, and unexpected, rejecting what he called the "spots of time" that lyric poetry has traditionally sought to capture. "Each movement/ of utterance is the true one; likewise none is true." Strung on the separate wires of this paradox, the point is not to merely record verbal artifacts but to make poems that feel a part of a living system, alive themselves and parcels of a greater whole. From "Clepsydra," Ashbery hoped to capture "the way music passes, emblematic/ of life and how you cannot isolate a note of it/ And say it is good or bad/ ... one cannot guard treasure/ that stalled moment. It too is flowing, fleeting."

Besides Stevens, Ashbery is the most Frenchified of American poets. He has translated Pierre Reverdy, Max Jacob, Pierre Martory, and others, and like the Dada and Surrealist poets he admired, he has written extensively about art. One of his aims was "to produce a poem that the critic cannot even talk about." So, being Surrealist and Romantic at once, making everything a part of his poems and nothing alone their primary subject matter, he has achieved a wide audience and a measurably strong contingent of detractors. Like the Abstract Expressionsists, Ashbery's poems can feel incomplete, a kind of "organized chaos," as he calls them. Meghan O'Rourke, a poet as well as the culture editor for *Slate* and poetry editor for *The Paris Review*, said he is "a kind of radio transistor through which many different voices, genres, and curious archaeological remains of language filter, so that the poems are like the sound you would hear if you spun through the FM/AM dial without stopping to tune into any one program for long." In this manner, he is Cubist, a maker of collages, borrowing voices and then inventing their parody, B-movies, newspaper headlines, comic books, a soup of artfully strained musical noodles. In this strategy he may also recall Apollinaire. Consider these lines from his poem "Fragment":

> The young man places a bird-house
> Against the blue sea. He walks away
> And it remains. Now other
>
> Men appear, but they live in boxes.
> The sea protects them like a wall.
> The gods worship a line-drawing

Of a woman, in the shadow of the sea
Which goes on writing. Are there
Collisions, communications on the shore

Or did all secrets vanish when
The woman left? Is the bird mentioned
In the wave's minutes, or did the land advance?

Among his influences he counted Raymond Roussel, who declared
that his books had been composed not out of experience but out of verbal
games. Since an Ashbery poem is "a snapshot of whatever is going on in
my head at the time," he tried not to set any goals for his work and insisted
on music, but never the expected rhythm "I would prefer not to think I
have any special aims in mind," he said, "as I might then be forced into
a program for myself." This springing back and forth has kept Ashbery
from being pinned down to any one expectation or definition, save his associations with the New York School poets Frank O'Hara, Kenneth Koch,
James Schuyler, Ron Padgett, and others with whom he has collaborated
or praised or been influenced by. His work and free-wheeling tone seem to
represent what Wallace Stevens called "the hum of thoughts evaded in the
mind" and keep his readers fastened fiercely and attentively to the present,
focused wholly on the moment in front of them; but at his best, he speaks
deeply to the moments that unite the sensibilities for all his readers. His
famous book *Self Portrait In A Convex Mirror*, which won the Pulitzer
Prize and made him the Daddy Mack in American poetry, ends with this
beautiful and representative stanza:

We have seen the city; it is the gibbous
Mirrored eye of an insect. All things happen
On its balcony and are resumed within,
But the action is the cold, syrupy flow
Of a pageant. One feels too confined,
Sifting the April sunlight for clues,
In the mere stillness of the ease of its
Parameter. The hand holds no chalk
And each part of the whole falls off
And cannot know it knew, except

Here and there, in cold pockets
Of remembrance, whispers out of time.

The love of the city and its beehive rhythms characterized the loosely connected New York School, with O'Hara being the easiest, loosest, and most urban of the group. His surrealism, especially in the landmark volume *Meditations in an Emergency Ward*, is also the most acutely felt and legitimately and openly demonstrated:

The white chocolate jar full of petals
swirls odds and ends around in a dizzying eye
of four o'clocks now and to come. The tiger,
marvelously striped and irritable, leaps
on the table and without disturbing a hair
of the flower's breathless attention, pisses
into the pot, right down its delicate spout.
A whisper of steam goes up from the porcelain
eurythra. "Saint-Saens!" it seems to be whispering ...

Born in Baltimore, O'Hara settled in New York in 1951, where he worked for *Art News* and joined the staff of the Museum of Modern Art, eventually becoming associate curator for the exhibitions of painting and sculpture. Among the New York poets, great inspiration came from the paintings they encountered and the explosion of the arts scene in the 1960s, with artists such as Pollock, Jasper Johns, Franz Kline, Larry Rivers, and Willem de Kooning being discussed and defined by the poets they inspired. James Schuyler wrote, "New York poets, except I suppose the color blind, are affected most by the floods of paint in whose crashing surf we all scramble ... In New York the art world is a painter's world; writers and musicians are in the boat, but they don't steer."

O'Hara's authenticity is derived from his avoidance of polish or his ability to grandly finish; his poems feel rapidly written, haphazardly gathered, but wholly and deeply felt. "I historically belong to the enormous bliss of American death," he wrote in "Rhapsody," which was a title taken from a 1954 movie starring Elizabeth Taylor. Indeed, no American poet has made his fragments, jottings, diary entries, and daily observations of the city seem more important or clearly defined. He is the finest lover of the cityscape since Baudelaire—and even more deeply immersed in the rhythms and pace of city life. Like E. E. Cummings, he is also a poet capable of wild joy; he revised his stream-of-consciousness observations less and less as he continued to write. He called his poems "living facts," and what mattered to him was the fit of the language to its particular occasion. His method was "I do this, I do that," he said, and then he pinned down the event in his poetry. Here is an example, taken from "Les Luths":

> I want to hear only your light voice running on about Florida as we pass
> the changing traffic light and buy grapes for wherever we will end up
> praising the mattressless sleigh-bed and the Mexican egg and the clock
> that will not make me know how to leave you.

Ashbery said, "The poem is the chronicle of the creative act that produces it." This attitude, so clearly adapted from the Surrealists, merges the process with the product and holds that the creation of poetry is a living process; each poem is a part of a vast semantic canvas and, as such, must be read as a portion of the whole. This is particularly true for O'Hara, for most of his work escaped critical attention until after his death in 1966. It wasn't until 1971 and the publication of his gigantic *Collected Poems* that his accomplishment came into focus.

The New York poets also echo the French Surrealists in their reliance upon one another and their collaborative spirit. Their books were made with covers designed by their friends in the arts community; they wrote books together and reviewed those books. Ashbery and Schuyler wrote a novel, *The Nest of Ninnies*, and occasional musical collaborations were entertained with Cage and others. Translations of the French poets they admired were accomplished with guidance from one or the other, sometimes over long distances. The fascinating things about the groups of New York poets—and there were two, the first comprised of O'Hara, Barbara Guest, Ashbery, Koch, and Schuyler; and the second of Ron Padgett, Ted Berrigan, Alice Notley, Joe Brainard, Dean Young, and others—was that none of them were from New York City. They were all immigrants or exiles to that great metropolis. Koch was from Cincinnati and Padgett from Tulsa. Between them and their counterparts, they would translate the work of Jacques Prevert, Reverdy, Apollinaire, Valéry Larbaud, Blaise Cendrars, Tristan Tzara, and others, exposing these poets to an American audience, often for the first time.

CHAPTER 23

Breach and Convergence: The Spanish Revolution

A s the French assimilated through the Beats and the New York School, the magisterial and earthen poetry of the Latin American and Spanish schools were also made accessible through the efforts of a handful of dedicated translators. Where the French Surrealists had found their inspiration in Charles Baudelaire, the Symbolists, and Sigmund Freud, the Spanish had diverged from the nihilism of André Breton and his fellows and taken as their champion the self-centric Walt Whitman, the voice of the underdog and the unexplored wilderness, the lover of the primitive impulse. Pablo Neruda, in an interview with Robert Bly in 1966, described the difference:

> Poetry in South America is a different matter altogether. You see, there are in our countries rivers which have no names, trees which nobody knows, and birds which nobody has described. It is easier for us to be surrealistic because everything we know is new. Our duty, then, as we understand it, is to express what is unheard of. Everything has been painted in Europe, everything has been sung in Europe. But not in America. In that sense, Whitman was a great teacher ... He was not only intensely conscious, but he was open-eyed! He had tremendous eyes to see everything—he taught us to see things. He was our poet.

The breach in influences may be as simple as the terrain the poets existed upon. Poets are made from the memories of their people. For the French, the city was where the Symbolists and Surrealists yearned to be—Paris, the great

---

jewel of Europe. The Beats and the New York poets were clustered on opposite sides of the United States, in San Francisco and New York, where they helped to sustain and encourage each other. Baudelaire's city had been filled with night scenes in which the gaslights and their reflections lit the wounded, poverty-strafed parades of prostitution, crime, and solitary despair. The city of the modern poet was a city of crowds, brightly lit billboards, taxicabs and shows, transformed into a Mecca of possibility and promise, an electric garden.

Prior to this, the Romantic hero was a swashbuckling adventurer, a poet turned freedom fighter, or an intellectual giant immersed in meditation by a soft lapping lake. For Baudelaire, Stéphane Mallarmé, and Arthur Rimbaud, the poet was a fallen vagabond, a clown, and a magus, whose black clothes were stained with tobacco and mud, his senses addled by opium, absinthe, and loneliness. The Symbolist poem was an archipelago of fragments that bordered on silence, a poem about being a poem, suggestive, evasive, sequences of intense moments artfully rendered.

Whitman's hero is not solitary, nor does he speak of the vicissitudes of his own self. He is an *I* that is a *You*, his *He* is a *We*, one among many, a wanderer whose love of the cosmos is complete and unending. He lives in the eternal present—for men are the same as they have always been—and his rhythm returns to the Bible, even to the origins of the spoken word, a poetry that must be heard. Mallarmé's song of myself is the song of the solitary wrecked man in the face of a corrupted universe. Whitman's *Song of Myself* is a celebration of a democratic and free community, a fraternal yawp between man and his planet, man and the myriad things he may encounter—birds, plants, stars. Faced with this choice and armed with the new instruments of Surrealism, the Spanish-speaking poets walked out of the closed room of the dialectic and into the blazing Whitman sun.

At the core of the Spanish Surrealism is empathy, and it is political, avowedly leftist, and aimed at the dictatorial state. Francisco Franco's soldiers shot Federico Garcia Lorca in cold blood. César Vallejo died of infection and poverty fighting the same battle on behalf of the Spanish refugees. Miguel Hernandez rotted away in Franco's prison, eventually succumbing to tuberculosis. Even Neruda, the world traveler and Nobel Prize winner, lay dying in a Chilean hospital while doctors ignored his condition, too afraid of Augusto Pinochet's hatchet men to care for their country's greatest poet. The sense of overriding sorrow (and hopefulness in spite of it) merged with a feeling for folk songs and sensual imagery, creates a type of poetry that is unforgettable and unlike any other.

In his poem "The Dictators," translated by Robert Bly, Neruda wrote, "An odor has remained among the sugarcane … / a penetrating petal that brings nausea … Hatred has grown scale on scale,/ blow on blow, in the ghastly water of the swamp,/ with a snout full of ooze and silence." He is comparing the corrupt dictators to the menace of the crocodile—hidden away, but the people smell it, they know it means to kill them. In the last sentence of his *Memoirs*, Neruda described the death of his friend and elected President of Chile, Salvador Allende: "That corpse, followed to its grave only by a woman who carried with her the grief of the world, that glorious dead figure, was riddled and torn to pieces by the machine guns of Chile's soldiers, who had betrayed Chile once more."

Neruda was born Neftali Ricardo Reyes Basoalto in July 1904 in Parral, Chile. Within a month of his birth, his mother died of TB, and his father moved Pablo and his brothers to a small mountain town and remarried. Tall and lonely, the precocious boy began to write poetry at age ten. His father never cared for his writing, and so to cover the publication of his first poems when he was fourteen, the boy "looked for a last name that would throw him completely off the scent. I took the Czech name from a magazine, without knowing it was the name of a great writer (Jan Neruda, 1834–1891) loved by a whole nation, the author of elegant ballads and narrative poems, whose monument stood in Prague's Mala Strana quarter."

A principal of the Girls' School, Gabriela Mistral, a Nobel Prize-winning poet herself, encouraged him to develop his talent, and by 1934 he published *Twenty Love Poems and A Song of Despair*, which sold millions of copies in the Spanish-speaking countries and made a celebrity of the poet. An unrequited love affair, coupled with the young poet's fascination with Santiago and the Imperial River, made the lines come alive; Marisol, his country lover in the enchanted countryside, and Marisombra with her gray beret and gentle honeysuckle eyes watching him as they made love in the city's hideaways below the university buildings. Consider this last stanza of "Body of a Woman …" translated by W. S. Merwin:

> Body of my woman, I will persist in your Grace
> My thirst, my boundless desire, my shifting road.

Dark river-beds where the eternal thirst flows
and weariness follows, and the infinite ache.

Later, the young lover continues to follow his beloved, and the land-scapes begin to merge in the topography of the bodies. In "I have Gone Marking ...," again translated by Merwin, the poet begins:

I have gone marking the atlas of your body
with crosses of fire.
My mouth went across: a spider trying to hide.
In you, behind you, timid, driven by thirst.

And the intermingling continues, tied up in the processes of the Natural World, making sex and its bylaws suddenly governed by "a sad wind" at one with the "light of the universe" and arriving "in the flower and the water." Sex in its purest form can transform the whole world; here are the facts from the last two stanzas of "Every Day You Play":

How you must have suffered getting accustomed to me,
my savage, solitary soul, my name that sends them all running.
So many times we have seen the morning star burn, kissing our eyes,
and over our heads the grey light unwind in turning fans.

My words rained over you, stroking you,
A long time I have loved the sunned mother-of-pearl of your body
Until I even believe that you own the universe.
I will bring you happy flowers from the mountains, blue bells,
dark hazels, and rustic baskets of kisses.
I want
to do with you what spring does with the cherry trees.

At the age of only twenty-three, Neruda was appointed by the Chilean government as consul to Burma, where he lived in abject poverty for a time, since as honorary consul he received no salary. From Rangoon, he was posted in Sri Lanka, and his political beliefs began to form as he identified with the poverty, colonial rule, and political oppression of the South Asian masses who were heirs to a proud and spiritually advanced ancient culture. During these years from 1925–1935, he worked on the first two volumes of *Residence on Earth* and abandoned the lyrical syntax and conventional conceits of the love poems, leaping instead into a highly evolved personal voice, streaked with disintegrating visions and chaotic blues shouts developed from his close reading of the Surrealists, who were dominating European thought. His travels went from Indonesia to Argentina, where he met the poet Lorca. The two became close friends when Neruda was sent as consul in Barcelona, Spain. Lorca introduced him to the incredible circle of poets known as The Generation of '27, including Rafael Alberti and Miguel Hernandez, who were involved in the radical politics of the Communist Party. The outbreak of the Spanish Civil War in 1936 ended the revelry of the poets, creating an international crisis. Lorca was executed by the Nationalist troops, Alberti and Hernandez headed to the front, and Neruda journeyed in and out of the country gathering money and trying to mobilize support for the Republicans. His book *Spain In My Heart* was printed by Republican soldiers on improvised presses and passed among the troops, just as Che Guevara would later read poems from Neruda's *Canto General* to his bearded guerillas in the Sierra Maestra. Neruda was the great leveler of animosity, and his poems are a clarion eagle cry for freedom in all its forms—physical, political, spiritual—as illustrated in this excerpt from "I'm Explaining a Few Things, translated by Nathaniel Tarn:

Spain emerges
and from every dead child a rifle with eyes,
and from every crime bullets are born
which will one day find
the bull's eye of your hearts.

And you will ask: why doesn't his poetry
speak of dreams and leaves
and the great volcanoes of his native land?

Come and see the blood in the streets,
Come and see
the blood in the streets.
Come and see the blood
in the streets!

Neruda returned to Chile in 1943 and was elected a senator (like W. B. Yeats) in 1945. He campaigned for the leftist candidate, Gabriel Gonzalez

---

Videla, in the election of 1946, only to find President Videla setting up death camps for his political enemies. Betrayed, Neruda composed an open letter critical of Videla and, as a consequence, he was expelled from the Senate and forced to flee, hiding in the houses of friends to avoid arrest. Eventually, he was rushed out of Chile, crossing the Andes Mountains on horseback at night with the manuscript for *Canto General* rustling in his saddlebag. This epic poem, which also contains one of his finest works, "The Heights of Macchu Picchu," is a history of Latin America, its exotic flora and fauna, its wars and chieftains, its triumphs, and its dismemberment by dictatorships preying on the divided classes of the populace, usually lighting on the injustice visible to all but the wealthy.

Robert Bly called Neruda a poet whose "imagination sees the hidden connections between conscious and unconscious substances with such assurance that he hardly bothers with metaphors—he links them by tying their hidden tails. He is a new kind of creature moving about under the surface of everything. Moving under the earth, he knows everything from the bottom up (which is the right way to learn the nature of a thing) and therefore is never at a loss for its name ... He has few literary theories ... and has written great poetry at all times of his life." Bly called the fifty-six poems of *Residence On Earth*, books I and II, "the greatest Surrrealist poems written in a Western language," and it is hard to argue.

From 1952, when his exile ended, to his death in 1973, Neruda published twenty more books and found his poems translated into many languages. He continued to travel the world, lighting down in Russia, Cuba, China, and Mexico to accept awards and praise, only to return to his house on Isla Negra, facing the Pacific Ocean, full of giant shells and his wild collection of carved mastheads wrenched from ships the world over.

> I am here, watching, listening,
> with half of my soul at sea and half of my soul on land,
> and with both halves of my soul I watch the world.
>
> And even if I close my eyes and cover my heart over
> entirely,
> I see the monotonous water falling
> in big monotonous drops.
> It is like a hurricane of gelatin,

like a waterfall of sperm and sea anemones.

I see a clouded rainbow hurrying.

I see its water moving over my bones.

THE DEEP SONG AND DUENDE

When Neruda speaks of Lorca in his *Memoirs*, he does not speak of *duende*, the Spanish obsession with death; rather, he said that he had never met a brother who "loved laughter more" or "known anyone else with such magical hands." Trained as an attorney and a musician, Lorca wrote plays, poems, and songs with equal facility, as well as essays detailing not only his own creative process but attempting to capture the source of all great creative endeavors: the bond between the reader and the poem, the listener and the song. Not published until 1931, Lorca's book *Poem of the Deep Song* was his first major incursion into the soul of the Gypsy-Andalusian-Flamenco cosmos, written when the poet was twenty-three years old. It is full of images provoked by the *cante jondo* ("deep song") and comes from a musical tradition that developed among peoples who fled into the mountains in the fifteenth century to escape the Spanish Inquisition.

The composer Manuel de Falla said, "The historical events that have influenced our songs are three: the Spanish Church adopting the Byzantine liturgical chant, the Saracen invasion, and the arrival of numerous bands of gypsies; they are the mysterious, wandering folk who gave deep song its definitive form." Most students of Spanish folk music believe that an antecedent to deep song—combining native Andalusian, Arab, and Hebrew elements—existed prior to the arrival of the gypsies from India in 1477, who were driven from their homeland by a hundred thousand horsemen and then forced into the mountains by the Catholic Church. *Cante jondo*, in the 1880s, went from the seedy tavern to the cabaret and, in the process, changed from the plaintive, solitary cry of the Andalusian soul into the commercially viable music hall spectacular of flamenco.

Lorca believed the deep song echoed the sad laments of the gypsy diaspora and was "deeper than all the wells and seas of the world. It comes from the first sob and the first kiss and lives in the wide night steeped with stars. This deep song shoots its arrows of gold straight into our hearts." Lorca was keen to preserve the songs be heard. "The artistic treasure of an entire race is on the road to oblivion," he said. "Old men are taking to the grave price-less treasures of past generations."

Lorca's most famous book, *Gypsy Ballads*, was published in 1928, and his widening celebrity, coupled with his increasing despair over his secret homosexual identity, caused his parents to send him to New York City for a year. Lorca was also distraught over his failed love affair with the sculptor Emilio Aladren and believed (wrongly) that the wildly controversial film *Un Chien Andalou* (*The Andalusian Dog*, 1929) released in Paris was a vi-cious satirical attack on him. *Un Chien Andalou*, which was written by Luis Buñuel and Salvador Dalí without a thought of Lorca, had also made house-hold names out of his countrymen and former schoolmates, further alien-ating the young Spaniard. In New York, his fame spread, but his despair deepened. His book *Poet in New York* is filled with the shocks of recogni-tion from the poet as he sees the prejudice, class divisions, and pollution as he moves inside the chaos of a futuristic metropolis, the city he felt was the industrial center of the world. Here is Stephen Spender and J. L. Gili's translation of the tenth stanza of "The King of Harlem," which is also a kind of refrain, repeated at the beginning and end of the poem:

> That night the King of Harlem with a very hard spoon
> scooped out the eyes of crocodiles
> and spanked the monkeys on their bottoms.
> With a spoon.
> The negroes cried abased
> among umbrellas and golden suns,
> the mulattoes were stretching gum, anxious to reach
> the white torso,
> and the wind blurred mirrors
> and burst open the veins of the dancers.

Lorca, like Neruda and Ruben Dario, the Nicaraguan poet who was Latin America's first modernist voice, also felt a creative debt to Whitman and cel-ebrated him in his "Ode to Walt Whitman." Here is the seventh stanza, again translated by Spender and Gili:

> Not for one moment, beautiful aged Walt Whitman,
> have I failed to see your beard full of butterflies,
> nor your shoulders of corduroy worn out by the moon,

nor your thighs of virginal Apollo,

nor your voice like a pillar of ashes:

ancient and beautiful as the mist,

you moaned like a bird

with the sex transfixed by a needle,

enemy of the satyr,

enemy of the vine,

and lover of bodies under the rough cloth.

Not for one moment; virile beauty,

who in mountains of coal, posters and railways,

dreamed of being a river and sleeping like a river

with that comrade who would place in your breast

the small pain of an ignorant leopard.

Most of *Poet in New York* was composed while Lorca was in residence at Columbia University during the Great Depression, 1929–1930. Upon his return to Spain, his friend, the great bullfighter Ignacio Sanchez Mejias, was killed in the bullring. His "Lament For Ancio Sanchez Mejias" is a beautiful and masterly achievement. With the refrain "at five in the afternoon" repeated throughout like a tonal chorus, the poem's sad glacial music slowly gains in anguish and momentum: "Nobody knows you. No. But I sing of you ... / For posterity I sing of your profile and grace ... / of your appetite for death and the taste of its mouth."

Lorca said, "There are countries that draw the curtains on death, that treat death as a finality roped off from the rest of life. But Spain is a country where the curtains are flung wide open ... and death is invited in the room ... A dead man in Spain is more alive as a dead man than any place else in the world." This recognition led Lorca to formulate an advancement to his theories and work on behalf of the tradition of the deep song. His essay "In Search of Duende" took the core feeling needed to transmit the deep song and found it surrounded by the grave, mystical, dark force known as *duende*. Lorca said, "The great artists of the south of Spain, whether gypsy or flamenco, whether they sing, dance, or play, know that no emotion is possible unless the *duende* comes."

The *duende* (the etymology comes from *duen de casa*, "lord of the house") has generally been considered in Spanish folklore something like a household version of the Yiddish *dybbuk*, a hobgoblin, a cunning trickster who stirs up trouble. There are two such meddling sprites in Lorca's tragic farces *The Love of Don Perlimplin* and *Belissa in the Garden*, but he used the term in special Andalusian sense as a phrase to represent obscure power during performance of a song or poem, part of the penetrating inspiration of all great art. Lorca described it, quoting Goethe on Paganini, as "a mysterious power which everyone senses and no philosopher explains." The Gypsy singer Manuel Torres said that "all that has black sounds has duende." Here is an excerpt from Lorca's *Poet in New York*:

> Well, then, before reading poems aloud before
> many creatures, the first thing one must do is to
> invoke the duende. That is the only way that
> everybody will immediately succeed at the hard task
> of understanding metaphor (without depending on
> intelligence or critical apparatus), and be able to
> hunt, at the speed of the voice, the rhythmic
> design of the poem.

In Ralph Waldo Emerson's great essay "The Poet," he wrote, "Art is the path of the creator to his work. Doubt not, O poet, but persist. Say, 'It is in me, and shall out.' Stand there, baulked and dumb, stuttering and stammering, hissed and hooted, stand and strive until, at last, rage draw out of thee that dream-power which every night shows thee is thine own, a power transcending all limit and privacy, and by virtue of which a man is the conductor of the whole river of electricity." Marcel Proust's perception about "the involuntary memory" is a kind of creative trance-state that allows for the unknown channels of thought that thread through the artist's creative moment to be felt when composing. Lorca believed *duende* was especially active during the live performance of a poem or song when defeat is possible. "The duende does not come at all unless he sees that death is possible," Lorca said. It speaks to an art that touches and transfigures death, that woos and yet evades it. The eminently quotable Jean Cocteau wrote, "All poets are mediums and work-hands of this mysterious force that inhabits them. I do not mean inspiration. Inspiration does not come out of the blue. It's something that emerges from our depths, our night, and a poet tries to lay out his night upon the table."

The fluidity of language and its ability to affect the human body is well-documented in the power of the Sufi dervish chant, in voodoo, and in hypnotism. "What the imagination seizes as beauty must be truth," Keats declared. In a culture permeated with death, the bullfight is not a sport, but "a religious mystery," or in Antonio Machado's words, "a sacrifice to an unknown god." There is a Portugese word *saudade*, which musicians speak of in fado and Brazilian street music, that is used to describe the deeply-felt nostalgia and sadness inherent in the chord progressions and melodies. There is no English equivalent that I'm aware of, but I have felt this presence in certain Blues singers, and if Aretha Franklin, Ray Charles, or Otis Redding do not possess *duende*, then it clearly does not exist.

In one of the best examples of *duende* in modern poetry "Sailing To Byzantium," William Butler Yeats imagined himself being transformed into a magical bird who might sing with a perfection denied the living writer, "to sing to lords and ladies of Byzantium of what is past, or passing, or to come." Art needs a living body to interpret it. "That's when the duende comes," said Lorca, "through the empty arch of the body, a mental wind blowing relentlessly over the heads of the dead, in search of new landscapes and unknown accents; a wind that smells of baby's spittle, crushed grass, and jellyfish veils, announcing the constant baptism of newly created things." Here is the last stanza of Lorca's "Ballad of One Doomed to Die," translated by Langston Hughes:

Men came down the street
to look upon the doomed one
who cast on the wall his shadow
of loneliness at rest.
And the impeccable sheet
with its hard Roman accent
gave death a certain poise
by the rectitude of its folds.

Lorca related a story of an eighty-year-old woman who won first prize at a dance contest in Jerez de la Frontera. She was competing against beautiful women and young girls with waists as supple as water, but all she did was raise her arms, throw back her head, and stamp her foot on the floor. "In that gathering of muses and angels, beautiful forms and beautiful smiles, who could have won but her moribund *duende*, sweeping the ground with

---

its wings of rusty knives." The people of the countryside, the poor with their Andalusian pain and inexpressible joy, were always on Lorca's mind and populated his poems. Duende for the people is balanced precisely between happiness and mortality and possesses "a longing without object, a keen love for nothing, with the certainty that death is breathing behind the door."

This love of the people spawned a special program. In 1931, Lorca was appointed as director of a university student theatre company. This was funded by the Ministry of Education and it was charged with touring Spain's most remote areas in order to introduce audiences to radically modern interpretations of classic Spanish theatre. As well as directing, Lorca was also an actor. While touring with the company, Lorca wrote his best-known plays, the "rural trilogy" of *Blood Wedding*, and formulated his theories about *duende* and performance while those plays were being produced for the first time.

When war broke out in 1936, the program was disbanded and Lorca left Madrid for Granada, one of the most conservative regions in Spain. Lorca was rounded up, along with his brother-in-law (who was also the Socialist major of Granada), and arrested. Executed shortly after by Franco's falange militia on August 19, 1936, Lorca's body was thrown into an unmarked grave. It was only after Franco's death in 1975 that Lorca's work could be openly produced, published, and discussed in Spain, though a heavily edited *Complete Works* had appeared in 1953. Today there is a statue honoring Lorca in Madrid's Plaza de Santa Ana, and according to David Crocker, a political philosopher who lives there, "the statue is still an emblem of the contested past. Every day the Left puts a red handkerchief on the neck of the statue, and someone from the Right comes around every evening to take it off."

> Between plaster and jasmines, your glance
> was a pale branch of seeds.
> I sought in my heart to give you
> the ivory letters that say always,
>
> always, always: garden of my agony
> your body elusive always,
> the blood of your veins in my mouth,
> your mouth already lightless for my death.
> from *"Gracela of Unforeseen Love,"* translated by W. S. Merwin

Though the Franco regime banned the work of Lorca in Spain, his work still found its way into the rest of the world and was highly influential. In 1986, Leonard Cohen's English translation of the Lorca poem "Pequeno Vals Vienes" reached number one in the Spanish single charts as "Take This Waltz," with musical accompaniment by Cohen. Many poets also found Lorca's theories of creation to be riveting. Edward Hirsch was inspired by his writing on *duende* to assemble the book *The Demon and the Angel: Searching for the Source of Artistic Inspiration*, which was published in 2002. Lorca's work has found a wide range of American translators, including Stephen Spender, Langston Hughes, Rolf Humphries, Ben Belitt, Christopher Mauer, Roy Campbell, W. S. Merwin, Carlos Bauer, Donald Allen, Edwin Honig, William Jay Smith, and many others. He has been namechecked by the Clash in *London Calling*, their definitive album, and scores of poets—including Robert Creeley, Jack Spicer, Pablo Neruda, Jorge Luis Borges, Octavio Paz, Allen Ginsberg, and others—have dedicated poems to his memory. Two San Francisco poets of very different tastes sent tributes in their own idiosyncratic styles. Creeley's "After Lorca" speaks to Lorca's great love and compassion for the poor:

The church is a business, and the rich
are the business men.
                When they pull on the bells, the
poor come piling in and when a poor man dies, he has a
wooden
cross, and they rush through the ceremony.

But when a rich man dies, they
drag out the Sacrament
and a gold Cross, and go *doucement, doucement*
        to the cemetery

And the poor love it
and think it's crazy.

Jack Spicer was another poet from San Francisco—part of the triumvirate that included Robin Blaser and Robert Duncan, followers of Kenneth Rexroth who found the Spanish Surrealists through Rexroth's immaculate

---

translations. Spicer's lectures and teaching of "Poetry As Magic Workshop" at San Francisco State College in 1957 were duly influenced by the concept of the poem as a dictation. "Poets seek magic," he argued. "They'll bend themselves like pretzels to get to it." His ideas about "dictating" seem awfully close to the Surrealist concept of automatic writing. "The trick naturally is ... not to search for the perfect poem but to let your way of writing of the moment go along its own paths, explore and retreat but never be fully realized (confined) within the boundaries of the single poem ... Poems should echo and re-echo against each other. They should create resonances. They cannot live alone any more than we can." His notion of dictation, similar to Yeats's, was a way for his ailing physical body to be uplifted by the winged role of the poet, a transmitter of mystic wavelengths and messages into art. The idea of *duende* entering the poet during these moments of heightened transmission were akin to his magic telekinesis. Spicer's books, starting with his first, *After Lorca*, and continuing through the insanely ironic *Book of Magazine Verse*, established the idea of a serial poem, made from several sections, a single poetic text like a scroll made from the flow of the author's life. This is from "After Lorca":

Dear Lorca,

These letters are to be as temporary as our poetry is to be permanent. They will establish the bulk, the wastage that my sour-stomached contemporaries demand to help them swallow and digest the pure word. We will use up our rhetoric here so that it will not appear in our poems. Let it be consumed paragraph by paragraph, day by day, until nothing of it is left in our poetry and nothing of our poetry is left in it. It is precisely because these letters are unnecessary that they must be written.

In my last letter I spoke of the tradition. The fools that read these letters will think by this we mean what tradition seems to have meant lately—an historical patchwork (whether made up of Elizabethan quotations, guide books of the poet's home town, or obscure hints of obscure bits of magic published by Pantheon, which is used to cover up the nakedness of the bare word. Tradition means much more than that. It means generations of different poets in different countries patiently telling the same story, writing the same poem, gaining and losing something with each transformation—but, of course, never really losing anything. This has nothing to do with calmness, classicism, temperament, or anything else. Invention is merely the enemy of poetry.

See how weak prose is. I invent a word like invention. These paragraphs could be translated, performed by a chain of fifty poets in fifty languages, and they still would be temporary, untrue, unable to yield the substance of a single image. Prose invents—poetry discloses.

A mad man is talking to himself in the room next to mine. He speaks in prose. Presently I shall go to a bar and there one or two poets will speak to me and I to them and we will try to destroy each other or attract each other or even listen to each other and nothing will happen because we will be speaking in prose. I will go home, drunken and dissatisfied, and sleep—and my dreams will be prose. Even the subconscious is not patient enough for poetry.

You are dead and the dead are very patient.

Love,

Jack

THE DEEP IMAGE

"I know I was not the only one who felt these things," Spicer wrote, and it was true; other poets took Lorca's idea of the deep song and the Symbolist theory of correspondences and formed a new school of poetry. Jerome Rothenberg and Robert Kelly coined the term "deep image poetry" to describe poems that were highly stylized and resonant with free-standing imagery that always had deeper symbolic significances. Later, Robert Bly, James Wright, Galway Kinnell, Diane Wakoski, and Clayton Eshleman began to apply the idea to concrete imagery without abstractions or ambiguous language, allowing the experiences and imagery to flow naturally from the moment, creating a kind of narrative.

Rothenberg translated a number of German and Spanish poets, including the first English appearances of poems by Paul Celan and Gunter Grass. His interest in tribal poetry and ethnopoetics echoes the interests of Breton and Lorca before him, and he gathered poetry from Africa, America, Europe, and the Far East into a groundbreaking anthology called *Technicians of the*

Sacred, which went far beyond the standard collections of folk songs and poems to include sonic poetry and texts for ritual events. He and Bly have probably done more through their translations, editing, and critical studies to further the cause of Spanish Surrealism and poetry from other cultures than any writers since the enormous contributions of Rexroth.

Other poets, such as Gary Snyder, Nathaniel Tarn, and David Autin, saw ethnopoetics as a link to poetry in performance. Their interest in anthropology and linguistics tied the tribal rituals to the oral traditions in which the speaking, chanting, or singing voice gives shape to proverbs, riddles, curses, laments, histories, prayers, prophecies, and all the instinctive remembered links from generation to generation inside the tribal structures. Bly has translated dozens of poets, including Neruda, Jimenez, Lorca, Machado, Rumi, Rilke, Kabir, Hafez, Transtromer, Ponge, and Vallejo—many appearing in English for the first time. The political struggles of many of these poets profoundly affected Bly, and in 1966 he founded, with David Ray, American Writers Against the Vietnam War. In his essay "On Political Poetry," Bly wrote: "The life of the country can be imagined as a psyche larger than the psyche of anyone living, a larger sphere, floating above everyone. In order for the poet to write a true political poem, he has to be able to have such a grasp of his own concerns that he can leave them for awhile, and then leap up, like a grasshopper, into this other psyche. In that sphere he finds strange plants and curious many-eyed creatures which he brings back with him. This half-visible psychic life he entangles in his language." Here are the last nine lines of Bly's poem "Romans Angry About The Inner World":

A light snow began to fall
And covered the mangled body,
And the executives, astonished, withdrew.
The other world is like a thorn
In the ear of a tiny beast!
The fingers of the executives are too thick
To pull it out!
It is like a jagged stone
Flying toward them out of the darkness.

Bly's sense of surrealism and the deep image replaced rhyme, pentameter, and argument as the organizing principles of the poem. The images themselves build meanings and paradoxes out of disparate realities. The poem, carefully and musically constructed, noses forward by leaps and breaks in the logic of perception; its discoveries are the property of the reader, who enters the poem as if entering a building for the first time, and each break in imagery trips a light that the reader follows from room to room. Bly's poems in *The Light Around The Body*, his second book (which won the National Book Award in 1968), have a detached, almost dreamlike aura.

> We think of Charlemagne
> As we open oysters.
> Looking down, we see
> Crowds waving from islands inside the oyster shell.
> The neck swings to bite the dog.
> When the fishermen take in the floats
> They find nets some giant fish
> Broke through at night.
> At dusk we leave. We start north with twenty dogs.
> A blizzard begins,
> Making us look down.
> And the miles of snow crust going past between the runners!
> Westward the ice peaks
> Like vast maternity hospitals turned white by oyster shells ...

Other writers—like W. S. Merwin, Mark Strand, Charles Simic, James Tate, and Russell Edson—took the deep image and dislocated it, appealing to the idea of a tribal mythology buried in each man's DNA, myths and symbols which tie us to one another and to the unconscious cross-cultural imagery embedded in our deepest longing for brotherhood. Merwin was particularly effective and consistent in his insistence that poetry regularly reverts "to its naked condition, where it touches on all that is unrealized." Here are the last two stanzas of his "Footprints on the Glacier":

> I scan the high slopes for a dark speck
> that was lately here
> I pass my hands
> over the melted wax
> like a blind man

they are all
moving into their seasons at last
my bones face each other trying
to remember a question

nothing moves while I watch
but here the black trees
are the cemetery of a great battle
and behind me as I turn
I hear names leaving the bark
in growing numbers and flying north

The bonds and family tree of American Surrealism are tied and branched by the most slender of mental threads and strangely buoyant connective tissue. Surrealism has become the language we all speak, the rose-colored lenses we peer through, the emerald sled we use to speed down the slopes of traditional forms and into a landslide of new meanings and visions. Because of these mutations and various predecessors, no one group can hold sway. Invariably, no one voice rose up to define the river's direction. Franklin Rosemont and the Chicago Surrealists are clear in their intent, but Rosemont's critical writings and essays feel like warmed leftovers from a buffet of Breton. Others directly related to the French, such as Lamantia, Ken Wainio, and Nanos Valaoritis, have admirably advanced the initial aims of their forefathers in Paris, creating work that contains echoes of the initial revolt but maintaining a contemporary vision.

Wainio is another San Francisco poet whose work contains elements of Dada, with its whiffs of revolt, but is Freudian in its relentless search for the divine inside the actions of the poem's parts. Each poem has definitive movements, but he is a mistrustful medium for the dictated word, feeling a need to blend tabloid headlines, overheard colloquialisms, and the occult into a strange brew of carefully considered theories and contemporary fables. Here is a late poem of his called "Getting Rid of the Ego":

It's like getting married in the rain. A coach will pull up
at the edge of the damn when the flood starts and the bride
throws her flowers at the drowned. If you don't believe this,
go to a monastery for ten years and study the light through a

---

The Rhythm Method, Razzmatazz, and Memory

keyhole. Without moving your eye from the door cut out a piece of sky and wait for somebody to come with a key.

The flood is well up by this time. The dead are getting married in rowboats and copulating on pieces of wreckage. If you still don't believe it, take out your keyhole and study the drowned. They are discussing the possibilities of islands and shaping tombstones into anchors. Their children hold their breath underwater and pray to the God of Rain. He is holding himself in a cloud making everybody worship the flood. He is quite fond of suffering and has never understood sociology. But the dead come with their pogo sticks and stare up at the seat of his pants.

If you still don't get this, go sit down in the nearest bar and study the runway of faces. If anyone comes up to you and demands your marriage certificate, take out your keyhole and blast them with a peak of stars. If they are still sitting there waiting for you to kill your ego, tell them the world is flat and has an edge like the table. Drop something transparent over the side and tell them it was the argument of Columbus on his way to the new world.

BETWEEN THE COASTS: A NEST TO REST IN

It probably seems from the tenor of this section that American Surrealists have congregated on the opposite coasts of New York and San Francisco, biding their time inside vast urban dreamscapes, but there are exceptions such as John Yau or Merwin, ensconced in Hawaii; or Bly in Minnesota; or Frank Stanford in Arkansas, whose career was cut tragically short by his suicide at age thirty. A prodigy who wrote more words than most of us will produce in twice the time, Stanford's life is a Hollywood movie waiting to be cast. He left behind a boiling gumbo of powerfully original poems filled with characters more perverse and swamp-haunted than any of Faulkner's degenerate Snopes. Stanford's unending dialogue with death never encroaches on the appetites of his figures; rather, like Lorca's *duende*, it seems to be the catalyst bristling in their beards and bellies, propelling them in all their relations with brothers, coon dogs, magnolias, and water pumps. Voodoo occupies the same space as the Bible, which is "thick as pigment." "I have seen doors," he wrote, "through which death comes and goes." Here's an excerpt from Stanford's poem "The Light the Dead See" from his first book *The Singing Knives*:

> There are bookshelves I threw together
> I took the lumber
> From a horse thief's barn
> And there are books the dead light their stoves with
> Books howling like pines on a ridge
> Cats in heat
> Deserted and cold like a handgun or a spoor
> A gar looking for a wife in a swamp

Another maverick, for whom Surrealism served as a nest he could rest in while he whittled his poems and pronouncements and hung them on the sleeping brow of the world, was a young North Carolinian named Amon Liner. Wallace Stevens once boasted to his wife, "I believe that with a bucket of sand and a wishing lamp I could create a world in half a second that would make this one look like a hunk of mud." Liner created a parallel universe that mirrored our own, and then, as if to entice us to look, he stepped into it and disappeared at the tender age of thirty-six. Diagnosed with a congenital heart condition as a child, Liner spent his entire life with the wind of the wing of death hovering overhead. Cornered in that box, he fought his way out with five books of remarkable inventiveness and dexterity and one masterpiece that belies any description—a prophecy, I believe—called *The Far Journey and Final End of Dr. Faustwitz, Spaceman.* His books merged a frantic technical prowess with a fascination for pop culture, regional colloquialisms, science fiction, and fantasy all swirled in a soup of Surrealism. Fred Chappell called him "the one true genius I have ever met." Almost as surely as you hold this book in your hands, dear reader, I am sure you have not read the work of Liner. To excavate him will cost you nothing, but to savor his work will challenge all your notions of Southern poetry.

The Rhythm Method, Razzmatazz, and Memory

A MONDRIAN POEM ON THE DECLINE AND FALL
OF GREECE, CHILE, BRAZIL, AMERIKA,
THE WEIMAR REPUBLIC AND THE LANGUAGE OF PELLUCIDAR

ALL ART ASPIRES
TO THE CONDITION
OF MUSIC, that's
the line that generates
transformations like
spontaneous combustion;

ALL ART INSPIRES TO THE RHYTHM
OF THE DAY. That's the sun
that generates information
like spontaneous night.
Where the grass grows highest.
DEMOCRACY AND SOCIAL PLANNING

Even found poems, as:
IT'S THE REAL THING
poised against
NEW TRENDS IN INDUSTRIAL
ORGANIZATIONS must
dissolve into post-

UNHAPPY IN THE BEST OF TIMES.
Dream equals dream.
Poised against the backdrop
of bluecollar dissatisfaction.
Even A plus A equals double
overtime dissolves into

modern poem, as:
BACH PRELUDE TO
ABSTRACTION. All art
requires theory, something
to hang the bowler hat
of decay on. A meathook.

the post modern triple vision:
WARHOL'S EPILOG TO A POSTCARD
in triple time. All dreams
require satisfaction. At last,
something to maximize television.
TO MEET BASIC HUMAN NEEDS

All art desires the
proposition of decay.
DECAY FOR THE SAKE
OF DECAY. A fundamental
theorem. Like A equals A.
A flat A major A sharp A minor.

Ah, yr. icebox's generator.
WITHOUT CITIZENS THERE IS NO
CITIZEN ACTION. Action
for the sake of action. A hard
germlike fantasy. Green
under the minimum wage floor.

A piece of meat. Green
on the cement floor.
IT'S THE REAL THING,
THE DYNAMICS OF THE
CENTRAL CITY, Ah, yr.
muthas bruddas fada

ALL INFORMATION ACQUIRES
THE LOGIC OF THE INVISIBLE,
IT'S THE REAL THING,
THE DYNAMICS OF THE CENTRAL
CITY, NEW TRENDS IN INDUSTRIAL
ORGANIZATION, mondrian organization

---

la te do. Say it slow.
It sounds like music.
Say-it-fast, it's a snob
about to jet to the Old Country
to see the ruins. Of Beethoven's
skull. WORKPLACE OF THE FUTURE

charts. Color them slow
they resemble old boogiewoogie
left in the corner to rot;
color them fast, it's a current
of hot blood about to jet into the
sky, Prelude to a Sunny Day.

I found Liner's poetry to be irresistible, and also somehow inevitable, as one turns instinctively toward the rays of the sun in a shaded grove, the warmth in pockets between the tangled roots and the cool skin of the trunks. Like all Surrealists, Liner appears hidden at first, then his bone-white love of all things exposes his true nature and his hope, despite all evidence to the contrary. The tribute I wrote for him has a line, "There is no such thing as Southern poetry," which is a logical extension of his poem "Why I Do Not Write Southern Poetry." To press poems into categories or regions is largely to try and diminish them, to imply that a double standard exists, to segregate or ghettoize work that already shines forth with universal signifi-cance and regional reflection. To posit poems as academic vs. non-academic implies a different level of proof—that somehow performance is registered and calibrated with different instruments, that the judged in question must perform at a different standard or distance from his or her perceived target. These are the preconceived notions that poetry is dying to destroy. Liner wrote, "I do not know/ whether I shall starve or sing/ or if out of starving,/ I can sing the emptiness/ that fills me." His concerns are the concerns of the entire tribe, felt by one marginalized by his geography, his body, and the historical echoes that pressed his language out of him. Here is the last half of my tribute to Liner, "Death is a Fiction of Stone," from *The Lost Sea*:

There is no such thing as Southern poetry.
There is no such thing.
The individual cannot be forced
to flatten the night
with snowflakes of frozen honey.
Flesh and mud meditations
are what I seek, lullabies
of meat and smashed-up stars.
We cannot make time go down

The Rhythm Method, Razzmatazz, and Memory

scratching each other's back,

drinking martinis

in the back-lit poverty

of asphalt groves,

spending more money on the prison system

than the school system

while silence grins in the slums,

its eyeholes leaking lime-green dust.

Cathedrals of bees splinter,

a signal that the city has fallen

into flash bulbs of blood.

When the trees begin to speak

and the mind is on fire,

when the snarls of the white hounds

and the white-bearded weeds

swim through the poets

with television fins,

language, like a sonorous animal,

will evolve into its new skin.

Like a dead man walking backward

on glass stilts,

his lizard energy crackling

in the sad air,

a rain of salt statues will wrestle

with death in all its fictions,

in the distance

between necessity and despair.

We rest in the belly of language. We are born by distorting it. Surrealism is the funhouse mirror of our century, held up for our amusement and disgust. Its distortions have become the gold standard, the language we have commonly learned to translate splendidly. With it, poets, painters, admen, and rebel moviemakers have created a new world to replace that one that no longer seemed true. By looking into the layers of that mirror, we can find new ways of viewing ourselves, our work, and our world.

CHAPTER 24

Ekphrasis and the Ecstasy of Cinema

Throughout this section, we have found writers greatly influenced by the art of their time. At times the painters, in their willingness to experiment, have induced visionary language through their various approaches. Ekphrasis is the vivid description, through a poem or prose, intended to bring the subject before the mind's eye of the listener. It is the art of describing works of art, the verbal representation of a visual presentation. In some cases, ekphrastic poetry celebrates the power of the silent image even as it tries to circumscribe that power with the authority of the word, the persuasion of the language. The poem is made more beautiful by invoking the power of a particular painting or sculpture or movie and conversely defines the imagery by its description. Each made thing, the poem or the painting, is made more powerful by the focus of the other.

Ekphrasis found a welcome and crucial place among the Romantic poets of the mid-nineteenth century. John Keats's "Ode on a Grecian Urn" is one such example, as are Lord Byron's *Childe Harold's Pilgrimage* and Percy Shelley's "On the Medusa of Leonardo da Vinci in the Florentine Gallery." Because many of the Romantics celebrated nature in their work and spent countless hours describing it and its metaphysical qualities, they created greater respect for the Natural World among the populace. The American Transcendentalist movement was a logical progression and found its voice through the essays of Ralph Waldo Emerson and Henry David Thoreau. As far back as the second century A.D., the Greeks composed ekphrastic works for sculptures, paintings, and buildings, many of which survived the Byzan-

The Rhythm Method, Razzmatazz, and Memory

tine Middle Ages and reached the West during the Renaissance. In an early textbook on style, Aphthonius's *Progymnasmata*, the word ekphrasis could be found and certainly applied to Virgil's description of the hero Achilles's shield at the beginning of the *Aeneid*. But ekphrasis can be about any visually powerful scene or subject. Throughout this section, we have focused on artists whose contributions to Surrealism were manifested by their search for an imaginative center in their work and by the influence of the painters and visual artists whose work paralleled the literary artists' experiments and were often the mitigating catalyst for the literary movements.

The sources of inspiration for a working and alert writer can be myriad but are often visual, and the power of description in the process is often the combustible starting point. The visual artists—and, by extension, the movies—that have inhabited my own work have been crucial to my ability to layer imagery inside the musical structure of a poem. Indeed, the structure of a poem can mimic the energy in a painting. Consider this poem by Katherine Graham, inspired by Marc Chagall's painting "The Woman with the Blue Face":

> The woman
> with the blue face dressed in white queen for a day takes for her husband this
> man green in the spring of his fire his body so next to hers he is
> inside her another part of her becomes his green splendor in the red
> snapdragon garden of her belly and in the darkness of their together
> the horse gallops across the rooftops of the village the shadows of
> his hooves are midnight crescent moons on the ceiling of quiet desires
> let us listen to the music laughter drunk full in our cups and let the
> bull flick his tail at the fly and let the fish stumble up the stairs
> spawning and let the bird fly yellow into night let the angel fly blue
> forever into white as the neck of a swan parts the darkness as Moses
> parts the sea as our hearts adjust to the vastness like a marble sized
> teacup in the galaxy of a saucer its center heavy and hungry it drinks
> all things in and it splits apart and becomes many instead of one

I can never visit a museum without a notebook to record my thoughts, and I have found that to describe the action in a painting is to give life to an alternative work of art. Words work in concert with images, and the theory of composition aptly described becomes a theory for life, or as Czeslaw Milosz has written, "I have always aspired to a more spacious form/ that would

---

be free from the claims of poetry or prose." Milosz advised stillness for the poet as Auguste Rodin advised Rainer Maria Rilke: Seek in stillness the images to build your words around. Allow the active imagination to fill in around the forms your mind has conjured. "To refine, to clarify, to intensify that eternal moment in which we alone live there is but a single force," said William Carlos Williams, "the imagination." Williams's poems are often sheer descriptions, lyrics in which familiar objects are clarified and presented in a fresh context, such as "The Yachts," or a red wheelbarrow, or a flowerpot "gay with rough moss." Williams's struggle in his art involved finding the poem between the struggle of opposing images and their unseen polarities. "Between two contending forces," he said, "there may at all times arrive that moment when the stress is equal on both sides, so with a great pushing, a great stability results, giving a picture of perfect rest."

Since cinema is first about the picture in the frame—the objects and the lights that fall upon them—it is not surprising that many famous directors were first photographers (George Stevens or Stanley Kubrick) or painters (Salvador Dalí or Jean Cocteau or Jean-Pierre Jeunet), first learning to fill the empty frame with balanced compositions. Early on, without sound— from the extravagant silent vistas in the first films to the comedic master- pieces of Charlie Chaplin, Buster Keaton, or Laurel and Hardy—filmmakers made the symbolic and transferred layers of images, signifying by gesture, motion, or edit, the loves, laments, and hopes of their stories. The last mel- ancholy dance of Fred Astaire and Ginger Rogers in *Swing Time* conveyed the sadness of their lost affair in one spinning, perfectly choreographed scene without a word between them.

Sometimes curiosity is its own reward. At the end of the 1960s, movie- makers became more experimental and less refined, letting the camera do the work. In *Easy Rider*, there is a simple panorama in the commune scene, just after planting and before the meal prayer, that is encyclopedic in its almost religious stillness; and later in the cemetery acid scene, the camera reels and dodges, creating the same vertigo in the viewer as the actors are experiencing. *Easy Rider* is filled with these moments of New Orleans *mojo santeria*, distilling its trippy and distorted iconography in chalky re- ligious chunks. The ending still stuns after repeated viewings, with its sud- den chicken-fried Alabama deathbed conclusion in full gory display. The movie's authenticity and gritty color palettes were highly influential, and as one of the first independent films to go guerilla budget and make a bundle, it inspired a whole generation of poverty-stricken genuises to take a chance. So much great art is created out of the excitement of necessity, with only oneself to rely on.

The art of cinema may be the strongest medium in the history of the human species. It affects our bodies and our subconscious in ways that we are only beginning to understand. An audience entranced by a movie goes into a dreamlike state and is transported. Like water that finds its way into the rock and freezes, tearing it apart, so too do the light rays of a memorable film enter our memories and freeze all other events from that time, a touchstone etched forever in the seduced watcher's psyche. Every other event from that moment and the surrounding moments are measured against the emotional impact of an unforgettable film, so powerful with its combination of images and music and visceral tones that it creates physical responses for the audience decades later. It is no wonder that Hollywood—built by East Coast immigrants with grand ideas, including the desire to shoot film day and night in the perfect sunny weather—has reached such mythical proportions in only a hundred years.

Sydney Pollack said, "directors' lives are linear, moving quickly to the end and transparent, but when you're directing a film you have several lives and many possibilities for that life, living through the lens of others. It's like mining clay; you gather great quantities and then make many statues." He's talking about the cutting room, where the edits the director carefully chooses determines the quality of the story he can tell. These choices go beyond and define the performances of the actors, the personal chemistry, even the corrosive effects of time, erecting a single gallery with many sculptures, each telling the same story together with such vigor that time cannot diminish it.

Our memory and our imagination are our greatest tools as poets, and the movies capture memories for us, freezing events in time. Federico Fellini said, "For me the things that are most real are things that I have invented. I seem to remember a certain continuity in the feeling of expectation, things happened in a very natural manner and I went along with them. The same can be said of my films. I never decided to make one film over another. It was as if I were a train and the stations were films. It was as if they were ripe and ready to be plucked in a sense, as if they'd already been made." All films aspire to the condition of music, the same dynamism attached to the confirmed refractions of the past blended note by note, scene by scene, into a coherent whole.

At different periods of our lives, we define ourselves by the reflections we see on the screen's giant mirror. What man would not like to take these elements and refine himself, defined by the passivity of Spencer Tracy, the swagger and insouciance of Marlon Brando, the belligerent bluster and concerted simmer of Al Pacino, the menace and sweep of Robert DeNiro, the suave composure of Cary Grant, the macho bloviation of George C. Scott, the meticulous slither of Peter Sellers, the precision and sentimentality of John Wayne, James Woods's slimy dissembling, Christopher Walken's snide stutter, the carnal and confused Russell Crowe, the kinetic athleticism of Tom Cruise, the quirky metaphysics and blue Zen torrents of Jack Nicholson? Many of these actors emerged from the maverick visions of directors in the opposition, operating outside the expectations of both the studio and their audience.

> *All films aspire to the condition of music, the same dynamism attached to the confirmed refractions of the past blended note by note, scene by scene, into a coherent whole.*

American cinema was affected by its European counterparts in France and Italy—directors like Jean-Luc Godard, Bernardo Bertolucci, Luis Buñuel, Vittorio De Sica, Roberto Rosselini, Ingmar Bergman, Luchino Visconti, Jean Renoir, Michelangelo Antonioni, and especially Fellini. These men made the experience of film-making a fresher, more exalted undertaking that broke out of the old frames in a more seamless, grittier anti-fashion. Each brought a different style to their films; camera placement and cinematography were tools to be exploited as a painter would, one frame at a time.

The camera is a discoverer, an uncoverer; it recovers our truest essence and says it plain. The new generation of film-makers in America were more sophisticated than the studio bosses of yesteryear; they wrote their own scripts and were shooting scenes straight out of their brains, trusting their intuitions. Interiors became more important than graphic symbolism; the inner emotional life of the character began to drive the storytellers, and in that realm, improvisational and succinct, anything was possible. Roger Corman and John Cassavetes would hand the camera to anyone, make

The Rhythm Method, Razzmatazz, and Memory

movies out of their own pocket in a couple of weeks, and release them to great acclaim and profitability. Actors and movie stars became dark and imperfect and looked like the guys and gals next door. "Cinematic success is not necessarily the result of good brain work," said Francois Truffaut, "but of a harmony of existing elements in ourselves that we may not have ever been conscious of, as accidental coincidence of our own preoccupations at a certain moment of life and the public's perception."

In this arena, Surrealism so assimilated itself into our culture that it was no longer recognizable. Cultural and iconic imagery that would have been dubbed surreal became commonplace. Now to be called surrealistic, an image or idea has to be so over the top as to be insane, utterly illogical, nonsensical, or hyperreal. In fiction, Surrealism morphed into magical realism, such as *One Hundred Years of Solitude* by Gabriel García Márquez. The theatre of the unexpected, or absurd, bled into movies and advertising. Almost all advertising copy today contains some type of surreal imagery for the purpose is to stop the ceaseless consumer in his tracks and cause him to focus on the product at hand. Thus, a piano playing by itself on the beach, or a person walking away in the sand leaving no footprints, or a beer can becoming a train and blasting through the countryside are images that are not "real" but designed to make the observer stop and shift, feel the abnormality, and be attracted by its sudden pull, to take stock of this product and return to it in the retail marketplace.

A SHORT HISTORY AND DEMONSTRATION OF SURREALISTIC TECHNIQUE IN THE CINEMA

Man Ray began in Paris by taking portrait photos of some of the more famous itinerants of the 1920s—Igor Stravinsky and Pablo Picasso, Ernest Hemingway and Gertrude Stein—many of them lodging in Paris for a short time. "I felt like a doctor," said Ray, as his subjects sought him out and posed, "but these people came to me at their most powerful, not in sickness but in greatness, and I became aware of my own power as a photographer. Everybody who came in my studio was photographed automatically." Whether they were Sinclair Lewis or James Joyce or T. S. Eliot or Georges Braque or Henri Matisse or Constantin Brancusi, it made no difference; somehow, in three or four exposures, the transmission of a shared moment was captured, and those illuminated portraits gave Ray the confidence to stretch the artistic possibilities of his photography and then his paintings.

His Ray-o-graphs were made by laying found objects directly onto the celluloid paper and then hitting them with a bright light, capturing the outline and detail of the thing without benefit of a camera. This led Ray and his cohorts to consider making films. "In my own village of Calanda, where I was born ... the Middle Ages lasted until World War I," said Luis Buñuel in 1932. Indeed, until just a few years ago, parts of Spain were so poor that the streets were still dirt, ruts of mud when it rained. Buñuel had one of the first phonographs and would point its speakers into the square out of his garage, blasting Wagner at the peasants who were hearing the music for the first time. Some of the towns didn't make it into the twentieth century until the late 1970s.

At La Residencia, a type of centralized university or academy in Madrid, the young Buñuel, whose father had sent him to study agriculture, met the two-headed artistic dragon of Salvador Dalí and Federico Garcia Lorca, and the three budding artists became inseparable. Together, they pulled pranks on the unsuspecting local patrons and thought up outrageous art projects that would make them famous. One of Spain's most renowned artists, Joan Miró, set up an exhibition for Dalí in Paris, which was wildly received and opened the door for other artists. Buñuel followed soon after and spent several years as an assistant director for a French film studio, until he decided to make his own film and his mother paid for him to produce it. Thus was *Un Chien Andalou* born into this world.

Buñuel sought out his old friend Dalí, and they decided to make a movie that was composed entirely of irrational images that raced back and forth in time. It was 1927, and the two men sequestered themselves in a hotel room and began to exchange dreams and fantasies and unreal possibilities. They aimed to shock rather than please their audience, and they succeeded. Audiences were aghast when confronted by the picture. At its first showing, Buñuel stood behind the screen as the film was projected and played a series of records, mainly Wagner, to serve as a kind of soundtrack, since this was the era of silent movies. His jacket pockets were filled with stones the size of potatoes just in case the crowd had a nasty reaction. Thankfully, the audience, whose members included Picasso and Braque and Cocteau, cheered wildly at the conclusion, so Buñuel discreetly emptied his pockets into a large potted plant. (Later, when *L'Age d'Or*, the second collaboration of Buñuel and Dalí, was premiered, it was met with riots and gunfire; paint was thrown on the screen, patrons were arrested, and the film was banned in France for fifty years, finally escaping censorship in 1980.)

Un Chien Andalou became a very influential piece of film. Charlie Chaplin owned his own copy and would have it screened for friends. Every time the famous eye-slicing scene came on, his Chinese projectionist would faint, according to legend, and have to be revived. The iconography of the film is simple enough (it only lasts sixteen minutes) but very powerful. At the outset, in black and white, of course, a man is standing with his back to the camera, sharpening a razor. The man is smoking a cigarette and sporadically tests the sharpness of the razor on his thumbnail. Eventually satisfied, the man walks onto the adjoining balcony and stares out at the city. He seems agitated and looks up to see a sliver of cloud pass over a full moon. He then walks inside behind a woman who seems resigned to her fate, holds her eye open, and then slices across it slowly with the razor, its insides gushing out onto her cheek. This is one of the most notorious scenes in cinema history, one which served to define early Surrealist strategies. This, along with André Breton's famous dictum that "the simplest surrealist act consists of dashing down into the street, pistol in hand, and firing blindly," caused no small scandal in polite society and firmly cemented Surrealism as an outsider art, produced by renegades with no moral equilibrium.

If Surrealism is a tear in the fabric of the culture, or "reality in collision with the eyes," as Antonin Artaud said, then Un Chien Andalou accomplishes both things at once, literally and figuratively. The woman whose eye is cut in the first scene is the same woman who reappears over and over throughout the rest. The man who does the cutting, Buñuel himself, disappears and does not return, replaced by the clown. Despite these convulsive sections, the film has a peculiar propulsion. It moves seamlessly from image to image until they seem to be a continuation in the observer's mind, linked by the rising and falling strains of the orchestra in the background. It feels like a dream, but a dream in rhythm—and that's the key to its visual effectiveness. One could not exist without the other. The contrasts waltz around the frame out of season or sequence, but in time with the flow of the violin.

The sexual obsessions and fantasies in Un Chien Andalou careen around and against the corrosive figures of death and disfigurement; this seems especially ironic considering that the film is the seminal experimental film of the

1920s—in many ways the last and best of its kind. Talkies began in the 1930s, and with them came the need to make films that catered to their audience, those which entertained and soothed the observer. It would be decades later before cinema regained its confidence enough to challenge its patrons. However nonsensical *Un Chien Andalou*'s creators wished to be, their film has a resonance that still exists, a poignant lyricism in spite of their best efforts to confound. Artaud predicted sound would be the death of cinema. It turned out to be merely a sucker punch from which the studios eventually recovered.

The 1930 film *L'Age d'Or* was not built out of serenity or deliverance but a sense of desperate foreboding and chaos. The two friends, Buñuel and Dalí, who had collaborated so magnificently on *Un Chien Andalou*, could now agree on nothing and, upon the film's completion, saw each other only twice more for the rest of their lives. Film in 1929 still had few preconceptions. For two decades, filmmakers had done whatever they pleased, followed their own instincts and dictums, and tried to ply the audience with unexpected mysteries, unsteady and unpredictable territory that bent their preconceived notions of reality in spectacular ways.

By the mid-1930s, when talkies changed the landscape, the studios in Hollywood and elsewhere began to make pictures to play on the heartstrings of their patrons. Roy Rogers and Shirley Temple became the biggest stars in the world, and the independent auteur was forced to work for someone else or toe the line. The front edge of this delicate conundrum was creeping in when *L'Age d'Or* was conceived and released. Skewering everything from Catholic piety to sexual fetishism, this movie is a gleeful fever of Freudian neurosis and bizarre, humorous satire that provoked riots, was denounced by Mussolini's ambassador, earned its backer a threat of excommunication, and was banned by the French police all within two weeks of its premiere. Seventy-five years later, it seems relatively tame and more absurd than scandalous, and it's hard to separate the parody from the polemic, less shocking perhaps than laugh-out-loud nuts.

Lauded by generations of filmmakers—from Alfred Hitchcock to Fellini to David Lynch—you can feel *L'Age d'Or*'s modern echoes in Fellini's *Satyricon* and *La Dolce Vita*, in Lynch's *Blue Velvet* and *Wild at Heart*, and in the comedic sketches of The Monty Python players, particularly in their satirical Holy Grail feature. Renowned movie critic Pauline Kael called it "deliberately, pornographically blasphemous," but that must have been in

The Rhythm Method, Razzmatazz, and Memory

one of her more pious moments. It did serve, however, to keep the Surrealists out of the theatre for years.

When *L'Age d'Or* opens, with its clinical language and footage of scorpions wrestling in the desert, it dislocates the audience, hoping to suspend the tension before its lovers and deteriorating clergy are introduced in all their social complexity. It is clear that the film's creators considered the scorpions' anti-social behavior to be congruent with the Parisian society that they hoped to sting. Since the scorpion is the zodiacal sign of the testicles and the anus, and as such merges sex and death, it thereby bolsters the French word for orgasm—as *le petit morte*, or "little death." The scorpion's tail also parallels the film's structure, five prismatic sections with a sixth denouement, administering its final dose of poison in the last act. Whereas *Un Chien Andalou* was well-received and profitable, *L'Age d'Or* was accepted with only grudging respect by the avatars of the Surrealist movement, suspicious of public acceptance and flattery. The first film was a short artistic dream, albeit a violent one, and so *L'Age d'Or* was stubbornly fixed at sixty minutes, too short for a feature, too long for an artistic short, and so trenchant as to be unclassifiable.

Surprisingly, this revolutionary gob of spit was funded by a Parisian aristocrat who had already funded a film by Man Ray and was also a direct descendant of the Marquis de Sade. The production, although hampered by the deterioration of the relationship between Buñuel and Dalí, took only three weeks and was edited quickly, but it still went way over budget and cost about eight times more than their first film. Upon its release, Dalí disavowed *L'Age d'Or*, claiming it lacked subtlety and was more overtly political and dogmatic than he had intended. Clarity and method and calculation had replaced the automatism and fantastic spontaneity of their previous collaboration, but Dalí had been largely absent from the new project, having to deal with a bankrupt sponsor and being in the first throes of his lifelong obsession with Gala Éluard, whom Buñuel detested.

The targets of the film were clearly the social climbers and its clerical upper crust, as opposed to the individual maladjustments that may have contributed to the civilization's decline in the first place. But there is no doubt that sexual repression is the real target, and the film defines long-suppressed desire as a destructive social force. In this way, the film could be viewed as a conciliation between Freud and Karl Marx, a way of bridging the gulf between their sometimes oppositional philosophies.

For the first time, Surrealism and its techniques were taken seriously by the public at large, and the results were not pretty. Bourgeois society and the rising wind of the conservative right wing slammed down all the weights of censorship at once, making Buñuel and Dalí household names but banning their film for the next fifty years from presentation in France.

Jean Cocteau's strategies for his surrealistic films were similar to those of Buñuel, but they differed in the way the camera was employed. Cocteau, being a painter, was less concerned with story and fixed his eye on the pointed image alone. This is Cocteau describing his first film, and his experience making it, at the movie's premiere in January 1932: "In *The Blood of a Poet* I tried to film poetry the way the Williamson Brothers film the bottom of the sea. It meant letting down the diver's bell deep inside me, like the diver's bell they let down in the sea. It meant capturing the poetic state. Many people believe that this poetic state does not exist, that it's a sort of voluntary excitement. But even those who think they are the furthest away from the poetic state have known it. They only have to think of a great grief, or a great fatigue. They are curled up by the fire dozing, but they are not asleep. They immediately have associations that are not associations of ideas, or of images, or of memories. They are more like coupling monsters, secrets that emerge in the light, a whole equivocal and enigmatic world, quite capable of giving one an idea of the nightmare in which poets live, that makes their lives so moving, and that the public so wrongly interprets as exceptional exhilaration. Of course, nothing is so hard as trying to get close to poetry."

The movement of the characters in *The Blood of a Poet* was created by laying the sets flat on the ground, making the actors and backdrops essentially crawl across them. When filmed from above, the effect makes the actors' steps appear labored, confused, without a central equilibrium, taking the one rule that governs everything—gravity—out of the equation. When the action is filmed in slow motion and then sped up, the actor seems to be dragging himself with great effort through the world on the other side of the mirror. "Slow motion is vulgar," Cocteau has said. Later in his introductory statements at the film's premiere, he added, "I would prefer a wheelbarrow to a Rolls Royce because they keep changing shape and engine."

The second half of the film centers on a public square in the village. A statue is reduced to dust by children confusing its chalky contents for snow, as they throw everything they can find at each other in a ferocious snowball fight. This action is filmed in rapid motion, making the boys' movements frenetic, their behavior frenzied and out of control. One child is knocked unconscious, perhaps killed, bleeding profusely from his mouth and left to his fate as his classmates scatter. A man and a woman appear, seated at both ends of a table over his still body and proceed to play cards. When the man is defeated, accompanied in his defeat by hilarious onlookers festooned on the balconies in operatic finery and ostrich feathers, a star appears on his temple and fills with blood. The woman turns into a statue and walks regally, if somewhat painstakingly, out of the square accompanied by a cow with a map of Europe on its back. The woman is blind; Cocteau has painted eyes on her closed eyelids, and so she moves unrealistically, with effort, in her darkness, as if she is asleep or afraid of falling.

Being that *The Blood of a Poet* was Cocteau's first effort, the film does lack a certain technique or refinement, but this lapse seems to actually serve his purposes. Unexpected lighting and jerky angles conspire with the filmmaker's intention to create a dream, a Freudian interior flooded with emotions straining to make sense of a life whose purpose is to create. The disjointed existence of the poet, or artist, seems ridiculous to those in the culture unable to experience or define it, no matter how much the public may enjoy the works this state enables its creator to produce. But for the artist, all habits, save the discipline needed for creation itself, are bad and to be avoided. This rails against all societal conventions of routine and conformity, the pallor of the ordinary. "My life is a long struggle against habits," Cocteau said, "against others, against myself ... a terrible mixture of chaos and order."

The image of the dying child is a repetitive theme in Cocteau's work. His 1929 novel *Les Enfants Terrible* describes an adolescent boy confined to a bedroom on account of a head injury, playing out a world of Surrealist fantasies with his sister as they become more and more obsessed with each other. The words *enfant terrible* sound as if they should mean a "dreadful child," but the phrase nowadays has little or nothing to do with children. It means someone who extravagantly defies convention, usually arising out of a cultural group or movement where the person has a provocative role. Twenty years after Cocteau's book was written, Jean-Pierre Melville cast convention to the winds, and his groundbreaking film of *Les Enfants Terrible* became one of the inspirations and sacred tests for the radical student uprisings in Paris in the late 1960s.

Life encroaches and shakes our confidence, disappointments pile up, luck rubs its legs on another, and we've no option; the drama drains away. Surrealism holds that anything is possible, that the sustained vigor of a note perfectly played does not fade away but races pell-mell across the landscape, creating unforeseen alliances, unsuspected associations, the perfectly achieved harmony for all of God's mistakes. Chagall's violin in the mouth of a horse is not absurd, but purposeful. Its strings will move with unrestricted speed back to the source. Magic is a turbulent mitosis, heaven and hell rusted together, because nothing stays where you put it. Even the magicians move quickly so as not to spoil the trick, and the trick is never letting the disappeared thing stay away too long, so that the mind may drift and fill the magic-suspended moment with a logical conclusion. Reason is the bridge that holds the brain in place. But what fun is there in that? The world is a comedy for those who think, a tragedy for those who feel.

Two recent hit movies of the popular zeitgiest, *Angels in America* and *Amélie*, both deploy Surrealistic techniques and imagery to support their narrative. On the surface, these films would appear to be as disparate as possible, but both are essentially love stories with happy endings. One sees life as an unfathomable force that exists between unspeakable tragedies; the other sees life as essentially benign, bouts of loneliness sandwiched between magical insights that unwittingly give evidence of the webbing that binds all cultures together.

In *Angels in America*, the central character is also the linchpin around which the story spins, a gay man in the Reagan '80s, dying of AIDS. *Amélie*'s central character also propels the action, except she is a doe-eyed French nymph with a secret life as a brilliant do-gooder too shy to confront the world on any terms but her own. *Angels* is distinctly New York, and *Amélie* is a postcard from Paris. The cinematography of *Amélie* is painstakingly arranged like frame after frame of calibrated paintings. As a matter of fact, a great deal of the most fantastic or surreal imagery is adapted from Central-American Surrealist painters, like Marcello's pig lamp, pulling his own cord and snuffing the light, or the paintings of animals that populate the walls of the apartments. Even the choice of Zorro as the heroine's alter

The Rhythm Method, Razzmatazz, and Memory

ego and the horse escaped from his pen and racing the bikes in the Tour de France are deliberate decisions by Jean-Pierre Jeunet to make the film hyper-real to his audience, choosing icons they will sympathize with. By contrast, *Angels* gets its more gritty feel from the anguished artistry of Robert Mapplethorpe or Man Ray, quickly and effectively juxtaposed against the classic masters of religious ecstatic painting, particularly in the appearances of the angels—the statuaries and columns and fountains—all capable of coming to life or pulsing like Rainer Maria Rilke's statue in the poem "The Archaic Torso of Apollo," who says, "You must change your life." Religious artists are, by virtue of their subject matter, beyond the pale of this world in their execution and in the ambitions and abilities, both of the characters they portray and the painters who breathed life into them, such as William Blake, Caravaggio, Hieronymus Bosch, El Greco, Diego Velázquez, Henry Fuseli, and Michelangelo.

We have been conditioned to believe that our external reality is true, but does not match our internal reality; however, there is an infinite sea of potential. Our brains are lit by what we see and by what we think we see, making the process of the past just as real as the lived moment viewed by the eyes. The brain processes 400 billion bits of information per second, but we're only aware of about 2,000 of those. We spend the majority of our time eliminating waste, disposing of random sensory projections, accepting the symbols and images that occur the most or serve our bodies best. The integration of reality is always slower than its actuality. We need patterns to promote the reality we want most, and routines are formed, expectations established, leaving the unconscious acceptance of the lowest common denominator.

But the universe is essentially empty, with cell particles disappearing and reappearing over and over at the subatomic level. A particle can be in one or more positions at the same time, but it is fixed by our brain into a single place. When we look away, there are waves of possibility; when we look back, the particles of experience are fixed. "Atoms are not things," said Werner Heisenberg. "They are only tendencies." The real trick to life, that which the Surrealists understood intuitively and without benefit of physics, is not to be in the know, but to be in the mystery. Most of our assumptions about the world are proven over and over again to be false, but the tangible reality of the body is almost always true—gloriously, mysteriously present.

This section on cinema began with the sounds of angel wings and so shall it reasonably conclude, with that half-breed, earthly interloper, the angel. The angel is an expert without experiences who lives among us, envious and disgusted at once. In *Wings of Desire*, directed by Wim Wenders, the angel is the vantage point of the audience and, through those surreal and violently attentive eyes, we get one of the most exquisitely detailed films about human behavior ever made. The action unfurls in Berlin before the wall fell, and in many ways it stands as a love letter to that bizarre, multilayered metropolis, textured with riddles and unsolvable dichotomies, a peculiar island floating like a buoy upon the contradictory currents of the Cold War. Berlin was where the line was drawn, and the absurd dance of detente and mutually assured destruction was played out eyeball to eyeball by the Cold War powers. Above this teeming game of political musical chairs, the skyline is alive and aligned with angels muttering, prowling on rooftops, and perched atop majestic pillars, listening attentively to the human conversations. These are the Rilkean angels. The greatest German poet of the twentieth century was Wenders's inspiration; for Rilke, the city was a terrifying place in dialogue with the sacred.

Wings of Desire is a fantastic collaboration, improvised from the talents of Wenders—whose love affair with Berlin and ideas of guardian angels inspired the whole thing—and the actors Bruno Ganz and Otto Sander—who had previously acted on stage together. Brainstorming from the monologues that were intermittently written by Peter Handke, who submitted them in no particular order with no particular strategy or story in mind, the director and his actors nosed through Berlin, inspired by Rilke and lead by the idea that angels could be anywhere, do anything, and subsequently grow tired of their divinity, envying the emotional dynamism that drives their human companions and clients. "Every angel is terrifying," said Rilke, "for beauty is nothing but the beginning of terror." They terrify us because they move among the invisible orders, the zones between life and death, and are the first of the divine order to intervene in human affairs—meddlers *par excellence*. In 1925, Rilke wrote to his Polish translator, Witold von Hulewicz, "The angel of the *Duino Elegies* has nothing to do with the angels of the Christian heavens. The angel of the *Elegies* is that creature in whom the transformation of the visible into the invisible, which we are accomplishing, already appears in its completion ... therefore, terrifying for us, because we,

The Rhythm Method, Razzmatazz, and Memory

its lovers and transformers, still cling to the visible." Paradise becomes un-attainable as soon as we begin searching for it, and it is only visible in ret-rospect, once it is lost. The modern angels of Rilke and Kafka and Chagall no longer carry messages back and forth to the divine being, and we are turned back toward mortality by their silence. Thus, the angel inside us can only be found through our annihilation.

In *Wings of Desire*, we are witness to these transcendent moments when beings in transformation are shown en route, like the ex-angel played by Peter Falk, whose constant praise and love of life seduces the active angels and sends them in a tailspin. Soon, one of them is in love with a human and his downfall is inevitable. "Those who are willing to be vulnerable move among mysteries," wrote Theodore Roethke. So the body becomes our mode of perceiving scale; the sacrifice of the body is the passage to the marvel-ous—not its destruction, but its surrender. "The *duende* works on the body of the dancer as the wind works on sand," wrote Federico Garcia Lorca in his *Deep Song*. Therefore, the poet or the angel is most exultant (or visionary) at the point of deterioration, standing in the doorway of creation, half-di-vine, half-human, in transit.

In his essay on Goya, André Malraux talks about the artist's journey be-tween worlds: "All truly profound art requires its creator to abandon himself to certain powers which he invokes but cannot altogether control." So angels and poets are ephemeral like Berlin itself, created in innumerable choirs to celebrate the motion and jubilation of life, growing in numbers requisite to their praise. But as soon as the song is finished, the dissolution begins, back into nothingness, the cooling ember extinguished. When the figures of the Bible are given messages, the intermediaries are direct, even threatening: Jacob wrestling with the angel, for instance, or Paul blinded on his trip to Damascus, or Mary, whose surrender, "let it be," is half in sorrow, for she is unable to see directly the face of God. Standing on the lip of the holy well, they can feel the water, but its surface is black, its depth unknown. Out of it, angels emerge momentarily and then return from whence they came.

The angels in *Wings of Desire* move among the population, yet remain apart from them, condemned to listen to the millions and millions of voices internally transmitted as the humans speak to themselves and strive to reconcile their voices with their appetites, their visceral perceptions at odds with their tingling intuition. The angels sift through the cauldron of voices and try to calm the most strident or least hopeful, those on the verge of giving up. The angels perch on the rooftops and towers, above the rabble, observed only by the children, soothing the human pain or protecting the victims on occasion, lightening the load of the human coil. But they long to roam the earth, to be apart from their pure spirit.

Appropriately perhaps, they live in the enormous library, among humans communicating at their highest mortal level, aspiring to bridge the gaps in their learning or awareness. The humans are bundles of worry, their flesh a soup of questions encased in a fragile boundary of skin. They bump together and separate, unable to reconcile their various reasons or disguises or fierce clumsy defenses. Time wastes like an illness, and sudden moments of music give them no lasting peace. The angels move among them like clipped birds, nestling the humans' fevered heads in their cool feathers. The days slither away, hissing with a sameness that devours the patience of both worlds. The trapeze artist at the circus, waiting an eternity for a loving word, glides back and forth in her faux wings, and one angel cannot resist her sharp longing and tender looks. She hangs onto her swing, spinning in her thin membrane of air, gloriously alone and aching for recognition, floating like a wraith on the ceiling of the tent. The angel in love begins to shadow her everywhere, hanging in the net of her constant internal monologue. Her emptiness engulfs him. Then, like an infection, her longing is transferred, and as the angel falls in love, the film is suddenly shown in color, only for an instant, and both their fates are sealed. "What is wrong with peace," one old man asks, "that its inspiration doesn't endure?"

Berlin is a city steeped with refugees, each with a different definition of peace. But the circus makes citizens of them, and then they are lost to themselves, teeming with fantasies, a crowd united behind a single smiling face. The certainty of the circus makes heroes of the children, every tossed ring or blown flame or leaping tiger tears the blue veil from the commonplace and all is possible. The labyrinth of shared happiness brings our angel and his woman together in a concert hall with Nick Cave and his band, the Bad Seeds, behind them, singing "From Her To Eternity." The angel's decision to join her is final, and he descends, into her, with her, and without looking back. He dives into the abyss and is born, awakening from sleep for the first time. Every event, from the taste of his own blood to the warmth of a new hat, is his with the newness of a baby and the appetite and will of a man, energetically whole.

Poetry is just such a life force, bringing definition to the invisible objects that surround us. Surrealism, as a discipline for seeing, brings the disparate images into focus, making the artist, through his faithful creations, as transparent as an angel, a conduit and storehouse for all these articles of faith. Let us conclude our discussion with a simple poem, fashioned in some ways after Pablo Neruda's landbound mermaid. Mike White's poem "Murder" is universal, standing in for the exposed elements of the other invisible world:

The most torn angel
Came into town and
We were dazzled
And a little afraid

His one shredded wing he held
To his side like a secret
And for all our asking
He would not speak of God

An angel fully broken
So that when we finally
Led him up the road
(Gathering stones as we did)

He trusted us
Like a serious child
And asked again for nothing
But water and homecoming

PART 3

Learning to Speak

THE SYNTHESIS OF MUSIC AND THE POEM

I didn't know what to say, my mouth
could not speak,
my eyes could not see
and something ignited in my soul,
fever or unremembered wings …

—PABLO NERUDA, *LA POESIA* (TRANS. BY DAVID WHYTE)

INTRODUCTION

The Long Blue Line: Memory and Sound

I would love to be a being of pure sound—to take everything I hear and return it as poetry, to make an orchestra of a single man. "We hear," said Ralph Waldo Emerson in *The American Scholar*, "that we may speak."

All art changes by touching other art. Poetry and music are mongrels; when properly fed, they gather things to them and are comprised of the things they gather. The poems and songs we have gathered within us change as we come upon others and our worldview is enlarged. Art also changes under the touch of other artists. A song has life only as long as a musician is playing it; every song has a future, waiting for a singer to come along who can fasten it to a moment in time or, failing that, make the song new, breathing into it a life that was missing before. Often a poet or songwriter doesn't even understand what he's done; he needs a translator to perform the piece and locate its position in time or focus its meaning. We, as makers, are compelled to open wide to persuasive voices that emanate from inside us, and though we hold ourselves to a certain creative standard, there are other interpreters who may locate the resonant core of the composition and then give everyone the capability to ride its shine.

"Sound brings us to our senses," said Henry David Thoreau. "But the music is not in the tune; it is in the sound." The poem and its sound have always walked together—one inside the other. The poet wears his music like a skin, and his poem is the force the music exerts. To produce a perfect sound, one has to abandon oneself to the making of it. How many times have I told myself on stage: "Stop thinking, and sing."? In those moments, I must shut my-

---

self off from the subjective impulse. I cannot allow myself to be interested in how I am being received, in the tone and timbre of my voice, or in the contrary sounds wafting to me from the shuffling crowd. I am listening only for the first note of the next sentence, one spare note at a time, and then I let my muscle memory take over, giving way to the body's remembrance of the rehearsal repeated over and over until the melody is driven into the collective wellspring of the calm brain and the body's obedient mechanisms.

Although poetry is made of music, a poem and a song are not the same thing. A poem has a fictive covering, but a song and its singer are naked, and must be so. Poetry stops time and music depends upon time's movement. Poetry is created in isolation and rarely performed, but unperformed, its music is never tested and may be missing or malformed. Music, however, particularly jazz, is sometimes formed only when performed. Improvisation is the art of presence, and what did not exist a moment before is the testament the next performer is building his instant upon. Poets and musicians have fostered a symbiotic relationship in America; only in the last fifty years have they begun to become the same thing.

> *To have possession of your own voice is empowering, making both the audience and your own mind a focused unit, ready to proceed together.*

So how can we embody the role of poet-singer, and can they be the same? We all have a sound blueprint within us, a voice we would like to inhabit. One of the many aspects of speaking, or making our sound our own and proficient in its communication, is recognition of our individual strengths and weaknesses, and how to subdue weakness when facing a crowd. To have possession of your own voice is empowering, making both the audience and your own mind a focused unit, ready to proceed together. A poem's music, properly rendered, is only a small part of the poetry performance. A poetry reading should approach the level of good theatre. Every reading, however relaxed or low-key, is a confrontation between the music of the poem and the expectation or stillness of the audience. Poetry promises invention, originality, and dynamism. The audience wants to feel, in as intimate a manner as possible, their expectations met, their concerns treated with respect and careful enunciation. They do not want to be assaulted with indifference; they want to recognize themselves in the rendering of the

The Rhythm Method, Razzmatazz, and Memory

poets' world, as the poems have truthfully and openly confronted it. This is why the poet has to inhabit the poem. This is why music is so important.

Every poet in this section will confess that their poetry would probably not have been possible without the music that has helped to form their life. We are always gathering sound. Our ears are wide open, even when we are seemingly unaware. So why are some of the finest makers of poetry some of the worst readers of their own work? The same caution required to perfect sound in a poem is certain to suppress the music when applied to its delivery. But poetry must live in the air. The radiation of sound guarantees we are not alone, and we call the others to us by repeating our favorite sounds. The snake charmer opens his basket and calls its contents upward wth his flute. The rivers listen as they fall, drawn toward the ocean and its roar. This is the gospel. And the blues. And every sound we make is new. Let that be our ecstasy and our emphasis. "Art is the path of the creator to his work," said Emerson. Let's go together down that path and across a century of music and poetry.

The remainder of this book explores how sound is gathered by examining the last century's music and many of the poets who furthered our understanding of music through their poetry.

CHAPTER 25

The Troubadours and the European Diaspora: Singing Is an Act of Love

What we are, I know, is water. What we choose to make is love. Guilhem d'Aquitaine is said to have invented the idea of courtly love at the beginning of the twelfth century, when his habitual adultery was threatened by the success of the preacher Robert d'Arbrissel who persuaded the ladies of the court that the fires of hell lay in wait for adulterers. Guilhem responded with a series of poems, probably based on Arab or Persian prototypes, which argued that love was not a sin but a divine mystery and that the woman who inspired love was a goddess worthy of adoration. This brilliant counterattack was apparently successful.

The theme of ennobling love became popular with the wandering singers, poets, and entertainers of the time. However, many of their clients were married noblewomen, and most of their songs were in first person, which led to misunderstandings with the ladies and battles with their husbands. In addition, it had long been an offense, sometimes punishable by death, to address a love song to a married woman, as the song had long been known to be a kind of enchantment or spell. It was a sternly moralistic entertainer named Marcabru who solved the problem by claiming that beauty and nobility alone were not enough to make a woman into a goddess. She must, by definition, be unattainable.

From this innovation sprang the troubadours, a group of poets who each chose the wife of a feudal lord as the object of his affections and dedicated all his poetry to her. A troubadour did not want to possess his lady; for most, it was enough to see her or be given some token from her, such as a scarf

---

The Rhythm Method, Razzmatazz, and Memory

or glove. Even those who spoke of undressing their mistresses never mentioned consumption. The willingness of the lord to support his wife's troubadour, and even praise him, suggests there was little suspicion or thought of adultery; indeed, there were even female troubadours, though they were very few in number. (Of the 460 or so known troubadours, from which about 2,500 poems have survived, only about forty of them were women.) As the Crusades wore on, the troubadours became champions of the Christian cause, and while some of their patrons felt compelled to join the ranks of the righteous to fight Muslims, the troubadours became willing comforters of their bereaved and lonely noble inspirations. "Our vision of the Provencal Troubadour and his songs completely changed," wrote poet W. D. Snodgrass. "Gone is the wistful figure singing sweetly to a far-off idealized lady. By now, the last Troubadour songs have only two subjects: one, let's go crusading and kill lots of Moors; two, let's go get in the boss's wife."

This time during the twelfth and thirteenth centuries was the most fertile for poetry since the Greeks, and most modern forms can trace their roots back to the stanzas and syllable forms of the troubadours, brushing past the *rondeaux* and the *canzoni*. Ezra Pound, whose cantos were especially influenced by the troubadours, wrote in his *Spirit of Romance*, "Song did not again awake until the Provencal viol aroused it." A poet and scholar, Pound trained in Romance philology, taught and published essays on the troubadours, and haunted the *Bibliotheque Nationale de France* while transcribing the troubadour melodies. He even headed out on foot to investigate the haunts of these songbirds, logging nearly five hundred miles in the process.

The troubadours have inspired poets and songwriters from every walk of life, from Dante and Chaucer to the Renaissance sonneteers of Queen Elizabeth's court and straight through to the Romantics and the French Symbolists, including Paul Verlaine and Arthur Rimbaud. The meter, word play, puns, and formal sound effects of the troubadours led to almost all of the formal structural developments for poetry that followed. The word *troubadour* means finder or maker, and these composers represented a breakthrough of artistic expression in a society where the language of the Roman Empire was still dominant in the courts and cathedrals of Europe. Before the troubadours, knightly behavior was barbaric and bloodthirsty. It was only when desire for a woman's approval became the motive for valor that chivalry came into being, if only as an ideal, and this legacy affected all romantic literature that followed.

The troubadours were makers, but generally not singers, of songs. Honey-voiced *joglars* performed their works. And these makers of songs hailed from all classes. The first troubadour, Guilhem d'Aquitaine—also known as Guillem de Peiteus (born in 1071)—was one of the wealthiest and most powerful men of his day. Many were minor noblemen, yet even humbler stock could find fortune, such as the aforementioned Marcabru, who rose solely on the wings of his talent with the language. The movement quickly spread to northern France, Germany, and England.

> *The meter, word play, puns, and formal sound effects of the troubadours led to almost all of the formal structural developments for poetry that followed.*

Music is always spread, seemingly, by discord. Pope Urban II launched the first Crusade in 1095 in Clermont, France, and promised sinners that "whoever for devotion alone, not to gain honor or money, goes to Jerusalem to liberate the Church of God, can substitute this journey for all penance." Peitieus' father had fought in the early wars with Moorish Spain and captured several servant girls whose songs captivated the young musician. Later, as an adult, after a crushing defeat by the Turks, Peitieus heard the eastern Arab songs of the desert nomads. These combinations found a willing listener in the young Frenchman and he wrote the first known lyrics of the troubadour movement.

CHAPTER 26

American Gumbo: Music Brewed in Democracy's Melting Pot

Nearly every immigrant who came to America brought some type of folk music with them. It wasn't written down; it wasn't charted on crib sheets; it was passed along from memory. Europeans and Africans alike, who entered their strange new country for the first time, carried songs within them that helped them to remember the customs, personalities, relatives, and topography of the land they had left behind. Gradually, these songs began to morph together, and the instruments used to play them changed. Songs that had endured for centuries in a single form took new form inside the cauldron of American culture. The diversity of American music is not derived from the pop songs of the day, though the radio as an influence on our culture is immense. It is the roots of the music that gnarled into our family tree, and those seeds were gathered in foreign lands and carried across the water to germinate and cross-pollinate into mongrel forms in American soil.

Technological advances helped to fertilize the tree. Thomas Edison's phonograph helped to expose people to recordings of sounds they had never heard before. The advent of the railroad brought gangs of workers together—Irish, African, Chinese, and others—and the work song, with its call-and-response format, sent a rhythmic shiver up the line as thousands of miles of track were laid down in harmony, remnants of slave songs that would foster the Blues. One instrument that was carried from Europe in countless backpacks and trunks was the violin, which became a fiddle to folks in the Appalachian Mountains. In the summer of 1928, an old fiddle

---

player named Bascom Lamar Lunsford organized a festival in Asheville, North Carolina, to bring together Bluegrass and Country musicians in one place. That hoedown was designed to lure tourists to the mountains, but it served to spread the mountain music, via the tourists, all over the country.

The traditional Christian music that came from western Europe was transmogrified in America's prison songs and field hollers; it merged with the African slave experience to create a new spiritual music known as Gospel, played now not only with organs and pianos but with banjos and guitars and drums. As the experience of the American West began to be documented in the new twentieth century, songs were recorded, including Indian tribal songs. In 1910, John Lomax published a book of cowboy and herding songs, *Cowboy Songs and other Frontier Ballads*, one of the first volumes to gather up this dying tradition and give it new life in American living rooms. It seemed that every citizen was required to know all the words to "Home On The Range," and most could sing it by heart—not only a hundred years ago, but today as well. Soon, mail-order catalogs gave everyone the opportunity to own a musical instrument, and as folks moved west and north, the railroads carried the music just as surely as Edison's phonograph, allowing their traditions to mingle. Vaudeville and Wild West Revues employed musicians and helped spread their rural sounds into the city theatres, bars, and juke joints.

STEAL AWAY: THE BIRTH OF SOUTHERN GOSPEL

In Nashville, Tennessee, later known as the home of Country music, a small all-black school known as Fisk University was failing. In order to raise the money needed to keep the school afloat, one professor named George White organized his students to sing classical European church songs and then the group embarked on a tour to bring home the bacon. The formal western choral arrangements were not appealing to the mostly white northern audiences, but when the students began to sing the spirituals they had sung as children, the audience response was markedly different. These were the songs sung in the privacy of the slave quarters, passed among families during the Reconstruction, heart-felt songs filled with the sorrow and longing of an imprisoned people whose emotional harmonies were authentic and deeply moving.

In 1871, the Fisk Jubilee Singers began to sing the slave spiritual "Steal Away," a song used by the slaves as a sort of code, letting the other slaves

The Rhythm Method, Razzmatazz, and Memory

know that a secret gathering or meeting was going to take place away from the prying eyes of their masters. This song became the signature for the Fisk choir, and they soon added other spiritual hymns to their repertoire. The Fisk Jubilee Singers became wildly popular, saving the university and, even more importantly, spreading the inimitable sound of the black spiritual to thousands of people who would have never heard these songs any other way. The American Gospel tradition was born.

Other universities formed choral groups and followed suit. Many revivals and tent meetings were flooded with the new hymns and the feelings they engendered. Many rural country churches had congregations who sung by ear but also by eye, through the style of shape-note singing—taking the eight notes of *do-re-mi-fa-so-la-ti-do* and applying them by sight to fit the melody. The Vaughan School of Music in Lawrenceburg, Tennessee, established by James D. Vaughan, published shape-note hymnals that were distributed all over the rural South in the small churches. These hymnals taught the art of Gospel singing to any member who wished to learn. Many parents brought their children to the Vaughan School during summer seminars, and they carried the hymnals away with them. The rudiments of harmony, pitch, and tempo were taught in both schools and churches by traveling emissaries of the Vaughan School as well, and like encyclopedia or vacuum-cleaner salesmen, these songbirds went door-to-door selling the shape-note hymnals to make a living. Soon, James Vaughan discovered that teams of four salesmen, or quartets, were more successful selling books, as their deeper harmonies were deemed more impressive and appealing to the congregations they performed for. Thousands of Gospel and Barbershop quartets sprung up in the wake of these tune peddlers, prefiguring the late popularity of the 1950s and '60s pop sensations like The Drifters and The Temptations. By 1910, James Vaughan was selling over one million shape-note hymnals a year.

The church, particularly in rural settings, was usually the center of the community, and Sunday worship was the closest thing to social interaction that many isolated families were able to experience. The number of musicians whose first training came during church services, or as part of the choir, is incalculable. My first singing lessons came from the elders in the church choir when I was six years old, too small to be seen, too loud to be ignored. I was fed parts to sing and put in the back, but my voice cut through the arrangements. Eventually, I was given solo lines in an attempt to bring me in line or at least force me to harmonize with the others when I wasn't singing my own parts. The choir director finally, in frustration, gave me my own song to sing every Sunday and released the choir from my interference. I've been a singer ever since. I loved the response of the crowd when a particularly poignant and powerful sound was made, how all the voices merged and made a single, more joyful noise, how music rose from inside us but seemed to carry us when the congregation joined in. Singing has always been a form of worship—perhaps the highest form—because the singer must transform himself and his audience, making a sound that is not normal and sustaining it, hopefully at ease inside the sound.

> *The poet who wishes to make her poetry sing must recognize that the audience is with her, in concert with her best intentions and willing to be transported, to go where they are asked—as long as the place they are asked to go is authentic, filled with grace, and clearly marked.*

My poetic voice rose out of my singing voice. My sister and I would travel around the mountains as we grew older, performing at revivals, prayer meetings, reunions, funerals, etc. She would accompany me on the piano and I would try to raise a few amens from the faithful. We did standard gospel fare out of the old Broadman Hymnal, which was a staple in all the Southern Baptist churches at the time. "Amazing Grace," "All Hail the Power," "Onward Christian Soldiers," "The Old Rugged Cross," "Peace! Be Still!," "Shall We Gather at the River?," "Nothing but the Blood," "The Nail-Scarred Hand," "Sweet By and By," "There is a Name I Love to Hear," "Leaning on the Everlasting Arms," "I Wonder as I Wander," and the song I believe should be our true national anthem: "America the Beautiful." All these songs were part of the 500 or so contained in the Broadman edition, originally published in 1940 by Broadman Press in Nashville and available in round or shaped-note editions. I still carry this hymnal with me wherever I go, though I haven't graced a church in many years, and I pick it up and thumb through it and am able to find a still place in the center of whatever chaos or deadlines are surrounding me. My poems and songs were formed out of this community, in the preacher's

The Rhythm Method, Razzmatazz, and Memory

call and response, the remembered prayers and pledges. These things became more valuable to me in my absence from them, just as Eden was more precious to Adam after the fall. And in his travels, Adam carried Eden inside him, sharing the memory and perfection of it with any person who would aspire to feel that state of grace.

THE POEM AS KEY TO THE SACRED DOORWAY

Geography is history, and we are made from the circumstances of our surroundings. Southerness is otherness; our colloquialisms and speech patterns are distinct. For a poet who would be a performer, he or she could do well to listen to the cadences and measured delivery of the best preachers or soul singers. The effect is emotional and the delivery theatrical. The opening scenes of the movie *The Apostle*, starring Robert Duvall, show the fiery white acolyte soaking up the rhythms and phrases of the black preachers who move him. When the young preacher asked one of the old black ministers what his formula was for the perfect sermon, the reply was: "First I tells 'em I'm going to tell 'em, then I tells 'em, then I tell 'em I done told 'em."

I have never so much sung a song as attacked it, and in the course of the action I lose sight somewhere in the rendering of whether I am still attacking or being attacked. Somehow, miraculously, the sound is the same and the audience is roused, being composed of two poles and lost in the give and take within the song, unwilling to decide which side to inhabit. This is the dream spell, the incantation that the deep song of Federico Garcia Lorca makes in the still air, where the listeners, entangled, have no choice but to cry or scream or cheer, raising their own voices in response. The poet who wishes to make her poetry sing must recognize that the audience is with her, in concert with her best intentions and willing to be transported, to go where they are asked—as long as the place they are asked to go is authentic, filled with grace, and clearly marked.

Here are two different poems, both drawn from a Gospel experience, but their strategies make different interiors for the audience to inhabit. The first, "Vera Genera, 1939" by R. Flowers Rivera, takes on the voice of a six-year-old girl trying to make sense of the emotional swell and hothouse swelter of a typical Sunday service, some seventy years ago:

What I am certain of. It is hot.
Today's my birthday. I am six.
Rain and more rain. I can hear
What the stain glass hides.
Sounds like T. Ray peeing
Off the back porch when the night is
Dark and Fofo has all the sheets
Balled 'tween her knees. I have to pee.
Mama said to wait. I got better sense
Than to ask again. Reverend
Fox is shouting to the congregation.
Only big-tittied, rawboned women
Catch the holy ghost. I will have to
Wait. I got the right build but
My chest is flat. Two hoecakes.
Mama never falls out. Her eyes just cry
Quiet tears. One at a time.
I have to pee. Reverend Fox is
Calling for me to come. I move to go.
Mama's hands stay my way. Her eyes
Say *no*. She's shaking her head *not yet*.
We had to wait four hours but
Yesterday Miss Reena marcelled mama
Some pretty curls. The kind I can get
"Soon as you get a job." There's a stray
Piece sticking out at her temple. It could
Use one good bump with more
Heat. Reverend Fox says,
"God is calling. Who will listen?"
I look around. Mama pops my legs,
Faces me front. My panties feel damp.
I hope it's sweat. I try harder
To hold still, to listen. He booms,
"Give the glory to God." Six elders in dark serge
Suits and white gloves take their place
In the aisles. Two and two and two.

The Rhythm Method, Razzmatazz, and Memory

Right, middle, left. They pass the plates.
Glory is money. God is in a little room
At the back of the church. Behind a closed door.
I want to be a deacon, so I can see God, too.

Now compare the different strategy of the Native American poet Sherman Alexie, who takes the same subject matter (after a fashion) and creates a more intimate atmosphere, a love poem called "Rise," made of religious ceremonial gestures.

1.
We are taught to take the bread
into our bodies
as proof of Jesus's body.

The bread is metaphor.
The bread is Jesus transubstantiated.
The bread is simply bread.

I have taken all three
of those tenets into my body
though I am Spokane Indian

and also take salmon
into my body
as proof of salmon.

The salmon is my faith returned.
The salmon is simply salmon.
The salmon is not bread.

2.
Suddenly, we are wed
and I am just as surprised as you
that marriage has become our bread.

You, the Hidatsa Indian
from the North Dakota plains
who did not grow up with salmon

and me, the Spokane, who rarely trusts
the hands of the priest
as he delivers the bread.

During Eucharist, I am afraid
to close my eyes. I want to see
what has been set on the table before me.

Look, I don't know what
would help me believe
that we have become sacred.

Sweetheart, are we the salmon
rising from the mouth
of the river that cannot keep them?

3.
If that was Easter
then the church was full
as we stood against the wall

praying for an empty pew.
If that was Easter
then I rose that morning

in love with you
though I rise every morning
from the water, more or less

in love with you.
If that was Easter
then you were asked

to be the Eucharistic minister.
If that was Easter
then you surprised me

by placing salmon on my tongue.
Then I surprised you
by swallowing it whole.

Amen, amen, amen.

The Rhythm Method, Razzmatazz, and Memory

Alexie's poem incorporates the techniques of the religious antiphonal call and the response to the congregation by the minister and turns it on its head. He uses the tercet as a stanza form, and with rapid perspective shifts, from the opening line, "**We** *are taught to take the bread*," to "**I** *have taken all three*" in the third stanza, to "*the* **salmon** *is ...*" in the fifth, Alexie creates a jostling of point of view that continues through the second and third sections. In the second section, "**we** *are wed*" changes to "**You**, *the Hidatsa*," and then to "**I**, *the Spokane*," and repeats itself, again altering perspective: "**I** *don't know*" to "**we** *have become*," then gently rocking in the third with "**We** *stood*," "**I** *rose*," "**you** *asked*." The shifting focus makes the poem's core agile, as if a spirit is moving into and out of the person speaking, like surround sound on my stereo system, where the circling tones of the soundtrack never light down anywhere for long.

Rivera's speaker, though graphic in her descriptions, keeps the spotlight firmly on her sweet little self and her full-to-bursting bladder. Though she effectively paints the dramatic sense of the Sunday worship, she is not engaged by it. It is pouring rain, she has to pee, it is miserably hot, and all the adults are experiencing something that hides its face from her. The stained glass hides a storm, not the face of the Father, and the Holy Spirit has not possessed anyone; he is waiting out back for the deacons to give him his money. This levity balanced against the stern rules of engagement the child feels controlled by, and segregated from, allows for a humorous yet poignant conclusion. We go to church to find God, but the child believes the mystery of God is the same abstraction as the mystery of adulthood, and in that merger she will be allowed a glimpse—or so she hopes. But for now, the puzzle remains hidden and she waits for a body that the Spirit will find big enough to inhabit, a job that will let her purchase "some pretty curls." And knowing that "Glory is money," access to a deacon might be just the arrangement needed for God to invite her to the big house, the inner sanctum, waving her Bible like a backstage pass.

Alexie's use of the sacrament as a central tenet is but one of the strategies he employs to equate his earthly bride to the heavenly wedding of redemption. In communion, the body of Christ is consumed, making the God body one with the flawed earthly vessel and merging the sinner with the bride that is Jesus Christ, absolving the sin by recognition of the merger, "accepting the call to be saved," and asking forgiveness for sins. The speaker in "Rise" wants to believe that the symbols have significance. "I don't know what would help me believe that we have become sacred," he says, but he does "rise every morning from the water, more or less in love ..." exhibiting the faith in things unseen that God asks from his people—the recognition that he died for our sins and redemption is possible, that baptism in the river or pool allows the sinner to "rise" to the surface, utterly changed, and *saved*, a new being equipped for everlasting life with a higher power that can be counted upon. The speaker in "Rise" finds that higher power in his marriage, and both parties of that union take the body of the other as proof of their splendid, loving surrender. It is a beautiful poem, pragmatic and filled with religious symbols representing the natural world that God has given his subjects to nurture and sustain them.

The combination or overlap of symbols is very effective and serves both masters. If, as Walter Benjamin suggested, all poetry is in fact a translation of feelings and perceptions that are in some ways unsayable, then both Rivera, with her frustrated child, and Alexie, with his spiritual bride, make the feeling of worship a function of the everyday experience, the grace we bump against, without awareness, that nevertheless buoys us in the choppy water. Poetry should be built to give pleasure, to make us laugh, or to reassure us in our dark nights of the soul. At its best, poetry appeals to every faculty of the listener, heart and logical mind. The poet speaking to the audience should ask his listeners to do some thinking but should also give them access, a doorway by which to enjoy the poem. For Rivera, in this case, it is humor and description; for Alexie, it is meditative music and universal symbols that reinforce our notions of love. Both are worth listening to.

The Rhythm Method, Razzmatazz, and Memory

CHAPTER 27

Poetry and Performance: Preach the Gospel of Beauty

After Walt Whitman in the nineteenth century, American poetry lost its intensity. For some years, there were no live models to inspire the younger poets—that is, until the emergence of the Chicago poets Carl Sandburg, Edgar Lee Masters, and Vachel Lindsay. These poets used the techniques of vaudeville and the gospel church to create a fresh and exciting poetry bristling with a new American vernacular and a love of the underdog. William Butler Yeats had asked Lindsay, "What are we going to do to restore the primitive singing of poetry?" Lindsay's solution was to write verse that could be "two-thirds spoken and one-third sung." But he also proposed the "higher vaudeville imagination" and contended that "America needs the flamboyant to save her soul."

Born in Springfield, Illinois, in 1879, Lindsay was brought up in the evangelical tradition and because of his close association with Springfield, he, like Whitman before him, saw Abraham Lincoln as a type of Christ figure. "We must have many Lincoln-hearted men," he wrote in "On the Building of Springfield," and in "The Ghosts of the Buffaloes," he said, "Would I might rouse the Lincoln in you all."

Lindsay's extravagant sense of self and desire to aid his fellow man was probably nurtured in his proximity to the unjust. His father was a physician and instrumental in aiding his son's imagination and literary aspirations. He was also well off enough to live next door to the governor's mansion. Young Lindsay saw demonstrations and strikes, and these informed his growing sympathy for the impoverished among us. A promising artist, whose sketches sometimes accompanied his published poems, Lindsay's art career came to an abrupt end when, while studying in New York in 1905, he went into the street and tried to sell (or give away) copies of one of his poems. He took in only thirteen cents but considered the experience a triumph. Lindsay wrote in his diary, "Now let there be here recorded my conclusions from one evening, one hour of peddling poetry. I am so rejoiced over it and so uplifted I am going to do it many times ... the people like poetry as well as the scholars, or better." He was a modern minstrel or troubadour, singing not of his feudal lady, but of the radiance of beauty and the irrepressible spirit of certain American characters. His method was to carry with him copies of a pamphlet called *Rhymes To Be Traded For Bread*.

In 1912, he made a walking tour from Illinois to New Mexico, and on the way he composed his most famous poem "The Congo," which Harriet Monroe published in *Poetry*. The demand for his performances became steady, but he kept his sense of himself as a beggar and wrote *A Handy Guide For Beggars* (1916), in which he offered, among others things, such rules as: "Have nothing to do with money and carry no baggage. Ask for dinner about quarter after eleven. Ask for supper, lodging, and breakfast about quarter of five. Travel alone. Be neat, deliberate, chaste, and civil. Preach the Gospel of Beauty."

Audiences began to anticipate Lindsay's arrival in their town. Sometimes his performances had a curiosity value—when he donned fancy dress, for instance, or accompanied his poems with snatches of song and dance—and they always had the attraction of his inimitable delivery, a mixture of revivalist sermon and political stump speech. From 1913 to 1920, Lindsay rode the crest of a wave. His poetry won several prizes and he was not only traveling the length and breadth of America, but in 1915, he performed for Woodrow Wilson's cabinet "The Wedding of the Rose and the Lotus," written to celebrate the opening that year of the Panama Canal. The climax of his career came in 1920. *The Golden Whales of California* was published in January; in August, he visited England, where he converted a skeptical Oxford University to the higher vaudeville and was lionized. *The Daniel Jazz* was published in England to coincide with his visit, and he returned to the United States in time for the publication of *The Golden Book of Springfield*.

For the next four years, as he tramped endlessly from gig to gig, Lindsay experienced a series of symptoms eventually diagnosed as epilepsy. The

The Rhythm Method, Razzmatazz, and Memory

accompanying schizophrenia took the form of an increasingly acute per-
secution complex and produced the moody, unpredictable conduct that he
became known for, in public and private as well. In 1925, at the age of forty-
five, he married a twenty-three-year-old English and Latin teacher, Elizabeth
Conner; a daughter and a son were born in 1926 and 1927. In 1931, suspect-
ing his wife of infidelity and his fellow writers of some indefinable menace,
he committed suicide by drinking Lysol. He explained himself in unbearably
classic persecution-manic terms: "They tried to get me. I got them instead."
Here is an excerpt from Lindsay's 1926 poem "A Curse for the Saxophone":

> Twenty thousand pigs on their hindlegs playing
> "The Beale St. Blues" and swaying and saying:
> "John Wilkes Booth, you are welcome to Hell,"
> And they played it on a saxophone, and played it well.
> And he picked up a saxophone, grunting and rasping.
> The red-hot horn in his hot hands clasping,
>
> And he played a typical radio jazz,
> He started an earthquake, he knew what for,
> And at last he started the late World War.

SANDBURG'S ONE-MAN BAND

In 1921, Carl Sandburg wrote to a friend, "I am reading poems and singing
Casey Jones, Steamboat Bill, and medleys. This whole thing is only in its beginnings, America knowing its songs ... It's been amazing to me to see how
audiences rise to 'em." In 1910, Sandburg had bought his first guitar and decided to add music to his repertoire as a lecturer and political organizer. He
quickly discovered that the addition drew a much larger audience. Sandburg
developed a fairly specific methodology to his readings and performances.
He believed that a singer had to live with a song and ingrain it into his or
her being. He liked to act out a dramatic part in his show, to become "the
storyteller of a piece of action." When giving a one-man show, he first talked
about poetry and art, then read some original verses, and concluded with
15–30 minutes of songs and commentary.

Throughout the 1920s, Sandburg notated and collected the folk songs he
heard on his travels, eventually amassing a repertoire of more than three

hundred songs. This project would ultimately become the classic volume *American Songbag*, published in 1927. He narrowed down the selection to 255 tunes. He altered some, but otherwise he printed them as he heard them. In the introduction, he called the book "an All-American affair, marshaling the genius of thousands of original singing Americans." The collection quickly became a standard in households across America.

Sandburg's poetry also broke new ground with its prosaic underpinnings and organic free verse structures. "Artists who honestly relate their own epoch to older epochs understand how art today, if it is to get results, must pierce exteriors and surfaces by ways different from artists of older times," he said. His famous *Chicago Poems* treated the overgrown industrial behemoth with an almost maternal indulgence: "Let me be the great nail holding a skyscraper through blue nights into the white stars." In 1913, he wrote to a friend, "You might say at first shot that this is a hell of a place for a poet, but the truth is it is a good place for a poet to get his head knocked when he needs it. In fact, it is so good a place for a healthy man who wants to watch the biggest, most intense, brutal, and complicated game in the world—the game by which the world gets fed and clothed—the method of control—the economics and waste—so good a place it is from this vantage point that I think you will like it."

No matter how popular he became, Sandburg continued to tour the country giving ballad concerts and writing children's books and several collections of poetry, as well as a Pulitzer Prize-winning biography of Lincoln. He enjoyed extraordinary acclaim as he grew older. The governor of Illinois declared "Carl Sandburg Day" on his seventy-fifth birthday; the King of Sweden decorated him; the United States Congress asked him to address a joint session in 1959; and in 1964, he received the Presidential Medal of Freedom. He got his sense of purpose from the modern working-class movement, and hoped his poetry would, through its lack of subtlety, find an audience as clear-eyed and unrelenting as possible. Here are two of my favorites, poems with vivid sound that have a clear voice and intimate tension between the homely images. These are poems that beg to be shouted or whispered and are just as effective in either mode. Sandburg's poetry and his songs intertwine, gnarl together, and overlap in surprising ways, speaking clearly across the great continental divides in American culture and reminding us where the seams are located.

The Rhythm Method, Razzmatazz, and Memory

JAZZ FANTASIA

Drum on your drums, batter on your banjoes,
sob on the long cool winding saxophones.
Go to it, O jazzmen.

Sling your knuckles on the bottoms of the happy
tin pans, let your trombones ooze, and go husha-
husha-hush with the slippery sand-paper.

Moan like an autumn wind high in the lonesome treetops, moan
soft like you wanted somebody terrible, cry like a racing car
slipping away from a motorcycle cop, bang-bang! you jazzmen,
bang altogether drums, traps, banjoes, horns, tin cans—make
two people fight on the top of a stairway and scratch each
other's eyes in a clinch tumbling down the stairs.

Can the rough stuff ... now a Mississippi steamboat pushes
up the night river with a hoo-hoo-hoo-oo ... and the green
lanterns calling to the high soft stars ... a red moon rides
on the humps of the low river hills ... go to it, O jazzmen.

DEATH SNIPS PROUD MEN

Death is stronger than all the governments because the governments are men and men die and then death laughs: Now
 you see 'em, now you don't.

Death is stronger than all proud men and so death snips proud
 men on the nose, throws a pair of dice and says: Read 'em
 and weep.

Death sends a radiogram every day: When I want you I'll drop
 in—and then one day he comes with a master-key and lets
 himself in and says: We'll go now.

Death is a nurse mother with big arms: 'Twon't hurt you at
 all; its your time now; you just need a long sleep, child;
 what have you had anyhow better than sleep?

CHAPTER 28

Building the Bridge: Classic Blues and Bessie's Radio

I n the first two or three decades of the twentieth century, the prized possession in most homes was the wind-up Victrola, playing a vast array of music that emanated from the early records' deep wax grooves through the needle and out of the horn. Every time the machine wound down, the listener had to wind it back up, using a crank on the side, singing back the music he had just listened to as he turned the crank. By 1920, Americans were buying 25 million records a year, and the most popular recordings were ragtime and jazz. But the music that jazz was based on—the blues— began to emerge in popular culture during the 1920s. The first blues recording, "Crazy Blues," was released by Mamie Smith to wide acclaim. A trio of women followed, each with their own distinctive charm: Bessie Smith, Ida Cox, and the sly and slinky Ma Rainey. Bessie Smith combined gospel chops with a weary blues tone and a vivacious vibrato to become one of the biggest recording stars of the decade, influencing a whole generation of singers, most notably Billie Holiday.

Classic blues is called "classic" because it was the music that seemed to contain all the diverse and conflicting elements of African-American music, plus the smoother emotional appeal of the "performance." It was the first Black music that appeared in a formal context as entertainment, though it still contained the harsh, uncompromising reality of the earlier blues forms. It was, in effect, the perfect balance between the two worlds, and as such, it represented a clearly definable step by the African-American back into the mainstream of American society. All of the great classic blues singers were

The Rhythm Method, Razzmatazz, and Memory

women. Ma Rainey, Bessie Smith, and the others became professionals at early ages; Ma Rainey started when she was fourteen, Bessie Smith before she was twenty. The majority of all the formal blues in the 1920s were sung from the point of view of women.

However, the great country blues singers (which we'll discuss later in this section) were almost always men. They were wanderers, migratory farm workers, or men who were street performers going joint to joint in search of work. And the country blues singers were not recorded until much later, during the great swell of blues and "race" recordings, when the companies were willing to try almost any black singer because of their newfound market. But the first recordings were classic blues; the ladies brought the blues into every living room in America.

Mamie Smith's initial recording of "Crazy Blues" on February 14, 1920, was not expected to be a success, but from the outset it sold 8,000 copies a week for almost three years. Classic blues became big business, and the lyrics were saturated with sex, like Ida Cox singing, "When your man comes home evil, tells you you are getting old,/ that's a true sign he's got someone else baking his jelly roll." Or Sippie Wallace telling the girls, "don't advertise your man." Hoodoo, too, is a big part of the Blues. Ma Rainey's "Black Dust Blues," for instance, tells about a woman who is angry because Ma took her man. "Lord, I was out one morning, found black dust all 'round my door," the song begins, but the speaker starts to get thin and develops trouble with her feet: "Black dust in my window, black dust on my porch mat ... / Black dust's got me walking on all fours like a cat." The subject here is "throwin' down" on someone; in African magic, the feet are considered to be a specifically vulnerable entry point for evil. Magical powder sprinkled in socks or shoes might bind the evil spell; in love spells, socks might be tied together.

Ma Rainey was the link between the harsher, more spontaneous country or primitive styles and the smoother, more theatrical style that conquered radio. Ma Rainey had toured for years with the Rabbit Foot Minstrels, and her vaudeville skills were honed to a razor-sharp edge. She passed her knowledge along to the first superstar black performer of her time, one who would be the highest paid singer in America—Bessie Smith. In 1923, long before microphones and amps and digital equipment, Bessie made her first recording with the Columbia Gramophone Company. She hollered her vocals into a funnel, and sheer sonic vibrations were converted into grooves on soft black wax. The record was "Down Hearted Blues," and it would be an immediate smash.

Born dirt-poor in Tennessee with seven siblings, Bessie's father, a Baptist preacher, died when she was an infant. Her mother died when she was eight. Slavery had ended just thirty-one years before she was born, and it still stained everyone and everything. Bessie's first recording sold 800,000 copies in six months, and she was instantly known as the "Empress of the Blues." She would go on to make 200 more records for Columbia, and when she died, she had been paid a total of 28,575 dollars.

She was nearly six feet tall, weighed over two hundred pounds, and walked around with her money stuffed in her clothes. Bessie was not to be trifled with. One man who tried to rob her stabbed her in the stomach, but she chased him down and tackled him, holding him until help arrived, and only then she collapsed. Once, to convince her husband she'd been hit by a car (and not on a two-day tryst with another man), she threw herself down two flights of stairs. The chorus girl who slept with her husband? The dancer exited the train in the middle of nowhere, at full speed, with Bessie's foot firmly planted on her behind. Bessie met her demise on the mythic Highway 61 near Clarksdale, Mississippi, not far from the devil's crossroads. The car her husband was driving plowed into a parked truck in the dark beside the road. Bessie's arm came out of its socket at the shoulder. A white doctor drove by and stopped, but instead called for an ambulance, supposedly to keep from bloodying his white car. Rumors spread thick as mosquitoes in the scorching heat of the Delta. With Bessie gone, so too died the era of classic blues; it simmered and stopped. Jazz was hot, and the new sound washed over the old like a white wave on the sand. Here is Myron O'Higgins's tribute, "Blues for Bessie":

> Let de peoples know (unnh)
> what dey did in dat Southern Town
> Let de peoples know
> what dey did in dat Southern Town
> Well, dey lef' po' Bessie dyin'
> wid de blood (Lawd) a-streamin' down
>
> Bessie lef' Chicago
> in a bran' new Cadillac;

The Rhythm Method, Razzmatazz, and Memory

didn' take no suitcase

but she wore her mournin' black (unnh)

Bessie, Bessie,

she wore her mournin' black

She went ridin' down to Dixie (Lawd)

an' dey shipped her body back

Lawd, wasn't it a turr'ble

when dat rain come down

Yes, wasn't it a turr'ble

when de rain come down

An' ol' Death caught po' Bessie

down in 'at Jim Crow town

Well, de thunder rolled

an' de lightnin' broke de sky

Lawd, de thunder rolled

an' de lightnin' broke de sky

An' you could hear po' Bessie moanin',

"Gret Gawd, please doan lemme die!"

She holler, "Lawd, please hep me!"

but He never heerd a word she say

Holler, "Please, somebody help me!"

but dey never heerd a word she say

Frien', when yo' luck run out in Dixie,

well, it doan do no good to pray

Well, dey give po' Bessie

to de undertaker man;

ol' Death an' Jim Crow (Lawd)

done de job, hand in han'

Well, Bessie, Bessie,

she won't sing de blues no mo'

Cause dey let her go down bloody (Lawd)

trav'lin' from door to do'

Bessie lef' Chicago
in a bran' new Cad'lac Eight
Yes, Bessie lef' Chicago
in a gret big Cad'lac Eight
But dey shipped po' Bessie back (Lawd)
on dat lonesome midnight freight

Lawd, let de peoples know
what dey did in dat Southern Town
Yes, let de peoples know
what dey did in dat Southern Town
Well, dey lef' po' Bessie dyin'
wid de blood (Lawd) a-streamin' down

The Rhythm Method, Razzmatazz, and Memory

CHAPTER 29

Satchmo: Embodying the Role

A figure of universal significance, perhaps the first American musical entertainer with global recognition, Louis Armstrong towers now over the most durable and original American art form like a colossus. He's the King Kong of jazz. Wynton Marsalis defined his appeal, saying it lies in the sound of his horn: "In its pure spiritual essence, it was the sound of America and represented the freedom that America is supposed to offer." But Armstrong's incredible charisma—animated and gleeful, with the music pouring out of him—gave every performance a patina of greatness. He not only revolutionized the role of the solo instrument inside the complete ensemble sound, but through his arrangements, varying the rhythm and the balance of textures, he experimented with and mastered every form of American music. As a singer, his sound is unmistakable; he was a grunting, gargling, scatting, purring, thundering, shouting, laughing, body-punching, exuberant fountain of feeling. From deep in his torso came the warmest squawling growl, which was meticulous in its percussive placement, always echoing the punch of the brass section. His stage manner created the colloquialisms for the front man and for the individual performers that followed him. And he did it for almost fifty years, having a number one hit in 1964, more than forty years removed from his first recordings. His singular rendition of "What A Wonderful World" is one of our most beloved and recognizable performances. Satch set all the ground rules.

Between 1925 and 1928, he embarked on a project that codified the art of jazz improvisation, organizing sixty-five recordings with small units

---

of five and seven performers, what he called the Hot Five and Hot Seven. These records, with their funky names—"Potato Head Blues," "West End Blues," "Muskrat Ramble," "Cornet Chop Suey," "Weather Bird," and "Heebie Jeebies"—changed the way popular music was organized and developed, making performers more willing to experiment, taking jazz beyond the chugging ragtime beat that was in vogue at the time. Impetuous and yet remarkably disciplined, Armstrong's wit showed itself in more than fifty film roles and countless television appearances.

Born on August 4 (a date he shares with myself, Percy Shelley, Orson Welles, and Roger "The Rocket" Clemens) in 1901, Armstrong was the son of a domestic servant and part-time prostitute named Mayann. When his father took off, Armstrong was raised by his grandmother in a Storyville New Orleans brothel. In extreme poverty, Armstrong was sometimes reduced to stealing from the shops and produce booths, which probably meant he had the attention of the neighborhood police when he made a fateful mistake on New Year's Day in 1913. With all the fireworks and smoke bombs going off, young Satch took out his revolver and began to fire it into the air. Not yet thirteen, he was sent to the Colored Waif's Municipal Boys' Home. A rough place indeed, Armstrong nonetheless attracted the attention of the music teacher Peter Davis by exhibiting an uncanny knack for harmonies, probably derived from singing on the street for change, but also through the early exposure to the music jumping out of the dives, dance halls, honkytonks, and street funerals of Storyville. Jazz got a papa when Davis made the boy the school bugler and gave him his first cornet. By the time he was released, Armstrong had made himself a musician.

Not quite eighteen, the newly-freed teenager married a younger prostitute and joined the trombonist Kid Ory, working in his band on a Mississippi steamboat. Within three years, Satch had made enough of a name for himself that he was summoned to Chicago to play second horn in Joe "King" Oliver's Creole Band that was headlining at the Lincoln Gardens. Armstrong dropped his marriage and New Orleans like two hot rocks and never looked back. King Oliver's patronage and endorsement gave his young charge the confidence he needed to move forward. With a new lease on life, a new wife (Lil Hardin, once a Fisk University student and King Oliver's piano player) and a new horn, Satch joined the Fletcher Henderson Orchestra in New York City. Henderson's glamorous and urbane orchestra was transformed from a glossy dance hall outfit into a swinging and inventive large ensemble by the presence of the budding new firebrand; the group embodied a fresh concept crucial to the later evolution of Swing music.

By 1925, Satch was a bandleader in his own right, changing the face of Jazz on the strength of the Hot Five and Hot Seven recordings. Though these records were highly influential, Satch didn't find true commercial success until the 1930s, with his smooth delivery of "Ain't Misbehavin'." After getting busted for marijuana possession in Los Angeles and surviving a contract dispute with gangland managers in Chicago, Armstrong lit out for Europe and was greeted by ten thousand fans in the Denmark airport. He would stay in Europe for the next four years.

Upon his return to America, Satch had no band and no management. The manager of the Lincoln Gardens, Joe Glaser (reputedly a former employee of Al Capone), signed Armstrong to a management contract, and the two men stayed together for decades. Armstrong then embarked on the movies, and while playing the Cotton Club, he found his third wife, Lucille Wilson, who was the love of his life. In the 1940s, when bop was at its height, some younger players began to see Armstrong as an anachronism, but his All-Stars, through occasional collaborations with other artists, was still the highest paid band in jazz.

Armstrong's popularity soared after his appearance in *High Society* with Bing Crosby, Frank Sinatra, and Grace Kelly, and he became Jazz's true international ambassador, bringing his unique sound to every port in the world, including West Africa in 1956. His protest song from 1929, "Black and Blue," (What did I do to be so black and blue?/ How will it end, ain't got a friend/ My only sin, the color of my skin/ What did I do to be so black and blue?) was performed in Ghana to more than 100,000 people.

Louis Armstrong had grown to transcend the art that made him. Whatever grief he had taken for his stereotypical roles in the 1930s or for his stage persona that was viewed as mugging or pandering by younger black players, Satch realized that race was the wound that made America imperfect. And when he spoke out against the mistreatment of black children in Little Rock during segregation, even President Eisenhower took notice, condemning the actions of the white citizens. Satch canceled his Soviet tour for the State Department, and his activities were subsequently monitored by the CIA for the rest of his life.

After 1959, when Armstrong suffered a heart attack, he was forced to slow down, but his playing still contained all the colorful tones and nuance of the younger Satch. His late popularity, due to the Number One hit "Hello Dolly," reminded the public how important his contributions had been. A second heart attack claimed the Ambassador of Love in New York on July 6, 1971. Here's Fred Chappell's tribute "The Highest Wind That Ever Blew: Homage to Louis":

Ever, ever in unanimous voice we drift:
But not you, baby, not you, Satchel-Gator-
Dippermouth. Punch them pepper lead-notes,
Louis. Ride it, fiercemeat, yon and hither.
Birthday morning I put the record on.
Hot Five, hot damn. What a way to never
Grow Old! I couldn't count how many times
You saved my life.
                Tuning my tiny Arvin,
I'd gasp to glimpse through the mindless crackle one gleamiest
Corner of a note you loosed. Once more tell us
About Black Benny and Mary Jack the Bear;
Red-Beans-and-Ricely Ours, *all ours,*
Let's hear the Good News about Fats Waller.
"You got millions in you and you spend
A nickel": that's what the Message is, okay,
I hear you, shall I ever understand?

What's in that Trumpet is the Tree of Life,
The branches overfreight with cantaloupes,
Peacocks, mangoes, and nekkid nekkid women.
And all around the tree a filigree halo
Like a silver lace mantilla. And limb to limb
Zip little silver birds like buckshot dimes,
Kissing and chucking each other under the chin.
Curst be he who worships not this Tree,
Cause you S.O.L., baby   I mean
You   outtaluck ... It's summertime forever,
Believe to your soul; and this is the River of Jordan.
Everyone was born for a warmer climate

And a jug of wine. You born for it, sweet mama,
And me, and even the blackbox boxback preacher,
He born for it. Up on the Mountain of Wind
I heard in the valley below a lonesome churchbell
Calling home, home, home, home,
And the last swell of the hymn dying at sunset.
Everywhere in your trumpet I heard that.
I'll follow it like a fire in air, I will,
To the purple verge of the world.
                    Rain aslant the wind,
The cozy lovers wind their wounds together.
The weepy eaves peep down into the rooms.
Wind and water drive against the windows
Like a black blind moth in the dark. They sigh
And settle and snuggle. A lemon-colored sun
Warms their innermosts, memory
Of the trumpet-bell uplifted like a sun
Where they'd paid a buck to see the greatest man
Who ever lived, man playing with fire
In air, pursuing his soul in a hovering sun;
Had a tune would melt the polar cap to whiskey.
This dreamshot sun the mellow lovers dream,
It warms them amid each other, the rain goes cozy.

And me too, man, I had me a woman livin
Way   back o' town.
Would wait till the blue-gray smoke of five o'clock
Came down and fetch my bourbon and Beechnut chewing gum
Along the cindery railroad track, counting
The chemical raw smells the paper mill
Dumped into the Pigeon, and the railroad ties.
From tie to tie I whistled *Potatohead Blues*,
Even the clarinet part. It made me happy.
It made me nostalgic for that present moment.
I could have walked like that forever, I could
Have snagged the ballhoot freight to New Orleans

And clung to the windy boxcar singing, *singing*.
I could have lugged my trombone and learned to learn ...
I learned, anyhow ... There's something in the woman
More than in the horn to teach you the blues.
Yet still you need to tune, it fixes a pride
On the joy of Traveling Light, there's courage in it.
Father Louis had told me all already.

What's whiskey without the jazz?
Nothin but gutache, nothin to look back on.
Whiskey alone don't fill you that honeysuckle
Sunlight in your vein, it ain't the gin
That makes you shine. It's the man in the cyclone of flame
Who keeps on saying *Yes* with a note that would light
Up the Ice Ages. He's the silver sunrise
In the pit of the body, dawnwind jiving the trees.
Thoreau was right: morning is moral reform,
Gimme a shot. And please play *West End Blues*,
I need to hear the wistful whippoorwill,
To hear the railroad ties hauling the lovers
As they walk down the line, walk down the line
With nineteen bottles of whiskey in each hand,
Going to meet the woman and hear the man.

I've had the warm May nights in the feathery grasses,
Wind poling woozy clouds across the moon,
And the glare light slicing out of the honky-tonk,
Oblong light with a frizzly shape of woman
Troubling its center, one hand on her slouch hip,
Trumpet-flutter in the jukebox behind her
Like a pinwheel of copper fire. She watched the moon.
She too knew that something pulled between them,
The moon and trumpet revolved on a common center
Of gravity which was — where? who? when? how?
Which was *some*where and some*thing*, mystical
But surely palpable, a hungry force
Obtaining as between sharpeyed lovers.

The Rhythm Method, Razzmatazz, and Memory

Fire's in the blood, my father told me; wind

Whips it forward, seizing every atom

In the veins till bloodfire, bloodfire takes the body

Whole, jerks the form of a man along

On that windriver bloodfire, helplessly

A new creature in the Planet of Green Night,

Half funky animal, half pure music,

Meat and spirit drunk together under

The cotton moon. And not one man alone,

Ever, but everyone in reach of the trumpet:

An armada of fireships destroying themselves

To essence pure as wind in the fever nighttime.

Papa Louis Armstrong has refashioned us

For our savage reverend assault upon the stars.

This may seem a ridiculous idea, but I believe only a country boy could have written this "Homage to Louis." I say this because, being a country boy, I have felt the enormous longing that Chappell described, the need to transform, the wish to escape mediocrity. The intellectual and curious country boy also maintains an astute study of the Natural World, whose organic signposts light the way for lovers and dreamers and singers of the "Good News," the liberation of the body in thrall to truthful rhythm (and youthful puberty). "You got millions in you and you spend a nickel," Armstrong's horn tells Chappell. There is a world which you intuit that feels like this, a horn winding its way like a linked chain of fire heavenward and that "bloodfire takes the body/ whole, jerks the form of man along/ ... helplessly/ a new creature in the Planet of Green Night,/ half funky animal, half pure music ..."

Paul Valéry has written that poetry is "a language within a language," meaning that poetry (through its use of music) may contain a code or understanding *inside* the normal meanings of the words themselves and that music (or poetry) can not only make an emotional statement convincing, it can also give an emotional content (and clarity) to statements of wild imagination. Satchmo wraps himself in his music to express his free interior, then Chappell wraps himself inside a formal poetic structure to express the free release of Satch's music as it unspools inside the poet's body. This "Homage to Louis" thus comes to us twice-told. The poet, listening to music, listens to

---

himself as part of the expressive act, and that listening becomes an essential part of the poem. Boris Pasternak believed that "poetry searches for music amidst the tumult of the dictionary." Armstrong searches within the tumult of his tone, an expressive story shifting and twisting to the onslaught of chord changes and pinned to the consistent beat of the drum. At times, Armstrong scats, singing sounds (or notes) instead of words. He is following the music, just as Chappell—carried along by the horn—follows the poem; the reader follows both, listening as the poem is spoken, translating it as it is read.

> The poet, listening to music, listens to himself as part of the expressive act, and that listening becomes an essential part of the poem.

"In the world of imagination," wrote Richard Hugo, "all things belong. If you take that on faith, you may be foolish, but foolish like a trout." The young Chappell—for clearly the speaker who first encounters Satchmo is young and full-to-bursting with ideas—is also likely suppressed the way all cultures suppress young men until they have gained experience: "Hot Five, hot damn. What a way to never/ Grow old! I couldn't count how many times/ You saved my life." Most of the songs mentioned by Chappell come from Armstrong's Hot Five and Hot Seven recordings, including "Potatohead Blues," and "West End Blues," the latter which Armstrong's biographer, James Lincoln Collier, has called "Shakespearean, richly clothed, full of event, and rounded to a finish." The fifteen-second introduction by Satchmo's trumpet is majestic—four notes repeated in various combinations—and after the first chorus, Armstrong folds the trumpet under his arm and scats, his voice in dialogue with the clarinet, relaxed and calm and easy, as if he were just speaking to a friend of a sad event in the neighborhood. This makes the re-entry of his trumpet at the end so chilling. Armstrong holds that last long note, a high B-flat, hovering over Earl Hines's beautiful piano melody for an unparalleled amount of time, contrasting the short, scattered phrases, and creating a cry of moody enchantment, a heartbreaking moment of naked anguish, completely unexpected.

Music makes us do what it wants, or we interpret it as a clarion call to act upon our body's impulses. "What's in that trumpet is the Tree of Life," wrote Chappell, and then later he swore, "I'll follow it like a fire in air, I will,/ to the purple verge of the world." That horn gives a man courage,

The Rhythm Method, Razzmatazz, and Memory

gives whiskey its "honeysuckle sunlight in your vein," and gives the women a gravity, a "hungry force" to follow, with Armstrong's "trumpet-flutter in the jukebox behind her/ like a pinwheel of copper fire."

Armstrong's trumpet and charisma also give a white Southern poet the courage to talk in the slang of that era's black bluesmen, almost scatting himself as he joins Satch in his seductive and languid address of the world. "One touch of nature makes the whole world kin," said Ulysses to a pouting Achilles in *Troilus and Cressida*, and I use the phrase here to comment upon Jazz music's assault on a segregated America. "Everyone was born for a warmer climate," wrote Chappell, "and a jug of wine. You born for it, sweet mama,/ And me, and even the blackbox boxback preacher,/ He born for it." There may be moral flexibility in the trumpet of Louis Armstrong, but for Chappell it extends to every creature alike, and all those creatures—in full worship of sound—are "destroying themselves/ To essence pure as wind in the fever nighttime," and they are color-blind, because "Papa Louis Armstrong has refashioned us ..." No musician in American history tore down more racial barriers than Satchmo, and none has been more revered the world over for this ability to ignore the divisions of class and culture. For Chappell, this is music capable of complete transformation and redemption, readying the sympathetic and willing listener "for our savage reverend assault upon the stars."

"Everyone is dragged along by his favorite pleasures," wrote Virgil, and for Chappell, finding Louis Armstrong on his tiny Arvin radio in the remote North Carolina Mountains created a kinship, an essential recognition, complete with its shocks that invade the body and the brain. "The only kinds of music available to me in the North Carolina Mountains in 1948," wrote Chappell in his essay "Jazz-Poetry Shock Therapy," "were church hymns, some pretty good local folk and bluegrass, the tiresome Nashville country ballads, and the insipid pop tunes ('zippy-dee-doohah, zippy-dee-yay ...')." Most artists or writers I admire have the qualities of children, the willingness to stand still in the face of elemental awe, and the absolute openness to aspects of fresh thought, fresh rhythm, leaving themselves entirely free of premeditation, alive and vibrant, surrendering to the energy or sound of this moment, this *now*, without fear.

For Chappell, his "shock of recognition" was the otherworldly call of a black man's trumpet, accompanied by sympathetic instruments and players. Poetry was created in private to commemorate the communal creation of the music. Jazz is also improvised, created spontaneously, unlike the best poetry, which requires editing and gestation. Poetry in performance is most like the improvisation of jazz, with the constant give and take of the audience. Just as Louis Armstrong embodied the role of a single performer, so too can the reader of poetry embody her role in performance, choosing work that best represents her voice, appearance, or stance. Singers often change the keys of songs to suit their particular vocal range, allowing for their strongest and most authentic rendering of the song's lyric and melody. So too should the reader consider what best aspects of her poems can be illustrated through the performer's desired projection. I'm not talking here about persona but of appropriate pragmatic atten-

> *A poem carefully considered and patiently, clearly recited by the poet has an air of originality, even strangeness, and this is what keeps the poem alive and in motion no matter how many times one reads it.*

tion to strength and weakness. The greatest performances are accompanied not by waves of applause but by stunned silence, the byproduct of awe. What do we do when we hear the most pleasant music or recited poetry? We close our eyes, letting the mind wander (or follow), because music, or the rhythm of a well-made poem, can become a portal by which the mind may investigate other realms of thought and feeling, a sudden trapdoor to the subconscious, where the imagination is sovereign.

The narrative involved in improvisation is your whole life up to that point and your whole self invested in that moment of creation. Presence is defined by involving your entire self in each moment you speak, each surface you break, each random action given focus in the service of total creation. Poems are fixed in time, and many times a public poetry performance cannot convey a poem's form, but the best readers give rhythmic shape to a poem written with clear discretion. The Australian poet Les Murray has said, "The public reading is the real hope of poetry at the moment. Far more people will come to a reading than will buy a poetry book." This may be sad but true. Poetry has to compete with so many alternative types of entertainment now that greater significance is put on the poet to *perform*, not merely recite or recount. The carefully considered performer, who embodies his poetry,

The Rhythm Method, Razzmatazz, and Memory

will find his books being sold so that the electrified listener becomes an appreciative reader, anxious to see the shape of the poem on the page.

A poem carefully considered and patiently, clearly recited by the poet has an of originality, even strangeness, and this is what keeps the poem alive and in motion no matter how many times one reads it. Every poet has her own individual sound; we have a different weight, different configuration and appendages, different outlooks and unique desires. More importantly, we hear each sound inside the different chambers of our bodies with the prejudice of our own expectations and worldview. Poetry is the random accumulation of all these factors, transfixed in time, as each person brings her contributions to bear upon the waves of sound, and the vibrating and varied breath of her voice, the poet's last best instrument to string her poem like a web inside the listener.

CHAPTER 30

Bristol Hillbillies and Delta Bluesmen

The popularity of the blues and jazz artists in the 1920s led producers like Ralph Peer ever-deeper into the Southern states to hunt for new talent. During his search in late 1923, Peer ran into a grocery story owner named Polk Brockman, who told him about a local guy who'd won the town's fiddling contest. Peer decided to take a chance and record "Fiddlin' John" Carson, though he thought his country-tinged voice was "plu-perfect awful." He released the single in a limited run and sent the rest of the records to Atlanta, back to Polk Brockman's store. After a little radio exposure, every record sold out in two weeks, and country music found a home on the airwaves for good.

Flush with the newfound success, Peer decided he might need some more "hillbilly" talent, and he scoured the towns of Savannah, Charlotte, and Bristol, Tennessee. It was in Bristol that he found two acts that would establish country music as an industry—the Carter Family and Jimmie Rodgers. The Bristol sessions, recorded quickly and crudely with borrowed equipment hastily rushed from New York, would change the face of not only country music, but American popular music as well. The Carter Family—with the patriarch A. P.; his wife, Sarah; and cousin, Maybelle—recorded a catalog of songs that many poor rural families were already familiar with, so many folks knew the words before the songs tumbled out of their radios. Carter would put the family on the road, touring several weeks a year, as he searched far and wide for new songs to record. Carter, working single-handedly as a folklorist and oral historian, recovered hundreds of songs that would otherwise have been lost for posterity. He then

The Rhythm Method, Razzmatazz, and Memory

tried to record as many of them as he could, becoming country music royalty in the midst of his grail quest.

Jimmie Rodgers was a hub for many of the disparate styles swirling around in the American South and in the Heartland. His raw, true voice and unmistakable yodel combined vaudeville with hobo stomp-down train songs, sentimental ballads, country blues, and drawing parlor and bar tunes. "A thousand miles away from home a-waiting for a train," he sang, strumming a handful of accompanying chords on his beat-up guitar. Every country music cliché was embodied in the early performances of Jimmie Rodgers, and his influence on all the music that followed him was enormous. In just six years he recorded 120 records, and then he succumbed to that great destroyer of artists worldwide—tuberculosis.

The success of "race" and "hillbilly" records in the 1920s and '30s led record producers into the Mississippi Delta, where—among the last vestiges of slavery, the sharecropper cotton shacks, and deep poverty—a distinctly American music was being perfected in the juke joints and shanties. The blues' simple structure belies its hypnotic effect, and in the hands of masters like Charley Patton, Son House, Willie Brown, and Robert Johnson, it is perhaps the most moving art form in our cultural history. A howling wilderness only 150 years ago, the Delta, convoluted by cypress swamps and forbidden dunes, was carved with great effort and human blood into cotton, peanut, and tobacco fields, oppressing the working man, black and white alike. Out of these extreme working conditions, vivid narratives—of love, loss, death, and voodoo—bubbled up into the blues, a desperate endurance in response to a unique human experience.

If Son House was the plaintive gospel, drink-drenched disaster merged with the blues, Robert Johnson was the doomed Picasso incorporating a hedonistic, soulful cry of the human condition with consummate technique and a poet's sense of the language. When Son House and Willie Brown laughed at the young Johnson's ambition to be a traveling bluesman, the determined young artist headed out to the crossroads, to the intersection of Highways 49 and 61, heading west and north out of the Delta. There, like Daniel Webster before him, he supposedly sold his soul to the devil for the ability to play and sing the Blues like no other man. Several of his songs would reflect the mythic deal: "Hellhounds On My Trail," "Crossroads Blues," "Me and the Devil Blues," "Stones in My Passway," and "If I Had Possession

Over Judgement Day" all contain lyrics that describe a man haunted by his decisions and powerless to change them, doomed and strangely defiant. Thousands of artists would record versions of the twenty-nine songs he composed during his short career.

Contrary to most surviving accounts, Johnson did receive a measure of acclaim during his lifetime, but he was a feverish traveler, always ready to move to another place. For most of his later years, he would hole up in Helena, Arkansas, when not roaming about up and down the Mississippi River playing in levee camps, for road gangs, on courthouse steps busking, or in the juke joints dotted about the Delta countryside. Most of the great bluesmen from the era made their way through Helena. Sonny Boy Williamson, Willie Brown, Robert Nighthawk, Elmore James, David "Honeyboy" Edwards, Howlin' Wolf, "Hacksaw" Harvey, Johnny Shiner, and Memphis Slim were among the countless itinerants who flopped down and jammed in West Helena's many hot spots and nightclubs.

It was in one of these little joints that Johnson played, called Three Forks, just south of Arkansas in Greenwood, Mississippi, that he met his demise. He was known to love the ladies and, being fond of whiskey, he was easily poisoned by someone, perhaps the owner of the Three Forks, whose woman had been spending a little too much carnal time with the bluesman. After a set performed with Sonny Boy Williamson, perhaps the greatest harmonica player of all time, Johnson took ill, could sing no longer, and struggled, dying slowly for the next two weeks before his body gave up on August 16, 1938. One of the century's most mercurial and influential musicians was buried in a wooden coffin furnished by the county, just next to the highway, as his song "Me and the Devil Blues" had predicted: "You may bury my body down by the highway side/ So my old evil spirit can catch a Greyhound bus and ride."

Eric Clapton, The Rolling Stones, Led Zeppelin, The Red Hot Chili Peppers, and numerous other rock bands claim Johnson as an influence, and every blues artist that followed him found themselves affected by the long shadow he cast. His lyrics and guitar techniques are utterly original; they contain a power—hard to describe but haunting to every listener fortunate enough to hear them. "When the train, it left the station/ with two lights on behind/ Well, the blue light was my blues/ and the red light was my mind./ All my love's in vain."

It has been said that the blues ain't nothing but a good man feeling bad, but the blues feels like an absence, an ache, a place where the well of the

The Rhythm Method, Razzmatazz, and Memory

spirit is filled with dust, where the imagination has run dry, the life-force squandered. Willie Dixon wrote:

> I'm the moans of suffering women
> I'm the groans of dying men
> I'm the last one to start
> And the first one to end
>
> I'm a thousand generations
> of poverty and starvation
> I'm the dog
> Of the United Nations
> I am the blues
> I am the blues

Another poet has written, "I can't get no satisfaction," and this is the blues. When Federico Garcia Lorca spoke of the gypsy's despair and its *duende*, its black sound, I believe he was talking about a version of the blues. "Deep song sings like a nightingale without eyes. It sings blind, for both its words and its ancient tunes are best set in the night, the blue night of our countryside." Ralph Ellison also compared the blues to flamenco, gypsies to slaves: "an outcast though undefeated people who have never lost their awareness of the physical source of man's most spiritual moments." Without blues, there is no jazz. Without blues, there is no rock and roll. When Son House sings about the loss of his woman in "Death Letter," he is quickly assaulted by the deep "walking blues," the recognition of unrecovered love, spiraling past his understanding:

> I grabbed up my suitcase
> and headed down the road
> Lord, but when I got there
> she was laid out on a cooling board.
>
> Seemed like 10,000 people standing
> 'round the burying ground
> I didn't know I loved her
> 'til they began to let her down.
>
> I didn't feel so bad
> 'til the Good Lord slung me down

---

now I ain't got a soul
to throw my arms around

House is singing about irretrievable loss, loss that brings with it all the energy we commonly take for granted, that energy, Ellison said, "which mocks the despair stated explicitly in the lyric, and it expresses the great human joke directed against the universe, that joke which is the secret of all folklore and myth: though we be dismembered daily we shall always rise up again."

Langston Hughes knew the hot blue jet of deprivation in the heart of this music, and it informed all his poetry with a brooding sense of solitude, the singular beauty of corrosive sadness. He was just twenty-four years old when his first book, *The Weary Blues*, was published in 1926. Here's the first stanza from the title poem:

Droning a drowsy syncopated tune,
Rocking back and forth to a mellow croon,
    I heard a Negro play.
Down on Lenox Avenue the other night
By the pale dull pallor of an old gaslight
    He did a lazy sway

Already self-assured and mature in his poetic philosophy, Hughes used his poems to speak not only for himself but also for the entire black community. *The Weary Blues* is split into seven distinct sections with varying themes. The poems have a strong lyrical framework and were written to be accompanied by music. This first book's success allowed the young poet to attend Lincoln University, where one of his classmates was Thurgood Marshall, a future Supreme Court Justice. Ironically, forty-six years before the famous Brown vs. The Board of Education case, which in 1954 ushered desegregation into the American educational system, Hughes's dynamic mother argued and won her case against the school board of Topeka, Kansas, for refusing to admit her son to a nearby segregated white school because of the color of his skin. Here is the first stanza of Hughes's "I, too, Sing America":

I, too, sing America
I am the darker brother.
They send me to eat in the kitchen

When company comes,
But I laugh,
And eat well
And grow strong.

Because his father immigrated to Mexico and his mother was often away, the young Hughes was raised in Lawrence, Kansas, by his grandmother, Mary Langston, whose first husband had died at Harper's Ferry fighting under John Brown and whose second husband (Hughes's grandfather) had also been a fierce abolitionist. These adult figures engendered in the boy a keen sense of social justice. As a poet, he was also influenced by Paul Laurence Dunbar, Carl Sandburg, and Walt Whitman, and he recognized in them the poignant descriptions of men at work and of the speech patterns and colloquial expressions of common folk. In this spirit, Hughes invented a character named Simple, a black laborer, and in his name and dialect composed a weekly column for the *New York Post*. What Hughes said of the Blues is often true of his own work, that "the mood of the Blues is almost always despondency, but when they are sung people laugh."

He published more than three dozen books during his life, starting out with poetry and then expanding into novels, short stories, and plays. Many of his plays incorporated musical elements and song, such as the musical *Simple Heavenly*, and his three gospel plays, *Black Nativity*, *Tambourines to Glory*, and *The Prodigal Son*. Hughes authored music guides, including *Famous Negro Music Makers*, and the children's title *The First Book of Jazz*. He also wrote liner notes for albums by Harry Belafonte and Nina Simone, who recorded a version of his poem "Backlash Blues."

"What is poetry?" Hughes was asked near his death. He answered, "It is the human soul entire, squeezed like a lemon or a lime, drop by drop, into atomic words." He wanted no definition of the poet that divorced his art from the immediacy of life. "A poet is a human being," he declared. "Each human being must live within his time, with and for his people, and within the boundaries of his country." In 1958, Hughes crossed into the jazz world by reading his work at the landmark Village Vanguard in New York City, accompanied by Charles Mingus and Phineas Newborn. The collaboration eventually resulted in the album *The Weary Blues*, which united Hughes's voice and words with the music of Leonard Feather and Mingus. The second half of the recording is amazing, with Mingus and his band laying down an organic funky groove that Hughes's mellifluous voice glides upon like a kite or parasail riding behind a moving boat, tipping precisely atop the feathery tide of wind and water. Here are lines 31–35 of "The Weary Blues":

> And far into the night he crooned that tune.
> The stars went out and so did the moon.
> The singer stopped playing and went to bed
> While the Weary Blues echoed through his head.
> He slept like a rock or a man that's dead.

Since the time of Langston Hughes, the blues poem has become a viable form, often in the musical tradition of the blues: a statement is made in the first line, some slight variation offered in the second line, and a type of alternative, perhaps ironic, declared in the next or third line. Kevin Young is a contemporary poet whose book *Jelly Roll* is a series of bluesy observations and musical effects. He has also edited an anthology collecting many of the poets whose blues-inflected poems he admires. Here is "Locomotive Songs," an example of Young's blues impressions, wrested together in a series of haikulike poems, concurrently comic and tragic, like all true blues:

> We were hobos every year.
> It was cheap—
>
> Our mother each
> Halloween smudged our cheeks
>
> stuffed us in someone
> else's clothes—
>
> We hopped houses
> like trains
>
> asking for sweets
>
> Much like last night,
> empty-armed, at your door
>
> I begged you

―――――――

Tonight the train horn
sounds like plenty

enough loud
to warm even the autumn—

The night air with a nip
that catches by surprise—

White light, blue
light, fog starting to rise

―――――――

She has me tied,
a tongue, to the tracks

Her new man's
elaborate moustache

Train comin fast

Can't cry
out to save my life

Drats

―――――――

I've heard tell
of a town where the train

bound for New Orleans slows
just enough, a turn

that folks place cars
good only for insurance in—

The train cashes them
coming round the bend—too late

to stop, too slow to derail—
That's how I feel

watching you & the station
being pulled away, one hand

hovering the emergency brake
the other

out to wave

When I spoke earlier in this section about embodying the role of the poet in performance, I used the example that the performer should choose material that they can best represent, the poems whose music fits the poet's ability to render it dynamically. It is also important to inhabit the country of your own identity. The audience wants to be entertained, of course, but also wants a feeling of intimacy with the poet, a chance to live inside, if only for the duration of performance, the poet's particular world, to share the act of creation. The poet who wants to speak down from Olympus upon the audience will find the wind howling at his back, the disdain of the listeners palpable. Let the audience share your life, show them your true self. Break down the third wall and find yourself rewarded.

CHAPTER 31

The Birth of a Blue Radio

The exodus from Mississippi and Louisiana began after World War II for black folks looking for better opportunities. Black blues musicians headed north as well, touching down in Memphis and Chicago. More than half a million people landed in Chicago in the early 1940s, seeking the jobs in the paper and steel mills supporting the war effort. In 1943, Muddy Waters followed Big Bill Broonzy to the Windy City, and by 1950, the Chicago blues scene exploded. Chess Records began to release their first blues records: Little Walter, James Cotton, and other musicians formed a band around Muddy Waters that would set the standard for high energy blues grooves and sophisticated arrangements. The poet laureate of the blues, Willie Dixon, began to write and help record songs containing the gritty vernacular of the street, penning songs for Muddy and Howlin' Wolf that would change American music forever. Their fierce rivalry attracted many young musicians to the Chicago scene, including Lightning Hopkins, Chuck Berry, John Lee Hooker, and T-Bone Walker. All would record for Chess and fill the radio with songs. Blues and country then had a baby and named it rock and roll.

The first stirrings of Rock and Roll were probably felt when Muddy Waters played his uncle's electric guitar. In 1941, two field recordists showed up in Coahoma County in Mississippi, close to Clarksdale and Stovall, on a mission to research the role music played in African-American life. The project had begun with John Work III, a young black musicologist at Fisk University. In his appeal for funds, he encountered Alan Lomax at the Library of Congress.

Lomax had returned to Mississippi to find Robert Johnson, who was already three years dead, paying back his Crossroads dues. When Lomax and his assistants inquired about talented bluesmen in the area, neighbor after neighbor pointed toward Stovall and repeated, "Find Muddy." When Muddy heard a white man was looking for him, he assumed it was a revenue agent sent to bust his whiskey still. Only after Lomax drank water out of the same cup as Muddy did the musician let down his guard. One of the primary rules of voodoo is to never drink from an opened container that you did not witness being poured. Robert Johnson had broken this rule to his great detriment. Local legend held that a woman who wanted to gain love and control a man by exciting his passion beyond all reason, might put menstrual blood in his drink. An enemy might put any manner of potion inside; a charm could make snake eggs hatch in his belly, a powder from a witch could cause madness, a root extract could make a man's legs swell up and his hands shake.

The recording equipment was set up at Muddy's cabin, a former shotgun sharecropper's shack, and among the sides he cut that day were "Can't Be Satisfied" and "Feel Like Going Home," which were soon issued by the Library of Congress as part of a folk music collection. Muddy got the confidence to hobo to Chicago when he heard Lomax's recordings of himself. When his performance was played back, Muddy said, "Man, I can sing." Two years and two more seasons of half-wages, weeding and pulling in the Delta heat, pushed Muddy north. He climbed off his tractor and onto a boxcar, riding those shiny rails toward Illinois.

Muddy's uncle, who preceded him to the Windy City, gave him an electric guitar soon after he arrived. The transition from an acoustic instrument was completely pragmatic; in rural Mississippi, the only sounds at night were the steady percussion of crickets and cicadas. In Chicago, there were clanging streetcars, trains, and automobiles growling past at all hours. Muddy took to the new instrument like Dr. Frankenstein to his monster, and this beautiful relationship remained in moaning high fidelity for more than thirty razor-toting, juke-joint-ruling years. His 1940 recording of "Rollin' Stone" was one of the first released from Chess Records, and it later became the inspiration for a rock magazine and a little white boys' blues band that called themselves The Rolling Stones, and whose biggest hit was called "(I Can't Get No) Satisfaction." Muddy and his blood brother Howlin' Wolf made Chicago the mecca of the blues. Their turf wars were like Bill Russell

The Rhythm Method, Razzmatazz, and Memory

and Wilt Chamberlain, titans of the Blues in bas-relief, and armed with the songs of Willie Dixon, the two men drug the blues into the light of day—and Leonard Chess got it all on tape, paying the men little to nothing for their Herculean labors. Here is an excerpt from the lyrics to Willie Dixon and Billy Emerson's "Dead Presidents":

Chorus: Give me some dead presidents
Give me some dead presidents
I ain't broke but I'm badly bent
Everybody wants them dead presidents

Now Lincoln, a penny, can't park your car
Washington on a nickel can't go too far
Jeff on two, good to play at the track
If you think you gonna bring some big ones back

Hamilton on a ten, can get you straight
But Jackson on a twenty is really great
And if you're talking about a poor man's friend
Grant will get you out of whatever you're in

Hundred dollar Franklin is really sweet
Five hundred McKinley is the one for me
And if I get Cleveland I'm really set
With thousand dollar Cleveland I forget the rest

Chester Burnett, a.k.a Howlin' Wolf, was in the possession of one of blues music's greatest vocal instruments. If Satan had decided to sing, he would probably have chosen Wolf's voice to express himself. Feral, huge, and raw, Wolf's amazing blues growl was reminiscent of Charley Patton but more powerful and refined. He learned to play guitar and blues harmonica simultaneously, sometimes using a rack-mounted harp. His stage presence was second to none, almost supernatural, as he stood over 6' 3" tall and weighed 275 pounds, screaming his lyrics with his whole body like a smokestack belching fire. Johnny Shines, who also traveled with Robert Johnson, said, "I was afraid of the Wolf, like you would be of some wild animal ... It was just the sound he was giving off!" In 1951, Wolf came to the attention of a young Memphis producer named Sam Phillips who recorded "Moanin' At Midnight" and "How Many More Years" and leased them to Chess Records. Released in 1952, they made it to the Top 10 on *Billboard*'s R&B charts. Chess eventually lured Wolf to Chicago in 1953; Wolf would live there for the rest of his life. Phillips later said that Wolf was his "greatest discovery" and losing him to Leonard Chess was his biggest disappointment in the music business.

Many of the songs Wolf recorded for Chess would become blues standards, and the Willie Dixon songs he chose to perform have been covered by rock and blues artists the world over. "Spoonful," "Little Red Rooster," "Evil," "Back Door Man," "I Ain't Superstitious," and others penned by Dixon were perfectly suited to Wolf's outsized persona. In an interview with Alan Paul, Bonnie Raitt spoke about her fascination with Wolf. "If I had to pick one person who does everything I loved about the blues, it would be Howlin' Wolf. It would be the size of his voice, or just the size of him. When you're a little pre-teenage girl and you imagine what a man in full arousal is like, it's Howlin' Wolf. When I was a kid, I saw a horse in a field with an erection, and I went, 'Holy Shit!' That's how I feel when I hear Howlin' Wolf, and when I met him it was the same thing. He was the scariest, most deliciously frightening bit of male testosterone I've ever experienced in my life." Here is one of Wolf's most famous songs, "Three Hundred Pounds of Joy," written by Willie Dixon:

> Now all you girls think your days are done
> You don't have to worry, you can have your fun
> Take me, baby, for your little boy
> You get three hundred pounds of heavenly joy
>
> This is it, this is it
> Look what you get
>
> You been sneakin' and hiding behind his back
> Because you got a man that you don't like
> Now throw that man, baby, out of your mind
> And follow me, baby, and have a real good time
>
> Hoy, hoy, I'm the boy
> You get three hundred pounds of heavenly joy
> I'm so glad you understand
> You get three hundred pounds of muscle and man

In 1941, a radio station no bigger than a little gob of spit began broadcasting blues by the harmonica virtuoso Sonny Boy Williamson and guitar player Robert Lockwood, Jr. The station, KFFA in Helena, Arkansas, called the show King Biscuit Time after the sponsor, King Biscuit Flour. Black laborers and sharecroppers in cotton fields would pause for lunch and listen to the first original blues show ever to feature live music on their airwaves. A young James Cotton began to mimic Sonny Boy from the age of nine years old, and a teenager named B. B. King used the inspiration of the show as a catalyst to leave the Delta cotton fields and head to Beale Street in Memphis. The desperately poor guitar-picking kid would play for change in the park and on the street corners, eventually landing a job with radio station KDIA alongside Rufus Thomas in 1948, touting their sponsor, the tonic Pepticon. Sam Phillips decided to record King and Thomas, along with Howlin' Wolf, for his fledgling record company, Sun Records. He also produced in tiny Sun Studios the Big Bang of Rock and Roll, putting to tape the four horsemen of the coming Rockalypse: Elvis Presley, Jerry Lee Lewis, Johnny Cash, and Carl Perkins.

B. B. King's popularity stemmed from his exciting radio show and, more importantly, from his innovations as a bandleader, incorporating horn sections into blues arrangements and touring incessantly, averaging three hundred performances per year, year-in and year-out, becoming the greatest ambassador of the Blues, his single-note hypersonic vibrato-picking style wringing authenticity from his sacred companion and ever-faithful sidekick, his guitar Lucille. His early influences were the bandleaders Count Basie, Louis Jordan, and Duke Ellington, so King took the sophistication of jazz discipline and poured it into a blues-band setting. His signature hit "The Thrill Is Gone" reflects these seemingly oppositional approaches and reconciles them beautifully. B. B., the Beale Street Blues Boy, became the undisputed King of the Blues by century's end, and with his superb musical instincts and soulful booming voice, he took a back seat to no man in the blues hierarchy. King held the blues in his arms like a woman he could not live without, and all the world was seduced by this singular love affair. Here's a tribute from Lyn Lifshin:

BB KING

how I call my
guitar Lucille?

Well I saw some guys
in a bar get into a fight,
really going at it

they started a fire,
then the building collapsed.

I ran back in to get my guitar
just minutes before, knew
I shouldn't have
done it

but she was there for me
and I named her Lucille,
the girl the men were
fighting over

CHAPTER 32

Swing Time and the Bebop Colossus

W hen the bottom dropped out of the U.S. economy in 1929, one could hear the cymbals crashing to the floor in the parlor socials in New York and Chicago, and a new hot style began to replace the clunky two-beat rhythm of ragtime. The blues, which had dominated radio in the 1920s, was buried in the rise of network shows. The notion of New Orleans jazz with simple, unvarnished idioms and straight-ahead arrangements was replaced by free-wheeling and free-thinking bandleaders and their orchestras. Louis Armstrong had opened the door for speed demons and virtuosos, giving the checkered flag to a generation of players with unforeseen technique. Duke Ellington, Count Basie, Jimmy Dorsey, Cab Calloway, Fletcher Henderson, King Oliver, and others moved away from collective improvisation and into complex arrangements with featured performers. A faster, smoother, more powerful music emerged for a mass market of young dancers. America began to swing. Most American households had radios by 1934, and live music broadcasts become the rage. Ballrooms were linked directly to radio stations. Prohibition was repealed in 1933, and the growing student audience recharged the demand for faster, more exhibitionist styles. The jazz big band became standardized to five brass, four reeds, and four rhythm players. The new bandleaders arranged for the brass and reeds to talk to each other in faster, more harmonically adventurous ways.

The clarinet sounds of Benny Goodman and Artie Shaw became staples of the new sound, and piano players like Fats Waller, Teddy Wilson, and the sonic whirlwind Art Tatum advanced the stride style to unheard-of levels

---

of sophistication and artistry. More advanced technology brought the microphone to the singer (not the other way around), and more subtle human nuances were breathily whispered across the hard-charging new chord changes. Billie Holiday established the new idea of what jazz singers would look and sound like; Sarah Vaughn and Billy Eckstine followed close behind. Innovative drummers like "Papa" Jo Jones, Art Blakey, Kenny Clarke, and the madcap Gene Krupa changed textures and rhythm signatures, becoming more than mere timekeepers. Ben Webster, Coleman Hawkins, and especially Lester Young—whose cool, airy tone and spacious phrasing became the rage—made the saxophone a leading instrument in the big band universe, paving the way for the hard bop giants that followed in the 1940s.

But the unparalleled King of Swing was Benny Goodman, who brought jazz out of its backwater status and into Carnegie Hall. Goodman was younger than all the jazz pioneers from the 1920s, and he resembled the new audience he was playing for, in demeanor and need for speed. His tightly disciplined improvisations were imitated across America. It was a sound and enthusiasm that made the Dust Bowl misery of the Depression melt into the mists of history. Here's Hayden Carruth's homage, "Sure, Said Benny Goodman":

"Sure," said Benny Goodman,
"We rode out the depression on technique." How gratifying
    and how rare,
Such expressions of a proper modesty. Notice it was not said
By T. Dorsey, who could not play a respectable "Aunt Hagar's"
    on a kazoo,
But by the man who turned the first jazz concert at Carnegie
    Hall
Into an artistic event and put black musicians on the stand with
    white ones equally,
The man who called himself Barefoot Jackson, or some such,
In order to be a sideman with Mel Powell on a small label
And made good music on "Blue Skies," etc. He knew exactly
    who he was, no more, no less.
It was rare and gratifying, as I've said. Do you remember the
    Incan priestling, Xtlgg, who said,
"O Lord Sun, we are probably not good enough to exalt thee,"
    and got himself

The Rhythm Method, Razzmatazz, and Memory

Flung over the wall at Machu Picchu for his candor?
I honor him for that, but I like him because his statement
    implies
That if he had foreseen the outcome he might not have said it.
But he did say it. *Candor seeks its own unforeseeable occasions.*
Once in America in a dark time the existentialist flatfoot floogie
    stomped across the land
Accompanied by a small floy floy. I think we shall not see their
    like in our people's art again.

Music can persuade without eliciting consent, which is why jazz was so important to the generation of writers who came of age in the 1930s and '40s. In a letter to me last year, Carruth wrote, "I regret that I haven't written more poems on jazz themes, since I consider jazz the most important cultural advance by far of western civilization after the Renaissance." William Matthews said that "Carruth is one of those poets for whom the inexpressible and the unspeakable are the best ambitions of language ... It's not that music is about desire ... It's that the love of music recapitulates desire ... and what musician hasn't felt the gap between what he can hear in his head and what he can play on his instrument?" In his poem "Freedom and Discipline," Carruth wrote:

Saint Harmony, many
years I have stript

naked in your service
under the lash. Yes, ...

"Freedom and discipline concur/ only in ecstasy," he continues near the end of the poem. He is trying his dead level best to assert that jazz, like poetry, expresses what is otherwise withheld from us; both expand our range of access to our deepest emotions, and how could that possibly be bad?

"Poetry makes nothing happen," W. H. Auden wrote. Our acceptance of that is to understand that our efforts as poets provide no panacea to poverty or bad governments, but our aspirations provide comfort and discovery, however small. Like jazz players, poets move from improvisational discovery to solitary contemplation in the blink of an eye, but our windows are open, the air is moving, and our experiments make us free, regardless of the compensation. We shore up these fragmented discoveries against disorder and chaos and open ourselves anew, after each failure and before the voices rustle up again. "He knew exactly who he was," Carruth wrote of Goodman, "no more, no less." Inherent in that statement is a satisfaction with the unknown, a humility in the face of darkness, and the courage to confront it anyway. "Be one of those people on whom nothing is lost," Henry James said. Candor seeks its own unforeseeable occasions. But candor is revealed through experimentation.

What Carruth admired about Goodman and the jazz artists of his generation was their fearlessness, turning swing from a verb into a noun, commencing on the journey even though you know that your best efforts may come to nothing. We will always be criticized for being artists and seeking a public forum. The ego embedded in that process is frightening enough, but without the faith that what we have to say is worthwhile, it would be impossible to surrender to the creative urge. It took Shakespeare two weeks to write *The Tempest*, and Ben Jonson chided him for taking that long. "I need the sea because it teaches me," wrote Pablo Neruda. "I move in the university of the waves." For our own private reasons, we commence the journey through poetry or music to find someone listening on the other side of silence, for whom our efforts were intended all along. "The poets," said Ralph Waldo Emerson, "they are free and they make free." The poems we make become one with the sum of all other created things and so there is no end to the making. "Sure, Said Benny Goodman" is a poem of praise for excellence, sure enough, but also for vigilance. The wellspring for that type of courage is rare but inexhaustible. Here's hoping we *do* see the like of these men in our people's art again.

The swing giants came and went quickly, but the best continued to change and record. Any style divisions too clearly delineated are artificial at best. The better jazz musicians won't be bound inside inflexible constraints and simply play their own music, regardless of trends or shifting public taste. To call Thelonius Monk strictly a bop player or Duke Ellington ex-

The Rhythm Method, Razzmatazz, and Memory

clusively a swing master does both men a disservice. Miles Davis changed styles (and the direction of jazz) at least three times, creating a shimmer of influence in his wake. Also, as new styles supercede old ones, the renegades of one era become the conservative defenders (or the old guard) of the next. Benny Goodman was the King of Swing in 1935 but was deemed a has-been by 1949, and he was only forty years old.

The musicians who comprise the bebop era differed from the swing artists in several substantial ways. From the outset, most jazz players would solo, even in ragtime, by keeping the initial melody strictly in mind. Most of the time you could name a song just from the echoes of the primary melody embedded in the solo's phrases. In bebop, the emphasis is on creativity and originality for the soloist who discarded the melody after the first chorus and would typically only return to it in the song's coda or conclusion. Bop solos are based almost strictly on the chord changes. Sometimes bebop composers would use "standard" versions of well-known songs to base their creation upon, only to shuffle the chord arrangements in wild and unpredictable ways. Also, the time-keeping and rhythm performers changed for the new bebop sound. In the swing era, the drummer kept time on the snare and hi-hat cymbal, keeping a lighter, more complimentary feel to the sound. Kenny Clarke shifted that function to the ride cymbal, making the snare and bass drum more improvisational, appearing at contrary and unexpected intervals—what players in the know called "dropping bombs." Even if the beat was in 4/4 time, the most consistent timekeeper in the band was the bass player, and few bop combos could function effectively without one. This made bop harder to dance to, which suited the musicians just fine.

Bebop players did not cater to their audience, considering it uncool to banter or tell jokes. Some bop musicians rarely addressed the audience at all, saving their allegiance and energy for the music itself, its improvisational demands enough entertainment for the true bop fan. As a consequence, many bebop performers were considered eccentric, aloof, even hostile to their audience, their loyalty reserved for the artistry of interpretation and the discovery of the live performance, frozen in the moment. In this context, no one was more reserved or eccentric than Thelonius Sphere Monk.

CHAPTER 33

Into the Mystic: The Art of Silence

With a style instantly recognizable, rebellious in nature, and iden- tified by its astounding rhythmic dexterity, Thelonius Sphere Monk accomplished something few artists ever dare. He decided he would develop his own voicing on the piano and revolutionize the ap- proach to his instrument, sticking to his agenda under every opposing circumstance. He took the Harlem stride piano style and brought beautiful harmonic surprises to his compositions, using unusual chord combina- tions and jarring, even jagged, idiosyncratic space and dissonance. He was completely indifferent to showy displays of technique and was described by *New Yorker* critic Whitney Balliett as using pauses so long "that the listener wondered if he had left the building." Balliett called the unexpected twists and suspensions of Monk's melodies "like missing the bottom step in the dark." To discover Monk for the first time requires the listener to cast his preconceived notions to the wind and to stand quietly inside a turbulence that jerks in stops and starts with Monk's one-of-a-kind timbres and tones, a sonic tunnel through which his haunted characters jump out of closets and from behind shades. A deeply entrenched proponent of Harlem stride piano, Monk's earliest influences were the great James P. Johnson, who lived nearby, and Teddy Wilson. His first and most enduring lessons, how- ever, came from the gospel church, accompanying his mother's choir.

Five-year-old Thelonius Monk moved from North Carolina to New York City in 1922, settling in a West Indian immigrant section on the poor side of 56th Street. Monk's mother decided he and his sister should play musical

The Rhythm Method, Razzmatazz, and Memory

instruments—she the piano, and Monk the trumpet. But his bronchial asthma soon caused the youngsters to switch instruments, and Monk became obsessed with the piano, displaying an amazing facility for it right from the beginning. With a couple of classmates, he formed a trio that won the amateur talent contest at the Apollo Theater in Harlem so many times that they were barred from participating. Monk's name and acclaim eventually landed him a house gig at Minton's Playhouse, host to one of the hippest and most discriminating audiences for jazz in the entire city of New York. With guitar player Charlie Christian, he began to experiment, composing his own music and trying it out with various collaborators.

Then bebop exploded in the middle of Manhattan, detonated by the most astounding group of musicians in American history. The roll call of names leaves one breathless: Bud Powell, Fats Navarro, Ben Webster, Coleman Hawkins, Charles Mingus, Clifford Brown, Max Roach, Gene Ammons, Sonny Criss, Ray Brown, Dizzy Gillespie, Charlie Parker, Miles Davis, Art Blakey, Kenny Clarke, Art Tatum, Lester Young, Sonny Rollins, John Coltrane, Dexter Gordon, Sonny Stitt, Roy Eldridge, George Shearing, Erroll Garner, J. J. Johnson, Howard McGhee, Tadd Dameron, and many others. Bebop would affect all the music that followed it, not so much as a revolution but as an evolution of freedom, where the old rhythmic ideas were discarded and subtly moved forward. It remains a golden age in the history and creativity of American music.

Monk was a central participant in the bebop evolution; his bohemian appearance and affection for shades and eccentric hats also defined the image and style of the postwar hipsters—musicians, actors, painters and poets alike. Monk personified cool detachment, even diffidence, but his playing always contained a spiritual warmth and sense of adventure. Arrested on a bogus drug charge in the late 1940s (the stash was Bud Powell's, but because of Powell's prior convictions, Monk took the rap), Monk lost his cabaret card and stayed out of circulation until the mid-1950s; but he had already composed a series of jazz songs that were to become classics. His "52nd Street Theme" had already been recorded by Bud Powell, Dizzy Gillespie, and Cootie Williams. Williams and several others had also covered "Epistrophy," "Well You Needn't," "Monk's Mood," and "Round Midnight."

The resurgence for Monk came with his third Riverside album, *Brilliant Corners*, which also featured Sonny Rollins, Ernie Henry, Max Roach, and

Clark Terry, with Oscar Pettiford on bass. To get some insight into Monk's thinking, some of the titles on the album are "Pannonica," "Bemsha Swing," "Ba-Lue Bolivar Ba-Lue's Are," and a gorgeous, one-take rendering of "I Surrender Dear." The title tune was so difficult that no single perfect take was finished (even after twenty-five tries), and the producer was forced to splice together the final performance that exists on the record. It nevertheless remains one of the pinnacles of jazz music and can only be buttressed by Monk's *Complete Blue Note Recordings*; the combination of the two albums is the best introduction a neophyte might have to approach the Monk canon for the first time.

The years of exile while Monk was imprisoned, then blacklisted, were not wasted by the composer. He spent long hours at the piano writing and became a sort of house husband for his two children while his wife worked to pay the bills. It made the later acclaim that much sweeter, culminating in 1964 when Monk was featured on the cover of *Time* magazine, one of only three jazz artists to have been accorded that accolade. Monk was at the peak of his fame during this time, touring the world and appearing at quite a few jazz festivals with his quartet, which featured Charlie Rouse on tenor sax from 1959 to 1970. After touring with the Giants of Jazz in 1972, Monk came home and abruptly retired, saying, "I don't feel like playing no more." Monk's final decade was interspersed with bouts of mental illness until his death in 1982. His legacy, however, remains secure, and he stands alongside Duke Ellington and Jelly Roll Morton as one of the greatest composers in jazz history. Here is "Misterioso," a tribute to Monk by Sascha Feinstein:

I.

One-fingering my way through
    the White Pages I stopped
        upon T. S. Monk, dialed,

and when a voice deeper
    than mine would ever get said
        Yeah I said nothing

for several seconds.
    I've blocked out my nervous
        words—something about

digging your music, until
a laugh said, "Hey, friend—
you talkin' 'bout my father."

You were in retirement then,
dying before I could see you
though I've heard so many gigs

in my mind: it's late, you look past
the whole room, your silence
inviting everyone into

your world like the talk
we never had, or those months
when performing didn't matter.

It's how I see you even now: not wanting
to play, just nudging the piano
like a rush-hour New Yorker—

hit a stray note, stare at it, wait
for the leftover sound to tell you
what tune to fall into, or who'll

survive your patience, who will leave—
wait for some polyester jacket to say,
Mr. Monk, it's really time to begin—

Those were the moods that kept us
keyed in to you more
than the elbow-dances off

the stand. Because so much
decision pressed itself into each
small move, because we wanted to say

We're listening, man, we've got the night,
and you, with your black fez & shades,
everything you didn't play.

Into the Mystic: The Art of Silence

II.

It's the silence that keeps me
awake, shaping bodies
from hanging suits,
my eyes pressed hard

to hear the crinkling night.
A Guinness, blinding
refrigerator bulb, headphones:
The London Collection

darkens my mouth to
the stout's charcoal.
Each six-note interval turns
the tune over itself like

flamed paper dancing to the chimney's
hot draw. Monk for a moment
holds on to his melody, then
breaks it: a blackened brick

cracked to its red core,
the building's plasterless skeleton
against the sky's blue sound.
What's left of the penitentiary

downtown rusts and glows
in the afternoon's warmth, iron
filings and brick paths
where men used to sing

the lives they never wanted.
Froth drips my foot
alive, eyes slowly
aware of the porch screen, the room

lit into a daguerreotype. Your silver
face, unfocused, unfolding,

The Rhythm Method, Razzmatazz, and Memory

white-flowered cotton
gown, hand rubbing

one eye, comes to life.
The headphones slip down as
flat-fingered chords reverberate
my neck. *Come back to bed,*

and I do, roses on the sheets
rich as Monk's rising sixths,
elevating, keeping time with the morning,
the breathing, now sunlit dust.

III.

Two sleeping pills from last night
linger this morning in my body,
everything behind the beat like
Ben Webster's wheezing tenor,
a horn with holes in it.
That's him playing, isn't it?
The piano player stealing Monk
licks. It's an old cut
And Ben's been gone for years.

Outside, these heavy boots slow
me down. Rochester February:
snow so high it covers
fire hydrants. All week
I've clipped out columns,
JAZZ GREAT IN COMA, as if
the act could keep him alive.

It's much colder than the night
I drank with a dancer from the Upper
West Side. We'd been at a party,
left early, and she pulled me into
a local bar. *Two Remy Martins*—
first hard liquor I'd ever had.

She sat real close, and cognacs later
dared me to take my shoes off,
slip the wintery sidewalk
to her apartment. We could
warm our feet with a nightcap.

Nobody noticed us and I never
felt any sting of cold.
She had a new stereo, music through
hanging beads that tinkled as she danced
from room to room to "Monk's Dream,"
until she wore nothing, took my hand
and left the record playing.

But upstate New York's no Manhattan
and these boots feel heavy enough
to drown a man in a river. Downtown.
I catch a buddy of mine, his *Times*
dappled from snow and wind.
"Hey," he says "that jazz guy
you like to talk about died last night.
I always thought you'd have to
make up a name like that."

Saxophonist Charles Lloyd calls the ability to stay focused in the middle
of a storm of music "restful alertness." That's the calm expression of a performer as the cascade of chords and ideas crashes through him. The capability to allow your thoughts coherence as quickly as they are born, patient
but immediate context derived from hour upon hour upon hour of obsessive
rehearsal, woodshedding, nurturing a solitary marriage to an inanimate
object. Slavish attention to your intuition. Monk, maybe more than any
other artist of the twentieth century, would sit unperturbed in the midst of
dramatic expectation and jerk the onrushing chord changes and rhythms
like a balloon artist twisting rubber filled with air into recognizable shapes.
I have always viewed Monk's assault on the rhythm track of most compositions as a form of violence. He tears apart every preconceived notion and
expectation of the listener. He stabs, parries, punches, and pummels the

The Rhythm Method, Razzmatazz, and Memory

piano, knowing full well he is on the verge of disaster and outwitting it with beautiful anticipation, a look of sweaty transcendence on his face and his right foot brushing the floor and the pedal in constant perfect sympathy with the bass and snare.

Sascha Feinstein's graceful elegy to Monk captures perfectly the audience's willingness to surrender to Monk's most eccentric impulses. "Those were the moods that kept us/ keyed in to you more/ than the elbow dances off/ the stand. Because so much/ decision pressed itself into each/ small move." The "elbow dances" he refers to were Monk's way of resting, while still demonstrating to everyone that the groove was *really cooking*. So he would stand, flap his arms slightly like a great cosmic Dodo with his mannered hat balanced atop his nodding head like a rooster's comb, and stagger about the stage (and even off the bandstand) in a relaxed frenzy. *Restful alertness*. Monk was way too cool to shimmy like Tina Turner, even if he could have turned the freighter of his intent listening around. His focus was frightening, so complete it sucked all the gravity of the room into it. "*We're listening, man, we've got the night*."

Feinstein's "Misterioso," whose title is taken from a Monk composition, is an exercise in listening; the speaker constantly catches the reader with his moments of stillness, the first being the phone call to Monk's apartment and hearing his son on the phone. Too nervous and timid to demand an audience with the king, the speaker doesn't give us the outcome of the conversation, but it's easy to figure out. Feinstein then brilliantly takes us to an imagined gig, having never seen the maestro in person, and sells it in his poem, capturing the awe and respect of the young men who are all born too late to feel the real Monk presence, breathlessly waiting and just as knocked out by everything he didn't play as by what he did. Monk's supreme adherence to rhythmic mayhem is surpassed only by his reverence for the negative space. "The piano ain't got no wrong notes," Monk famously said. But what you play has never been as important as where you play it, and the masters always remind us of that simple rule.

The use of negative space on a page is extremely important to the weight of the poem, just as stillness is essential to the dramatic weight of performance. Silence and the ability to manipulate it is one of the tender demarcations between the professional and amateur, the Brahmin and the beginning reader. Let me quote Ralph Ellison again, this time from *The Invisible Man*:

"Perhaps I like Louis Armstrong because he's made poetry out of being invisible ... Invisibility, let me explain, gives one a slightly different sense of time; you're never quite on the beat. Sometimes you're ahead and sometimes behind. Instead of the swift and imperceptive flowing of time, you are aware of its nodes, those points where time stands still or from which it leaps behind. And you slip into the breaks and look around ..." What to leave in and what to leave out makes the composition and performance of every art form succeed or fail.

"Literature is life with the boring parts removed," said Vladimir Nabokov, and Feinstein's "Misterioso" works because of what he chooses to include.

> The use of negative space on a page is extremely important to the weight of the poem, just as stillness is essential to the dramatic weight of performance.

Four person-to-person encounters inform the poem: the first a phone call; the second being caught by Monk's stillness in the middle of the night's tender twilight, immersed in the underwater world of music through headphones; and the third an erotic striptease by a chance encounter in the middle of a snowstorm. The last word is left to his friend, no jazz fan, who is convinced only of Monk's existence by the newspaper's account of his passing. Even at the conclusion of the poem, Monk's absence affirms him. Thelonius Sphere Monk: has any musician ever been more aptly or royally named?

Paul Blackmur said of Robert Lowell, "The whole push of the man is in the poems." There is the feeling that Monk said everything he had to say, then just stopped, opened the lid on his piano, and stepped in, dropping out of sight. In the best of Monk's work, just as in the best poetry, you get the feeling that the artist is using his work as an excavating tool or drill, trying to dig down to the more lasting essence of the self and hoping to emerge transformed before the air runs out. Each strike then becomes paramount because of the tremendous seriousness of the task unfolding in front of you.

THE SOUND BELOW THE SURFACE

When a listener is confronted by rhythm or the idea of the groove, one can always imagine the percussion player striking things, and consequently that contribution to music is viewed from the point of attack: At what interval does the strike take place? Does it resonate? Where do the other textures fit? And so on. When you try to incorporate some of the other ideas into the mix, say the contribution of the singer, for instance, and you think only in terms of attack, you are lost, because the singer's vantage point is predetermined by breath and is pushed out of the body, originating in the diaphragm and focused by the head or chest. It then comes out of the mouth. Several decisions and destinations for the passage of air through the mouth take place before sound occurs, so the variety, pace, and control of the breath is paramount. Therefore, all of the sound quality takes place way below the surface. Even for the percussionist, the sound is not on the surface plane, but below, under the plane; the tone is gathering underneath the attack and released behind it. An accomplished player seeks the sound beneath the surface, rather than investing all of their energy in mere attack.

The beginning musician or poet can become too wedded to the idea of timing alone, or the mere formation of the word, neglecting all the surface tensions created by the variety and congruence of his environment, his audience, his own internal purposes, etc. It is as important to feel the nuance of the word's sound—and to take into account that feeling—before you speak. To let the interior of the room, your own instrument (your breath), and the other sound textures in the room have their space, and to show consideration, is the mark of an accomplished performer—letting the silence work for you and through you, not positing all silence as a diabolical rival.

Just as the famous scientific example of a butterfly's beating wings shows one hemisphere affecting the weather patterns in another, so too do sound waves emanate and overlap in the atmosphere, their reverberations taking place whether we are conscious or unaware of their presence. Hearing is a form of touch. Sound moves to us and through us, constantly affecting our subconscious. It is omnipresent; even the wind which ceaselessly moves has obstacles that impede it—flags flapping, cars slapping and cutting. Trees, though stationary, still rustle against the wind's movement, and the leaves sizzle and shimmer, surrounding and invading the oblivious pedestrian with oscillations. The body is a chamber, cocooned in millions of fibers of sound, like the rocks bombarded by surf. Our ability to distinguish one sound from the other requires the body to stop, the mind to go silent, and the lungs, emptied of breath, to inhale the vibrations of the world.

Writing, then, and speaking aloud what you've written, is the end result of apprehension, not comprehension—capturing all the sounds the body has been surrounded by. Reading is fundamental, yes, but so is breathing, its rhythm a fundamental function of who we are. So the opposite of sound is not silence. Silence is present and heavy. The opposite of sound is stillness—all breath, all wind, all movement stopped.

One of my favorite poets, William Matthews, carefully and meticulously in love with language, has combined his passion for the making of poems with his passion for jazz, illuminating both concerns in unexpected ways by their union. It's as if the poems become a type of jazz in dialogue with the circumstances they are describing, making "the work of the body a body of work," as he wrote in his poem "Mingus in Diaspora." Matthews is often described as a wit, or witty, but that doesn't begin to define his sense of timing, the aptness of his work, knowing when to change the pace or when the last line is the right line, the time to close the lid. This requires restraint but stems from relentless curiosity and a buoyant belief that discipline, when applied to poetry, constitutes its own reward. "The power of music that poetry lacks is the ability to persuade without argument," Matthews has written. But the best poems hide their argument, as well as the seams in their form. The style is the mysterious bond between the audience and the poem's mechanics, slipping in and out of the reader, inviting him or her back to read it again and again, coaxing the imagination out like "energy in a spring." See how slowly Matthews builds the weight of "Mingus in Diaspora," from his 1995 collection *Time and Money:*

> You could say, I suppose that he ate his way out,
> like the prisoner who starts a tunnel with a spoon,
> or you could say he was one in whom nothing was lost,
> who took it all in, or that he was big as a bus.
>
> He would say, and he did, in one of those blurred
> melismatic slaloms his sentences ran—for all
> the music was in his speech: swift switches of tempo,
> stop-time, double time (he could *talk* in 6/8),
>
> "I just ruined my body." And there, Exhibit A,
> it stood, that Parthenon of fat, the tenant voice

lifted, as we say, since words are a weight, and music.
Silence is lighter than air, for the air we know

rises but to the edge of the atmosphere.
You have to pick up The Bass, as Mingus called
his, with audible capitals, and think of the slow years
the wood spent as a tree, which might well have been

enough for wood, and think of the skill the bassmaker
carried without great thought of it from home
to the shop and back for decades, and know
what bassists before you have played, and know

how much of this is stored in The Bass like energy
in a spring and know how much you must coax out.
How easy it would be, instead, to pull a sword
from a stone. But what's inside the bass wants out,

the way one day you will. Religious stories are rich
in symmetry. You must release as much of this hoard
as you can, little by little, in perfect time,
as the work of the body becomes a body of work.

In an interview with Dave Johnson in 1995, Matthews said, "When you read reviews of classical singing by critics lavish with jargon, you'll run across the phrase *breath control*. It doesn't refer to who can stay underwater the longest but to making, during the singing of a musical passage, a steady stream of right decisions about exactly how much breath to spend on each of the steps required to get from the beginning of the passage to the end. In great singing, good taste, technique, and emotional expressivity become the same thing: the fountain of breath on which the song is born aloft." This is the way well-written poems move, and in the undertow are the counter-melodies, vying for the reader's attention as he circles the poem and the poem's meanings circle and seep into him. Like two hurricanes tied at the tail or the symbol for infinity, the poem and the reader form a coil with one another, in a circulation that can last for a lifetime. Here's Matthews's "Unrelenting Flood":

Black key. White key. No,
that's wrong. It's all tactile;

it's not the information
of each struck key we love,
but how the mind and leavened
heart travel by information.
Think how blind and near-
blind pianists range along
their keyboards by clambering
over notes a sighted man
would notice to leave out,
by stringing it all on one
longing, the way bee-fingered,
blind, mountainous Art
Tatum did, the way we like
joy to arrive: in such
unrelenting flood the only
way we can describe it
is by music or another
beautiful abstraction,
like the ray of sunshine
in a child's drawing
running straight to a pig's ear,
tethering us all to our star.

We need to put everything in, singing or making love, the way Art Tatum played piano: hard, fast, and unusual, all presence and virtuosity pushing the length of the line to its most remote point and then releasing the pressure. In the first section, we talked about how to lead the reader by punctuation and spacing through the map of the poem, "stringing it all on one longing," as Matthews wrote. An incredible player who displayed blinding speed on the keyboard, Tatum was the type of piano player that intimidated mere mortals trying to match his facility. Due to the forbidding nature of his playing, his blindness, being black during the age of segregation, and his quiet personality, Tatum was barely known to the general public and never received the acclaim he deserved. But jazz musicians knew who he was. Charlie Parker got a job washing dishes in the joint where Tatum played just to listen to him on a nightly basis.

The Rhythm Method, Razzmatazz, and Memory

The incredible inventiveness of the jazz musicians from the 1940s and '50s continues to amaze even sixty years later, and their influence on the poetry of the time is incalculable. It is hard to imagine the Beat generation without jazz. At times, it seemed that the best work of Jack Kerouac in the groundbreaking *On The Road* novel, or William S. Burroughs's surreal riffs in *Naked Lunch*, or Allen Ginsberg's dithyrambic indictments of American society were extensions of the jazz records they admired. Many poets in the '50s set their poems to jazz accompaniment. Kenneth Rexroth, Lawrence Ferlinghetti, Kenneth Patchen, Langston Hughes, and many others attempted records with jazz as a backdrop, but it was a shotgun marriage. As Rexroth wrote in his introduction to Kazuko Shiraishi's *Seasons of Sacred Lust*: "Poetry read to jazz had only a brief popularity in America. It was ruined by people who knew nothing about either jazz or poetry."

The music did, however, break down social and cultural barriers, "leap-frogging the guard gates of the black literary community," according to Sascha Feinstein who, along with Yusef Komunyakaa, edited two anthologies of jazz poetry, demonstrating the music's significance in the formation of the black poetic voice, and indeed showcasing jazz's diverse role in the work of many contemporary poets, men and women alike. Feinstein has gone on to found and edit a remarkable journal of jazz writing called *Brilliant Corners*, after Monk's album, which continues to mark the trail that Jazz blazed through the literary landscape. As a force in the black literary community, jazz took its rightful place beside the blues as a language in itself, which opened the boundaries of black expression in fresh and original ways. The work of Larry Neal, Sterling Brown, Jayne Cortez, Amiri Baraka, Michael Harper, Askia Touré, and many, many others reflected their interest in a new literature, carved out of the black experience and filled with the echoes of black musical rhythms.

One of the first of these poets to combine Surrealism, jazz, and the Beat experimental sensibility was Bob Kaufman, known in France as the "Black Rimbaud." In San Francisco's North Beach, he was regarded as the first bebop poet, and he co-edited (along with William Margolis) the renowned *Beatitude Magazine*. Kaufman gave readings with jazz accompaniment and collaborated with many well-known writers of the day, including Ginsberg, Ferlinghetti, Michael McClure, Diane di Prima, Jack Micheline, and Gregory Corso. Many events, besides the immortal jazz concoctions of the time, were lodging themselves in the sensibilities of the poets. The breaking of the unions by the Taft-Hartley Act, the stoning of Paul Robeson, the founding of the state of Israel, the Wallace presidential campaign, the outset of the Cold War, the death of Stalin, the McCarthy Communist trials, and the first stirrings of a true and lasting civil rights movement all came home to roost in the American consciousness. None felt these seismic shifts more deeply than Kaufman, a half black, half German Jew, thirty years old in 1955 when he wrote "War Memoir."

WAR MEMOIR

Jazz—listen to it at your own risk.
At the beginning, a warm dark place.

(Her screams were trumpet laughter,
Not quite blues, but almost sinful.)

Crying above the pain, we forgave ourselves;
Original sin seemed a broken record.
God played blues to kill time, all the time.
Red-waved rivers floated us into life.

(So much laughter, concealed by blood and faith;
Life is a saxophone played by death.)

Greedy to please, we learned to cry;
Hungry to live, we learned to die.
The heart is a sad musician,
Forever playing the blues.

The blues blow life, as life blows fright;
Death begins, jazz blows soft in the night,
Too soft for ears of men whose minds
Hear only the sound of death, of war,

Of flagwrapped cremations in bitter lands.

No chords of jazz as mud is shoveled
Into the mouths of men; even the blues shy
At cries of children dying on deserted corners.
Jazz deserted, leaving us to our burning.

The Rhythm Method, Razzmatazz, and Memory

(Jazz is an African traitor.)

What one-hundred-percent redblooded savage
Wastes precious time listening to jazz
With so much important killing to do?

Silence the drums, that we may hear the burning
Of Japanese in atomic colorcinemascope,
And remember the stereophonic screaming.

Show me a hero, and I'll show you a tragedy. Kaufman's emotional and sensitive cultural antennae were so tuned to injustice that he began to square off with any authority figures he came into contact with, especially the police. He became the most arrested man in North Beach, waging a singular, personal battle with several officers, which usually concluded with nightsticks raining down on his skull at the courthouse. By 1980, the former lion had been reduced to a shadow of his younger self, the victim of an ailing liver and a brain diminished by drugs, beatings, and forced shock treatments undergone at Bellevue Hospital. Here is his poem "Michelangelo the Elder":

I live alone, like a pith in a tree
My teeth rattle, like musical instruments
In one ear a spider spins its web of eyes
In the other a cricket chirps all night
This is the end ...

I would die for poetry.

Certain jazz figures like Charlie Parker and John Coltrane, who came to be seen in quasi-spiritual terms for their otherwordly ability and struggles with drug dependency and mental stability, took on emotional significance for these poets. Parker always memorized the words of the song he was playing. He used the words to construct his solos, a counterpoint to the essential melody, a trampoline to bounce notes across, a crucial bridge of improvisation. Michael Harper has written eloquently of Coltrane and sees through him the black artists' struggle for transcendence in a hostile, impervious society with little need for jazz or poetry. Here is Harper's "The Book on Trane":

THE BOOK ON TRANE

In "Alabama" an off version of spiritual
J. Rosamond Johnson's hymnal holdovers

from his brother's gatherings in the field
James Weldon Johnson not allowed to beckon

his students into his Fisk 'sitting room'
because his wife has covered the furnishings

so James Weldon Johnson stood at the fence in Nashville
talking to his children in creative writing class

ex-slaves accommodating only the highest plane of service
refusing segregation as a supremacist covenant

enacted to prohibit any development
except the group areas acts (in the fields)

yet he has built a church on these vestments
passageway etched in exquisite pain

only tone remembers a scale untended
by the best technicians without the beloved's kiss

the vessel of song is the spiritual
the essence of singing the spirit itself "a love supreme"

The Rhythm Method, Razzmatazz, and Memory

CHAPTER 34

Sheets of Sound: John Coltrane's Musical Consilience

Listening to John Coltrane play sax is like watching a river flood out of its banks, the borders evaporating under the weight, force, and variety of the water's attack. The critic Ira Gitler described Trane's increasingly compact and layered phrasing as "sheets of sound," as his solos swelled with ever-greater intensity and density. His full-throated hailstorms of notes cascade like multiple series of waterfalls. "His continuous flow of ideas without stopping really hit me," Gitler said. "It was almost superhuman. The amount of energy he was using could have powered a spaceship." Trane played every solo as if it were his last. *Village Voice* writer Nat Hentoff said that Coltrane "legitimized the extended solo." Archie Shepp exclaimed that "Coltrane showed the rest of us that we better have stamina to sustain these long flights." Part of the sheer pleasure embodied in listening to Coltrane play comes off as catharsis for the player and the listener, an unbridled release of anger and fury, the pure fury of relentless discovery, the heat of the hunt, the endless varieties of the search for transcendence.

Pianist Zita Carno, writing in *The Jazz Review* in 1959, commented that Coltrane's range "is something to marvel at: a full three octaves upward from the lowest note obtainable on the horn (concert A-flat) ... there are a good many tenor players who have an extensive range, but what sets Coltrane apart is the equality of strength in all registers, which he has been able to obtain through long, hard practice. His sound is just as clear, full, and unforced in the topmost notes as it is down in the bottom." She described his tone as "a result of the particular combination of mouthpiece and reed he

---

uses plus an extremely tight embouchure that produces an incredibly power-ful, resonant, and sharply penetrating sound with a spine-chilling quality."

"The music," Trane said, "is the whole question of life itself." His wife, Alice, who accompanied him on piano in his last band, said, "His music is never complacent. He never stopped surprising himself." Part of Coltrane's ability to surprise himself came from an almost biblical preparedness, com-ing up through the ranks of some of the greatest combos in jazz history. He was born in Hamlet, North Carolina, on September 23, 1926. His father played several instruments and passed this love on to his son. At fifteen, young John learned E-flat alto horn and clarinet, switching to tenor sax while in high school. He studied in Philadelphia at the Granoff Studios and the Ornstein School of Music, becoming a pro at nineteen and playing in a Navy band based in Hawaii from 1945 to 1947. From 1947 to 1949, he ac-companied Joe Webb, King Kolax, Eddie "Cleanhead" Vinson, and Howard McGhee. He was with Dizzy Gillespie's band in 1949, and after the band broke up, Trane drifted from gig to gig in Philly, hooking up with Earl Bostic, Johnny Hodges, Jimmy Smith, and Bud Powell.

He first joined Miles Davis in 1955, recommended by Davis's drummer, Philly Joe Jones. As Davis made his triumphant comeback, Coltrane became the stormy counterpoint to Davis's emotional reticence. Davis, having been present at the inception of bebop, was looking for a different vibe, but the Trane was just leaving the station and gathering a head of steam. Davis was sometimes exasperated by his young charge. Defensively, Coltrane said that once he was immersed in a solo, he didn't know how to stop. "Try taking the saxophone out of your mouth," Davis said. But he knew Coltrane was unique, claiming that Sonny Rollins and Trane were the greatest tenors of all time and that playing with Coltrane was like hiring three sax players in one.

To make the onrush of sound even more urgent, Coltrane experimented by substituting larger numbers of chords and at times shifting the harmony virtually every beat (tricks he learned from the bebop masters Charlie Parker and Sonny Rollins), extending the reach of his instrument, revo-lutionizing saxophone technique, and perfecting the small group's sound and power. He told Wayne Shorter that his aim was to start in the middle of the sentence and progress to its beginning and end at the same time. "I'm not sure what I'm looking for," Trane said, "except that it'll be something that hasn't been played before. I don't know what it is. I know I'll have that feeling when I get it." At home, Trane would practice for hours, sometimes silently, just noodling his fingers over the keys. All the textures inside Coltrane's best playing reflect his immersion in the blues, particularly the blues attack of Dexter Gordon and the smooth full blues sound of Johnny Hodges, both influences as the young Trane assimilated all the colors and approaches of his many and varied mentors.

In 1957, Coltrane joined fellow tarheel Thelonius Monk's quartet, and this short-lived group became a classic. Trane learned to improvise around Monk's angular syncopated themes and rhythms, an acutely difficult challenge in a group expected to cohere around the always sphinxlike and mysterious Monk. "Miss one chord with Monk," Coltrane said, "and you feel like you're falling down an elevator shaft." Coltrane was hooked on narcotics and alcohol for much of the 1950s, and when a deepening religious conviction guided him away from his self-destructive behavior, his spiritual focus opened new vistas of possibility for his playing.

His return to play with Davis resulted in the seminal recording *Kind of Blue*, perhaps the best-selling jazz album of all time. Trane was now ready to begin his career as a leader, and over the next ten years his quartet—with McCoy Tyner, Jimmy Garrison, Elvin Jones, and later Rashied Ali—brought about a seismic change in jazz harmony. The group's even longer improvisations seemed bent on packing in every conceivable variation and inversion of an often conventional pop theme, and they made use of ever greater tonal distortion and timbral effects. In 1960, inspired by Sidney Bechet, Trane added soprano saxophone to his repertoire, making "My Favorite Things" an unlikely jazz hit.

John Coltrane took the idea of improvisations and relentless curiosity to extreme quasi-spiritual levels. Emerging from a background of religious training, the young musician collided with the temptations of secular blues music in his teens and was confronted with the choice of Howlin' Wolf and Jerry Lee Lewis before him: the need to play for the majesty of Heaven and the glory of the Lord, or to further the Devil's music, finding the deepest levels of the flesh and its groove. The Wolf's choice cost him the love of his mother, who turned her back on him. Jerry Lee, unlike his cousin Jimmy Swaggart, extended the vocabulary of Rock and Roll and acquired the moniker of The Killer, literally so, if some accounts are to be believed. Young Coltrane, better prepared and more intellectually adept than his counterparts, chose both paths at once. The music of the ecstatic congregations that surrounded him as a child and the indelible mark of voices giving free reign to their innermost emotional expressions of joy and worship sweltered through the horn of the young jazzman and became a trademark of his future compositions.

Rhythm and blues—with its honking and wailing tenor saxophones, exquisitely rendered by such masters as Coleman Hawkins and Illinois Jacquet—collided with the inevitable explosions of bebop and the olympic alto muscularity of Charlie Parker, creating a new country for an insatiably open and willing player, one who might take all of these elements and surrender himself to perfecting whatever problems might confront him. This infinite desire is evident in the classic Coltrane albums *Giant Steps* and the unforgettable *A Love Supreme*.

Coltrane expanded the lessons of western classical music and Igor Stravinsky by incorporating classical figures into unforeseen musical arrangements, illustrating their tonal similarities and building a bridge for the listener to both the jazz and orchestral worlds. All of the bebop giants took the concept of harmony more seriously than their predecessors. And this union of old and new found its nexus in the modern jazz explorations of Coltrane's quartet. Coltrane became a conduit for the decade to come and would expand the possibilities of all musical genres. He used dense, rapidly changing chords with complex extensions built on each note of the chord and played with remarkable dexterity. While Parker was a soloist of blinding speed and facility, Coltrane was a Bentley to Parker's Maserati, gliding through his solos with surprising tonal grace and astonishing textures, never landing in the same place twice. His first popularly accepted recording (a modal rendering of "My Favorite Things" from the musical play *The Sound of Music*), expanded the lessons learned from the Miles Davis Quintet, and gave a glimpse into what was possible for pop and avant garde expression, a hint of what the Great Trane was capable of, converting even Julie Andrews into a swirling Moroccan dervish.

Through constant evolution, Coltrane's techniques—and, later, his quartet—became a platform for introducing innovative ideas, constantly pushing the boundaries of what had been previously acceptable. By all accounts, Coltrane was relentless, putting the music under constant pressure. Like a boxer who needs to enter the ring already sweating, he would work himself

The Rhythm Method, Razzmatazz, and Memory

into a frenzy backstage and land on the bandstand flying, already lathered and ready to hit the arrangements with every conceivable combination of punches. He would impact a whole generation of composers known as "The Minimalists," including La Monte Young and Philip Glass, who used fixed constellations of tones and then pressed the arrangements into interesting mathematical permutations. Coltrane's advancement of his instrument was stunning; it was as if Lester Young was transported to India and given a blue coat of many notes, a plumage of ideas flying out of a single central theme, streamers that the bluesmen could never have conceived. This was a music that explored all emotional sensibilities and invited the listener to actively participate and engage with these deep-seated physical vibrations. *A Love Supreme*, taken in this context, becomes a mantra for all the spiritual musical movements that followed it—a magical *Om* trailing away from the repeated melody, inviting the trance.

Whereas *Giant Steps* was a leap toward independence as a musician and a man, *A Love Supreme* was a leap toward God by a man who had mortgaged his physical health, as a result of submerging himself in heroin and booze, and now felt compelled to praise his maker and seek the grace of transcendence and redemption. *Giant Steps* got its name from the fact that "the bass line is kind of a loping one," said Trane. "It goes from minor thirds to fourths, kind of a lopsided pattern in contrast to moving strictly in fourths or in half-steps." The foundations of *A Love Supreme* are almost childishly slight, and yet one hears a majestic outpouring of sound, couched in a language that is brutally violent, replete with split notes, multiphonics, and toneless breaths and chants. "It is a gift to God," Trane said, "a humble offering to Him. I feel this has been granted through His grace." After the album's enormous success, Trane headed down the path of the avant-garde, and his audiences dwindled as his health waned. Liver cancer would eventually overwhelm him at the age of forty. But he had been to the mountaintop. Indeed, if the mountain, under the weight of the sky, could speak, it would sound like Trane.

ARTISTIC CONSILIENCE: FIRES IN EVERY DIRECTION

Coltrane's approach and layering of tones served as remarkable example for me as a young poet. Under the influence of Rainer Maria Rilke, Wallace

Stevens, and Pablo Neruda, I wanted my poems to contain much, clusters of associations that hinted at the connectedness of all things but stated musically, matter-of-factly, gaining momentum as the narrative passed, the way songs do. Almost every pop song in the universe has the same basic structure: verse-chorus-verse-chorus-bridge(solo)-verse-chorus-outro(vamp)-conclusion; and the concluding vamp may be a separate section of music, but it is most likely the chorus or verse repeated ad infinitum with the hook or title sung over that chord progression to hammer it home, deep into the listener's inner ear. Coltrane created certain pieces that operated as hooks throughout the entire composition. In Miles Davis's *So What*, for example, two alternating chords spiral like kung fu throwing stars over and over in space as the intensity mounts and each instrument adds its variation to the mix. Layer upon layer of improvisation is laid neatly down across the bedrock of alternating chords, just as the sediments of Earth naturally commingle and cohere. *A Love Supreme* contains elements of the same technique. It is not surprising, therefore, to find other artists of the time employing similar strategies to their literary enterprises.

The collage techniques of William Burroughs, borrowed from the Surrealists, gathered life randomly, allowing the execution of the maker's immediate instinct to place the pieces just so, revealing a structure only after the maker stops. It was Paul Valéry who said that poems are never finished but merely abandoned, and thus their notch in time finds its beginning and its end, improvisation in its purest form. Jackson Pollock's drip technique and Willem de Kooning's abstract expressions came from the same wellspring. This collision of intentions and genres allowed for much collaboration among poets and jazzmen, painters and choreographers. Truman Capote and Norman Mailer wrote *In Cold Blood* and *The March on Washington*, respectively, books which merged journalism with long form prose, resulting in the nonfiction or historical novel. Hunter S. Thompson took this merger a step further in his gonzo missives, making literary journalism with its pants pulled down, as he covered the Hell's Angels and Nixon's presidential campaign. Just as Arthur Rimbaud had made Charles Baudelaire's dream come true a half-century before by making poems that operated as prose in his remarkable book *Illuminations*, many poets, such as Umberto Eco, Russell Edson, Robert Bly, and James Wright took Surrealism and injected its particular venom into the prose poem cluster to form a new animal. Michael

The Rhythm Method, Razzmatazz, and Memory

Ondaatje's *Collected Works of Billy the Kid* was neither fish nor fowl, constructed from anecdotes, journal entries, newspaper clippings, and lyrical prose musings to form a book of unique color that operated as biography.

Music then showed its ability to mutate as well, and the 1960s and '70s were a time of supreme experimentation and synthesis. Miles Davis's flirtations with rock bred fusion, which bred the Mahavishnu Orchestra. Steely Dan (whose name was derived from a William Burroughs novel) was a gumbo of existential poetry, extreme pop, cultural sensibilities, science fiction, and jazz. Bob Dylan merged folk and rock and French Symbolism. James Brown invented funk, an amalgam of jazz, blues, bop, and gospel refrains. Sly and The Family Stone merged psychadelia and pop, followed by Parliament and Mother's Finest, who took rock and funky soul to heights only a Mothership could reach. Tom Waits found a grumbling stew of barrelhouse blues and carnival dirges, German marches and Dixieland ragtime suites married to Louis Armstrong's rotted hellboy of a voice.

Rock poets emerged, shape-shifting out of the trail that Bob Dylan had blazed. Leonard Cohen—with a foot in two worlds, both literary and musical—fashioned harrowing love songs and hip, savvy poetry out of his Jamaican and Canadian backgrounds. Jim Morrison, Patti Smith, John Trudell, Jim Carroll, Nick Cave, and Exene Cervenka fought out of dire beginnings to become poets that spoke to the underdogs and disaffected youth of the emerging class-divided culture and its 1980s nihilism. The rock poets fronted bands and published books; singing their lyrics seemed essential to the impact of their narratives. The antihero was born.

John Coltrane has been written about in more poems than any other jazz figure. "It seems safe to say," wrote Joe Goldberg, "that Trane has replaced Charlie Parker as the Hipster Saint of Jazz." Trane's death on July 17, 1967, was followed by the explosion of rock and roll, the year of *Sergeant Pepper*, the assassinations of Bobby Kennedy and Dr. King the following year, and the era when bohemian animism devolved into disco chic and porn. Jazz became the haven of an increasingly immense minority. For sheer improvisational skill, there is still Sonny Rollins—after all these years, a master of the moment, where a horn and a man complete a cycle, like plugging a power tool into the wall socket to watch the sparks of sound fly forth, building a fire in every direction.

CHAPTER 35

This Land Is Our Land: The Real Folk Blues

John Lomax, who had already documented the fading Western songs of the nineteenth century, was commissioned by the Library of Congress to scour the country in search of valuable musical traditions and to record them for posterity. Along with his son, Alan, Lomax took the portable recording equipment in the back of his station wagon and made priceless recordings of artists as diverse as Leadbelly, the great Huddie Ledbetter, a folk singer they discovered in the Angola State Penitentiary in 1933. "When I blow my horn," he said, "the axes git to walking, and the gypsies git to talking." Helping Leadbelly secure a pardon from the governor, the Lomaxes booked him all over the country to wildly enthusiastic crowds. The fiercely proud performer got tired of performing in prison stripes and driving the Lomax car. He embarked on a tour of his own and landed in New York City, where he did gigs in union houses and speakeasy taverns, attracting the attention of a young Pete Seeger and his buddy Woody Guthrie.

Guthrie had left Oklahoma at the age of sixteen, after his mother was institutionalized with Huntington's disease, his father went bankrupt at the height of the Dust Bowl famines, and his sister died in a fire. Young Guthrie hoped that music would save him. The ultimate defender of the impoverished masses, Guthrie wrote songs that protested the ill treatment of those less fortunate and became the role model for the entire folk protest movement that emerged in the 1960s. Guthrie's guitar was a weapon; his songs approached the level of poetry and called the cavalry. On his guitar body, a phrase was written: "This machine kills fascists." Sitting in a truck stop

The Rhythm Method, Razzmatazz, and Memory

Guthrie heard Kate Smith's version of "God Bless America," and immediately penned one of the most patriotic and beloved songs of all time, "This Land Is Your Land":

This land is your land. This land is my land,
From California to the New York island;
From the redwood forest to the Gulf Stream waters,
This land was made for you and me.

As I was walking the ribbon of highway,
I saw above me that endless skyway.
I saw below me that golden valley;
This land was made for you and me.

I've roamed and rambled and I followed my footsteps,
To the sparkling sand of her diamond deserts,
And all around me a voice was sounding:
This land was made for you and me.

When the sun came shining, and I was strolling,
And the wheat fields waving and the dust clouds rolling,
As the fog was lifting a voice was chanting:
This land was made for you and me.

As I went walking I saw a sign there,
And on the sign it said "No Trespassing."
But on the other side it didn't say nothing;
That side was made for you and me.

In the shadow of the steeple I saw my people;
By the relief office I seen my people.
As they stood there hungry, I stood there asking
Is this land made for you and me?

Nobody living can ever stop me,
As I go walking that freedom highway.
Nobody living can ever make me turn back;
This land was made for you and me.

The Weavers, whose recording of Leadbelly's "Good Night Irene" became wildly popular, brought folk music to the radio, but their left-leaning politics caused them to be blacklisted by the anti-Communist hysteria of the late 1950s. The liberal college campuses across the nation embraced this traditional style of folk and bluegrass string bands, and the Kingston Trio, the Lost City Ramblers, and eventually, Peter, Paul and Mary, extended the folk revival to represent political causes—and this scene gained widespread popularity as the political mood of the country changed. The coffee houses sponsored hootenannies and gatherings of folk-songwriters like Joan Baez, Richie Havens, Pete Seeger, and a young Bob Dylan, who would play in Washington Square in New York City and in folk clubs like The Bitter End, honing their craft and attracting the young, hip, politically-energized students who would form the vanguard of the various revolutions in the 1960s counter-culture. This spiritual and political awakening found expression in the lyrics of the new troubadours, especially Dylan, who took Woody Guthrie as a model for his simple harmonica and guitar accompaniment, and as a setting for his lyrics, lyrics unlike any written before in American popular music, changing the expectation and possibilities for songcraft forever.

This folk revival caused producers to scour the countryside and resurrect the careers of some older blues musicians and folk performers who could fit in the format of the Newport Folk Festival, including spectacular flat pickers like Doc Watson, the rootsy songs of Mississippi John Hurt, a re-energized Sippie Wallace, and Son House, among others. The civil rights movement and new hippie values brought a diversity and freedom to the radio with formats never heard before or since. The inmates took over the asylum and rewrote the playbook, making any music with legitimate feeling and soulful emotional interpretation capable of finding an audience. All preconceived notions of what constituted pop music were swept away.

CHAPTER 36

Busy Being Born: Dylan, Hip Hop, and the Slam Movement

Equipped with James Dean's radical orphan sneer and swagger, Jimmie Rodger's hobo gospel, and Woody Guthrie and Leadbelly's sense of social justice, Bob Dylan understood the true radicalism and smoky insouciance of Elvis Presley and wanted to be present in the triangle of Blues and Beats and folk rebellion. An artist with the guts to fight the plantation owners and politicians (the combination that made the military-industrial complex that so frightened Ike), Dylan shouted in "Masters of War": "I just want you to know/ I can see through your masks/...And I hope that you die/ and your death'll come soon."

To the establishment, a poet was much less dangerous than a Beatle—especially with his antimedia stance—and Dylan's unwillingness to condescend to the audience helped him make grand pronouncements, even prophecies. Dylan understood how the Beats had broken open the status quo like an egg and all the king's horses would never put it back together with the same soft center. No war machine or soldier could pin down the civil rights and women's movements, the explosion of black rage and sexual expression. The youth became the new "unacknowledged legislators," and every facet of society was crystallized in this new light, shedding taboos and shadows and opening their minds and bodies to true revolution, the freedom of every person to say or do whatever they please, wherever they are in the world. Nothing would be the same as the blues burst out of the mouths of the poets and prophets, Gandhi and Martin Luther King, Jr. yielding to no injustice anywhere, no inhibition, no bayonet stronger than the will of the youth to believe in their new-found strength. Dylan was the voice of this resistance, transparent and mystical at once.

Around his slender neck, all the movements hung their heavy laurels. Under this burden, his songs turned fierce and, like Muddy Waters before him, the only way to make his voice large as the spirit that moved it would be to electrify. To make the regular chord Moby Dick fearsome, it had to have *power*, and the power chord required electricity. Split the electron and you create nuclear energy. Split open the placid society with an electric guitar and you have the energy that is "eternal delight," as William Blake said and Pete Townsend proved, with a roundhouse swing of his skinny right arm. When Muddy Waters electrified the Blues, the effect was cataclysmic, nuclear, the Blues on steroids, but when Dylan electrified, the protest from the folk singers at the Newport Folk Festival was deafening, self-defeating, and negative in the extreme. "They say sing while you slave and I just get bored. I ain't gonna work on Maggie's farm no more," Dylan sang. Like a black star, the movement collapsed in upon itself.

While Dylan's place in the pantheon of American musicians is secure, a debate still rages as to whether his work should be considered in the context of poetry. When asked that question in 1965, he famously answered, "I think of myself as more of a song-and-dance man." In 2004, *Newsweek* magazine called Dylan "the most influential cultural figure now alive," and he continues to be a viable force, having recently won an Academy Award and collected his first number one album, entitled *Modern Times*, on the *Billboard* charts. He has released more than forty albums in the last four decades, covering every conceivable style, and has created some of the most durable anthems of the twentieth century, with several now classic albums, including *Highway 61 Revisited, Blonde On Blonde,* and *Blood On the Tracks.* Proof of Dylan's relevance lies in part in the number of books published about him; here are a few recent ones: *Dylan's Visions of Sin,* by Oxford professor Christopher Ricks who makes the case for Dylan as a poet; *Lyrics 1962–2001,* a collection of Dylan songs presented in book form; *Keys To The Rain,* a 724-page Dylan encyclopedia; *Chronicles,* the first volume of his autobiography; and *Studio A,* an anthology of collected writing about Dylan by such esteemed writers as Joyce Carol Oates, Barry Hannah, Rick Moody, Allen Ginsberg, and others.

Christopher Ricks, who has also penned books about T. S. Eliot and John Keats, argued not only that Dylan's lyrics qualify as poetry but also that Dylan is among the finest poets of all time, on the same level as John Milton, Keats, and Alfred Tennyson. He points to Dylan's mastery of rhymes, which are often startling and perfectly judged; take, for example, this pairing from "Idiot Wind," released in 1975:

> Idiot wind, blowing like a circle around my skull,
> From the Grand Coulee Dam to the Capitol

"The case for denying Dylan the title of poet could not summarily, if at all, be made good by any open-minded close attention to the words and his ways with them," Ricks wrote in *Dylan's Visions of Sin.* "The case would need to begin with his medium." The problem many critics have with calling song lyrics poetry is that songs are only fully realized in performance. It takes the lyrics, music, and voice working in tandem to unpack the power of a song, whereas a poem ideally stands up by itself, on the page, controlling its own timing and internal music. Dylan's lyrics, and most especially his creative rhyme-making, may only work, as critic Ian Hamilton has written, with "Bob's barbed-wire tonsils in support." It is indisputable, though, that Dylan has been influenced a great deal by poetry. He counts Arthur Rimbaud and Paul Verlaine alongside Woody Guthrie as his most important forebears. He took his stage name, Bob Dylan, from the Welsh poet Dylan Thomas. (His real name is Robert Allen Zimmerman.) He described himself once as a "sixties troubadour," and when he talks about songwriting, he can sometimes sound like a professor of literature: "I can create several orbits that travel and intersect each other and are set up in a metaphysical way."

He has called Smokey Robinson his favorite poet and has been nominated for the Nobel Prize for Literature every year since 1996. It seems Dylan makes his own rules, but he has emerged as a nexus where every musical and literary movement intersected and took root. Here are lines 29–38 of Dylan's "Visions of Johanna":

> Inside the museums, Infinity goes up on trial
> Voices echo this is what salvation must be like after a while
> But Mona Lisa musta had the highway blues
> You can tell by the way she smiles

See the primitive wallflower freeze

When the jelly-faced women all sneeze

Hear the one with the mustache say, "Jeeze

I can't find my knees"

Oh, jewels and binoculars hang from the head of the mule

But these visions of Johanna, they make it all seem so cruel

FROM THE PAGE TO THE STAGE: ALGEBRA AND FIRE

"He not busy being born/ is busy dying," Dylan sang in "It's Alright, Ma." He has influenced all the music that followed him, from the Beatles to Eminem. In fact, it may be the rap artists who have most benefited from his example of lyrical intensity and social concern.

For all the various incarnations of hip hop music that have existed over the last thirty years, one immutable fact emerges: hip hop means empowerment. For rappers, a "dope" rhyme paired with your buddy's beats can move you out of the ghetto or, in less severe circumstances, give you a platform with which to state your beliefs or paint a picture of wrongs that need to be righted. Beck's famous hook "two turntables and a microphone" is an inventory for all that is needed by a rap artist to emerge creatively, combining an original viewpoint with an endless supply of sampled beats. Charles Ive's contention that "American music has already been written" was never more true. Rap artists sampled the chord progressions of a wide diversity of artists that preceded them. James Brown, Sly Stone, and George Clinton's publishing catalogues were assailed hammer and tong for the deep ore mines of funky grooves that flowed through them. Now the *Billboard* charts typically have several rap albums in the *Top 10* of any given week, and rap artists wield considerable influence in the music industry.

Since the protest raps of Gil-Scott Herron in the late 1960s and the rise of rap music in the culture in the '80s, the spoken-word movement is now a multimillion dollar enterprise, with an incredible amount of venues for poets and spoken-word performers to ply their trade. The revitalization of many urban areas—with a focus on their downtowns and city centers—the rise of rap and hip hop, and the burgeoning slam movement has created an environment for poets that is welcoming and wildly competitive. From the first slams in Chicago in 1986, fostered by construction

The Rhythm Method, Razzmatazz, and Memory

worker and poet Marc Smith at the Green Mill, to the multimedia Slam Olympics of the present day, even the sternest critics would be forced to admit that more people are listening to poetry, be it good or bad, than ever before. On any given day, in cafés and local watering holes, churches and student centers, poets are competing and cajoling one another with only their poetry as weapons. No longer is a poet automatically assumed to be an out-of-work bohemian; now there are poets from every walk of life, screaming their Whitman-esque "barbaric yawp" wherever they can find a stage. Most of the work runs the gamut of styles, from odes of unrequited love to protest monologues, decrying society's inequities. Like the rap artists, but with lesser financial leverage, poetry slams have become a cultural mainstay, a viable part of the entertainment industry, with poets perched on Broadway stages, television screens, radio programs, and movie theaters.

Whether we are mistaking poetry "performance" for the reading of true poetry, as some would suggest, is irrelevant. The fact that audiences are interested in the spoken-word helps maintain a sense of literary community in an atmosphere where fewer large publishers are talking the time to publish books of poetry and where book reviews of these collections have mostly vanished from the mainstream media. If the dire prognosticators of the NEA are to be believed, fewer people are reading books of any kind than ever before, even though more books are being published than at any time in history. It is probably unhealthy to speculate whether these extremes can be reconciled, but rather than lamenting the viability of any one style or group, we should find the atmosphere conducive to the art of poetry, strive to make the best poetry possible, and present it with the "right combination of algebra and fire," to quote Jorge Luis Borges.

It is true that many slam poets are better actors than poets, just as too many over-rated academic poets could stand to act a little better, or at least as if they cared whether the audience has been satisfied. We have spent the last hundred pages discussing a century's worth of music and musical performers in an attempt to delineate the aspects of their various strategies that might be assimilated by the poetry performer and add to their ability as a creator, both publicly and privately. With that in mind, let's review a few last reminders that might add to the performance of your poetry from the page to the stage.

1. Whether you are a published poet or a beginner, you have the same responsibilities to the audience: to give them every opportunity to understand your work and to respect their time.

2. The only poets actually selling books do so on the strength and quantity of their appearances at bookstores, universities, and libraries. Take into account the background and geography of your audience.

3. When reading with a group or another poet, be respectful of your allotment of time. There is no need to sully your name by hogging the time of others and going over your time limit. Treat others as you would like to be treated. Keep your performance tight.

4. Make eye contact with your audience—all of your audience—and pick out someone to occasionally refer to whose facial expressions (or lack thereof) may be a barometer for your performance. Practice by reading into a mirror and a tape recorder. If you don't know what you look like or sound like before you arrive, then every reading will be an experiment. That's a petri dish you don't want to land in. Be prepared, *always*.

5. Read slowly, carefully, and patiently, adding the necessary weight and pressure to emphasize line breaks and points of greater importance. Don't mutter or whisper. Test your microphone *before* you begin, and know the strength of it. Poor mic technique will create screeching distortions; keep too much distance and you will never be understood. If it's a small group, do without the sound system, but respond accordingly to the size of the room. Better to have it and not need it than the opposite.

6. Prepare your audience for the complexity or special requirements of your poem. Some background and explication may be necessary, but don't overdo it. The audience is always smarter than most poets give them credit for, and lord knows, the circumstances of every creation is not sacred or necessary. Let the audience in on vital details of your creative life and process. This will foster valuable intimacy.

7. Try to preface your remarks with humor, or share your humorous work first. Nothing wins a crowd faster than a collective belly laugh. Humility always wears well, and hitting the audience on the funny bone will win them every time.

8. Don't bring unfinished work and make guinea pigs out of your audience. Reading a well-rehearsed poem for the first time may be memorable for you and the audience, but no need to try a half-baked cake. No one will digest it properly.

9. If you have poems that you are known for, then certainly you should meet the expectations of your audience and read them. The poems may be old to you, but for every audience, pretend it's Groundhog Day (unless you've been there before) and give them what they want.

10. Have all your materials prepared beforehand. Nothing is worse than watching some fool nervously fumble through a jumble of pages, frantically trying to recall where they put a poem, or worse still, blithely ignoring the audience as they search book to book waiting for inspiration to strike.

11. Always assume that you need to seduce your audience, that they don't know who you are, and expect that you need to win them over. Even if you're relatively well known, your audience would appreciate a surprise. Be present and have a backup plan just in case you have misjudged your audience. Never let 'em see you sweat. Audiences are notoriously callous or overwhelmingly tender, but it depends on your preparedness.

Okay, now you're ready. Decide who you are and what you wish to project, and stick to it. Give your work its best chance to be heard, and read everywhere you can—wherever they will book you. Nothing succeeds like experience. I'll leave you with this little chestnut from my latest collection, *The Golden Ratio*:

LISTENING AS ANOTHER FAMOUS MAN
BADLY READS HIS POEMS

In the intervals between laborious searches
for page numbers and breathless meditation,
a man audibly chewing ice mutters
in his bourbon and two vigilant crickets
are engaged in musical foreplay downstage,
when suddenly the poem begins, the natty
monotone delivered like a phone conversation

with a mother-in-law about fertilizing her lawn,
and before the nodding audience knows what hit
them, the piece abruptly ends, and two nervous
claps clop unevenly from a candlelit corner.
Then the bloated quiet and rustling pages begin anew.
One night Aladdin shoes and self-deprecating jokes
to lower expectations. Another night, a soiled hair
shirt and uncombed freshly wakened beard bits keep
the local blue-voiced groupie mavens at bay.
The glamour of the cold page makes administrators
woozy with freshly-cut checks, and stunned
undergraduates change their majors to business law,
knowing now that Dad was right all along, and the
rhythm is lost or abandoned, and the canned comments
so scripted that they garner more interest than the text,
which becomes illegible in the mouth of its master,
a bowhead whale tumbling behind his massive girth,
 shoveling compliments in his maw like plankton,
Pulitzer riding on his snout like a hood ornament,
and all six-winged hope is drowned in his throat.
And no matter how mundane the personal experience,
the circumstance of each creation is sacred, pouring
his charm into our cups, which rattle on the bars
inside ourselves, trapped as we are,
fawning at the altar of fame, awkward and gawking,
like penguins baptized by a near-sighted priest.

BIBLIOGRAPHY

PART 1: LEARNING TO LISTEN

Atkinson, Brooks. *The Selected Writings of Ralph Waldo Emerson* (New York: The Modern Library, 1950)

Bettelheim, Bruno. *The Uses of Enchantment* (New York: Alfred A. Knopf, 1976)

Bloom, Harold. *Wallace Stevens: The Poems of Our Climate* (Ithaca and London: Cornell University Press, 1980)

Campbell, Joseph. *The Power of Myth* (New York: Anchor Books, 1991)

Clark, Tom. *Charles Olson: The Allegory of a Poet's Life* (Berkeley, CA: North Atlantic Books, 2000)

Creeley, Robert. *The Collected Poems: 1945-1975* (Berkley and Los Angeles: University of California Press, 1982)

Davis, Christina and Christopher Edgar, eds. *Illuminations: Great Writers on Writing* (New York: T&Wbooks, 2003)

Dickinson, Emily. *The Complete Poems*, ed. Thomas H. Johnson (Boston, MA and Toronto, Canada: Little, Brown, 1960)

Ellman, Richard and Robert O'Clair, eds. *The Norton Anthology of Modern Poetry* (New York: W.W. Norton, 1973)

Emoto, Masaru. *The Hidden Messages in Water*, trans. David A. Thayne (Hillsboro, OR: Beyond Words, 2004)

Hugo, Richard. *The Triggering Town* (New York and London: W. W. Norton, 1979)

Kermode, Frank. *Pieces of My Mind* (New York: Farrar, Straus and Giroux, 2003)

Koch, Kenneth. *Making Your Own Days* (New York: ouchstone, 1999)

Mac Liammoir, Michael, and Eavan Boland. *W.B. Yeats and His World* (New York: Viking Press, 1971)

Perkins, David, ed. *English Romantic Writers* (San Diego, New York, Chicago, etc.: Harcourt Brace Jovanovich, 1967)

Phillips, Rodney, ed. *The Hand of the Poet: Poems and Papers in Manuscript* (New York: Rizzoli International, 1997)

Plimpton, George. *Poets at Work: The* Paris Review *Interviews* (New York: Penguin Books, 1989)

Rilke, Rainer Maria. *The Selected Poetry*, ed., trans. Stephen Mitchell (New York: Vintage International, 1989)

—. *Letters on Cézanne*, trans. Joel Agee (New York: From International Publishing Corp., 1985)

—. *Letters of Rainer Maria Rilke, 1892-1910*, trans. Jane Bonnard Greene and M. D. Herter (New York: W.W. Norton, 1945)

—. *Selected Poems*, trans. Robert Bly (New York: Harper & Row, 1981)

Roberts, Stephen Morris. *A Space Inside a Space* (Laurinburg, NC: St. Andrews College Press, 1999)

Roethke, Theodore. *On Poetry & Craft* (Port Townsend, WA: Copper Canyon Press, 2001)

Sandburg, Carl. *Poems for the People*, ed. George Hendrick and Willene Hendrick (Chicago: Ivan R. Dee, 1999)

Sexton, Anne. *The Complete Poems* (Boston, MA: Houghton Mifflin, 1981)

Shenk, Joshua Wolf. *Lincoln's Melancholy* (New York: Houghton Mifflin, 2006)

Stevens, Wallace. *The Collected Poems* (New York: Alfred A. Knopf, 1999)

Whitman, Walt. *Selected Poems* (Avenel, NJ and New York: Gramercy Books, 1992)

Wicker, Christine. *Not in Kansas Anymore* (New York: Harper Collins, 2005)

Williams, William Carlos. *Selected Poems*, ed. Charles Tomlinson (New York: New Directions, 1985)

PART 2:
LEARNING TO OBSERVE

Apollinaire, Guillaume. *Alcools*, trans. Donald Revell (Hanover and London: Wesleyan University Press, published by University Press of New England, 1995)

Auster, Paul. *The Random House Book of Twentieth Century French Poetry* (New York: Vintage Books, 1984)

Bachelard, Gaston. *The Poetics of Reverie: Childhood, Language, and the Cosmos* (Boston, MA: Beacon Press, 1969)

Barnstone, Willis. *With Borges on an Ordinary Evening in Buenos Aires* (Urbana and Chicago: University of Illinois Press, 2000)

Baudelaire, Charles. *The Flowers of Evil*, ed. Jackson Mathews and Marthiel Mathews (New York: New Directions, 1989)

—. *Paris Spleen, 1896*, trans. Louise Varèse (New York: New Directions, 1970)

Baudelaire, Charles, Arthur Rimbaud, and Paul Verlaine. *Selected Verse and Prose Poems*, ed. Joseph Bernstein (New York: Citadel Press, 1990)

Bernard, Suzanne, *Le poème en prose de Baudelaire à nos jours* (Paris : Nizet, 1959)

Borges, Jorge Luis. *Dream Tigers*, trans. Mildred Boyer and Harold

Morland (New York: E. P. Dutton, 1970)

—. *Selected Poems*, ed. Alexander Coleman (New York: Viking, 1999)

Breton, André. *Poems*, ed., trans. Jean-Pierre Cauvin and Mary Ann Caws (Boston, MA: Black Widow Press, 2006)

Calvocoressi, Richard. *Magritte* (Oxford: Phaidon Press, 1990)

Cendrars, Blaise. *Selected Writings*, ed. Walter Albert (New York, NY: New Directions, 1966)

Cocteau, Jean. *The Blood of a Poet and the Testament of Orpheus*, trans. Carol Martin-Sperry (Marion Book Publishers, New York & London: 1985)

Cocteau, Jean. *Diary of an Unknown*, trans. Jesse Bronner (Paragon House: New York, 1988)

Cohen, Rachel. *A Chance Meeting* (New York: Random House, 2004)

Dalí, Salvador. *The Secret Life of Salvador Dalí*, trans. Haakon M. Chevalier (New York: Dial Press, 1942; San Antonio, TX: DASA Editions, 1986)

Dervaux, Isabelle. *Surrealism USA* (New York: Hatje Cantz, 2005)

Descharnes, Robert. *Dali*, trans. Eleanor R. Morse (New York: Abradale Press, 1993)

Éluard, Paul. *Letters to Gala* (New York: Paragon House, 1989)

Friebert, Stuart and David Young, eds. *Contemporary American Poetry* (New York and London: Longman, 1983)

Heiting, Manfred, ed. *Man Ray* (Köln, London, Madrid, etc.: Taschen, 2001)

Hirsch, Edward. *The Demon and the Angel* (New York: Harcourt, 2002)

—. *Poet's Choice* (New York, London, Toronto, etc.: Harcourt, 2006)

Jastrow, Joseph. *Freud: His Dream and Sex Theories* (New York: Pocket Books, 1954)

Lake, Carlton. *In Quest of Dali* (New York: Paragon House, 1990)

Lorca, Federico García. *In Search of Duende*, ed. Christopher Maurer (New York: New Directions, 1998)

—. *Poem of the Deep Song*, trans. Carlos Bauer (San Francisco: City Lights Books, 1987)

—. *The Selected Poems*, Francisco García Lorca and Donald M. Allen, eds. (New York: New Directions, 1955)

Mailer, Norman. *Portrait of Picasso as a Young Man* (New York: The Atlantic Monthly Press, 1995)

Malraux, André. *Picasso's Mask*, trans. June Guicharnaud and Jacques Guicharnaud (New York: Da Cappo Press, 1994)

Matthews, J. H. *Surrealism and the Novel* (Ann Arbor, MI: The University of Michigan Press, 1969)

McClanahan, Rebecca. *Word Painting: A Guide to Writing More Descriptively* (Cincinnati, OH: Writer's Digest Books, 1999)

Neruda, Pablo. *Memoirs*, trans. Hardie St. Martin (New York: Penguin Books, 1978)

—. *Selected Poems*, ed. Nathaniel Tarn (New York: Delta, 1970)

Neruda, Pablo and César Vallejo. *Selected Poems*, ed. Robert Bly (Boston, MA: Beacon Press, 1993)

Prose, Francine, ed. *The Lives of the Muses* (New York: Harper Collins, 2002)

Revell, Donald. *Invisible Green: Selected Prose* (Richmond, CA: Omnidawn, 2005)

Reverdy, Pierre. *Selected Poems*, ed. Mary Ann Caws, trans. John Ashberry, Mary Ann Caws, and Patricia Terry (Winston-Salem, NC: 1991)

—. *Selected Poems*, trans. Kenneth Rexroth (New York: New Directions, 1969)

Rimbaud, Arthur. *The Complete Works*, trans. Wallace Fowlie (Chicago and London: The University of Chicago Press, 1967)

—. *Illuminations*, trans. Louise Varèse (New York: New Directions, 1957)

—. *Illuminations and Other Prose Poems*, trans. Louise Varèse, rev. ed. (New York: New Directions, 1957)

Schroeder, Jean. *Pierre Reverdy* (Boston, MA: Twayne Publishers, 1981)

Shapiro, Karl. *Creative Glut*, ed. Robert Phillips (Chicago: Ivan R. Dee, 2004)

Sinclair, Andrew. *Dylan Thomas: No Man More Magical* (New York: Holt, Reinhart and Winston, 1975)

Steinmetz, Jean-Luc. *Arthur Rimbaud: Presence of an Enigma*, trans. Jon Graham (New York: Welcome Rain Publishers, 2001)

Villon, François. *The Poems of François Villon*, trans. Gallway Kinnell (Boston: Houghton Mifflin, 1977)

Wright, James. *Above the River: The Complete Poems* (Hanover and London: Wesleyan University Press, 1992)

PART 3:
LEARNING TO SPEAK

Bangs, Lester. *Psychotic Reactions and Carburetor Dung*, ed. Greil Marcus (New York, NY: Alfred A. Knopf, 1987)

Bishop, Clifford. *Sex and Spirit: Ecstasy and Transcendence, Ritual and Taboo, the Undivided Self* (London: Duncan Baird Publishers, 1996).

Boucher, David. *Dylan and Cohen: Poets of Rock and Roll* (New York and London: Continuum International, 2004)

McKinney, B. B., ed. *The Broadman Hymnal* (Nashville, TN: Broadman Press, 1940)

Cook, Richard, and Brian Morton. *The Penguin Guide to Jazz* (New York: Penguin Books, 2004)

Darton, Frederick J. H., ed. *Stories of Romance from the Age of Chivalry* (New York, NY: Arlington House, 1984)

Davis, Francis. *Jazz and its Discontents* (Cambridge, MA: Da Cappo Press, 2004)

Davis, Miles and Quincy Troupe. *Miles* (New York: Touchstone, 1990)

Dixon, Willie, and Don Snowden. *I am the Blues: The Willie Dixon Story* (New York: Da Capo Press, 1989)

Dylan, Bob. *Chronicles*, Vol. 1 (New York, London, Toronto, and Sydney: Simon & Schuster, 2005)

—. *The Essential Interviews*, ed. Jonathan Cott (New York, NY: Wenner Books, 2006)

—. *Writings and Drawings* (New York: Borzoi Books, 1981)

Fowlie, Wallace. *Rimbaud and Jim Morrison: The Rebel as Poet* (Durham, NC and London: Duke University Press, 1994)

Gordon, Robert. *Can't Be Satisfied: The Life and Times of Muddy Waters* (Boston, New York, and London: Little, Brown & Company, 2002)

Gray, Martin. *Blues for Bird* (Santa Monica, CA: Santa Monica Press, 2001)

Hampton, Wayne. *Guerrilla Minstrels* (Knoxville, TN: The University of Tennessee Press, 1986)

Hoffman, Mark, and James Segrest. *Moanin' at Midnight: The Life and Times of Howlin' Wolf* (New York: Pantheon Books, 2004)

Jones, LeRoi. *Blues People* (New York: William Morrow, 1963)

Kaufman, Bob. *The Ancient Rain* (New York: New Directions, 1981)

Kehew, Robert, ed. *Lark in the Morning: The Verses of the Troubadours*, trans. Ezra Pound, W.D. Snodgrass, and Robert Kehew (Chicago and London: The University of Chicago Press, 2005)

Komunyakaa, Yusef. *Pleasure Dome: New and Collected Poems* (Middletown, CT: Wesleyan University Press, 2001)

Maginnes, Al. *Film History* (Cincinnati, OH: WordTech Editions, 2005)

Massa, Ann. *Vachel Lindsay: Fieldworker for the American Dream* (Bloomington, IN and London: Indiana University Press, 1970)

Matthews, William. *The Poetry Blues: Essays and Interviews*, ed. Sebastian Matthews and Stanley Plumly (Ann Arbor, MI: The University of Michigan Press, 2004)

McClatchy, J.D. *The Voice of the Poet: Allen Ginsberg* (New York: Random House, 2004)

Montandon, Mac, ed. *Innocent When You Dream: The Tom Waits Reader* (New York: Thunder's Mouth Press, 2005)

Ritz, David. *Faith in Time: The Life of Jimmy Scott* (Cambridge, MA: Da Capo Press, 2002)

Shelton, Robert. *No Direction Home: The Life and Music of Bob Dylan* (New York, NY: Beech Tree Books, 1986)

Shinder, Jason, ed. *The Poem that Changed America: "Howl" Fifty Years Later* (New York: Farrar, Straus and Giroux, 2006)

Slonimsky, Nicolas. *Lectionary of Music* (New York, St. Louis, San Francisco, etc.: McGraw Hill, 1989)

Szwed, John. *So What: The Life of Miles Davis* (New York, London, Toronto, etc.: Simon & Schuster, 2002)

Touré. *Never Drank the Kool-Aid* (New York: Picador, 2006)

Troupe, Quincy. *Miles and Me* (Berkeley, Los Angeles, and London: University of California Press, 2002)

Young, Kevin. *Jelly Roll: A Blues* (New York: Alfred A. Knopf, 2005)

INDEX

The Rhythm Method, Razzmatazz, and Memory
